THE ANNUAL OF PSYCHOANALYSIS

THE ANNUAL OF PSYCHOANALYSIS

A Publication of the
Institute for Psychoanalysis
Chicago

Volume XVIII

Routledge
Taylor & Francis Group
LONDON AND NEW YORK

First published 1990 Analytic Press, Hillsdale, NJ.

2 Park Square, Milton Park, Abingdon, Oxfordshire OX14 4RN
52 Vanderbilt Avenue, New York, NY 10017

Routledge is an imprint of the Taylor & Francis Group, an informa business

First issued in paperback 2020

Library of Congress Catalog Number 72-9'1376

ISBN 978-0-88163-093-0 (hbk)
ISBN 978-0-367-60647-3 (pbk)

CONTENTS

III

OBJECT VERSUS SELFOBJECT STUDIES

IV

THEORETICAL AND HISTORICAL CONTRIBUTIONS

Contributors

Gerald Adler, M.D. Training and Supervising Analyst, Boston Psychoanalytic Society and Institute; Director, Medical Student Education in Psychiatry, Massachusetts General Hospital.

Bernard Brandchaft, M.D. Training and Supervising Analyst, Los Angeles Psychoanalytic Institute; Member, Core Faculty, Institute for the Psychoanalytic Study of Subjectivity, New York City.

James Callahan, Ph.D. Professor, Mathematics Department, Smith College, Northampton, MA.

Bertram J. Cohler, Ph.D. William Rainey Harper Professor of Social Sciences, The College, and Professor, The Committee on Human Development and Departments of Psychology, Education, and Psychiatry, University of Chicago.

Steven H. Cooper, Ph.D. Faculty, Boston Psychoanalytic Society and Institute; Assistant Professor of Psychology in Psychiatry, Beth Israel Hospital, Harvard Medical School.

David R. Edelstein, M.D. Assistant Clinical Professor of Psychiatry and Behavioral Sciences, Northwestern University Medical School; Faculty, Postgraduate Education Program, Institute for Psychoanalysis, Chicago.

Robert M. Galatzer-Levy, M.D. Lecturer in Psychiatry, University of Chicago; Faculty Member, Institute for Psychoanalysis, Chicago.

Fred M. Levin, M.D. Training and Supervising Analyst, Chicago Institute for Psychoanalysis; Assistant Professor of Clinical Psychiatry, Northwestern University Medical School.

J. G. Maguire, M.D. Training and Supervising Analyst, Institute for Psychoanalysis, Chicago.

Jerome I. Sashin, M.D. (deceased) Supervisory Analyst, Boston Psychoanalytic Society and Institute; Chairman, Research Committee, Psychoanalytic Institute of New England.

Estelle Shane, Ph.D. Founding President, Center for Early Education and College of Developmental Studies, Los Angeles; Visiting Lecturer, Department of

Psychiatry, UCLA.

Morton Shane, M.D. Director of Education, Training and Supervising Analyst in Adult and Child, Los Angeles Psychoanalytic Society and Institute; Associate Clinical Professor, Department of Psychiatry, UCLA.

Barry R. Silverstein, M.A. Professor of Psychology, William Paterson College, Wayne, NJ.

Steven M. Silverstein, Ph.D. Senior Instructor in Psychiatry (Psychology), University of Rochester Medical Center.

Robert D. Stolorow, Ph.D. Faculty, Southern California Psychoanalytic Institute; Member, Core Faculty, Institute for the Psychoanalytic Study of Subjectivity, New York City.

Mark Trewartha, M.D. Associate Clinical Professor of Psychiatry, University of Wisconsin Medical School, Madison; private practice of psychoanalysis and psychiatry.

Jerome A. Winer, M.D. Training and Supervising Analyst, Institute for Psychoanalysis, Chicago; Professor of Clinical Psychiatry, College of Medicine, University of Illinois at Chicago.

THE ANNUAL OF PSYCHOANALYSIS

I

DEVELOPMENTAL STUDIES

The Developmental Psychology of the Self and the Changing World View of Psychoanalysis

ROBERT M. GALATZER-LEVY
BERTRAM J. COHLER

Transformations in psychoanalysis and developmental psychology have produced a new psychoanalytic viewpoint in the past two decades. Tracking these large-scale shifts provides useful perspectives on current psychoanalytic controversies. In this chapter we show how the changing view of what constitutes adequate psychological explanation affects psychoanalytic work on many levels. We explore both what is achieved through these shifts and the problems they raise. We adopt a broad perspective, viewing the field from a distance, as it were, so that gross features of the landscape stand out. Some significant discriminations may be lost and strange bedfellows sometimes created; but the reward of a broad overview is a clearer picture of the development of our field and a clarification of controversies.

This exploration leads to the conclusion that many contemporary psychoanalytic controversies originate primarily in the worldviews of the disputants. We argue that much psychoanalytic debate arises from differences in worldviews, and we try to make these worldviews explicit so that discussions can move forward.

Our point of view is internal to psychoanalysis and developmental psychology. Partly because our task is already large, we have not addressed the important and closely related philosophical explorations into the nature of meaning, self, and evidence except as they have directly influenced psychoanalytic thinking. However, we are well aware that the hermeneutic turn in philosophy and the similar shift in psychology are intimately related.

The exploration of the structure of disciplines and their changes has taken two distinct paths in the postwar years. One continues the long tradition of philosophical analysis in which the propositions and methods of the disciplines are carefully scrutinized in terms of such issues as their logical interconnection and their epistemological status. Such analysis has been enormously fruitful in revealing the presence of implicit theories and assumptions and sharpening conceptual frameworks of a number of disciplines. The second point of view aims at the description of the processes through which disciplines evolve and attempts to identify the determinants and patterns of change in science. A major finding of the second point of view is that the evolution of scientific research and findings is far less driven by data and their deviation from available theory than was once believed.

In the more traditional view, a unitary scientific approach to truth gained ascendancy in physics with the scientific revolution of the 17th century (e.g., Gillispie, 1960; Butterfield, 1965), in chemistry with the Chemical Revolution during the 18th century, and more recently in the biological revolution of the late 19th century and the shift to a scientific study of psychology and other sciences of man. In this view, the major transition is from a nonscientific (metaphysical) to a scientific mode of thought. Once adopted, the latter mode of thought results in the correction and advancement of theories through their interaction with empirical data. This point of view holds that cognitive flux and shifting underlying viewpoints typify scientific history; Kuhn (1971) initiated a vast exploration in this direction. The basis of continuity in scientific investigation requires explanation from this point of view.[1]

Kuhn (1971) proposed that a central contributing factor to the continuity of approach of scientific communities lies in shared "paradigms," which constitute the communities' ideals of discourse. Often these are paradigms in the ordinary sense, that is, exemplary instances of the type of thing the community has in mind. Thus, classical mechanics, a field in which a very small number of mathematically expressible principles could be applied in unambiguous fashion to a very wide range of actual situations, has been the paradigmatic theoretical science for the

[1]The relationship between the standard philosophical position that scientific thinking should be explored in terms of logical processes dependent only upon some theoretical presuppositions and Kuhn's essentially empirical observation that theories are built through step by step extensions of existing ideas (in the direction of some, often vague, ideal whose only representation is its exemplars—if that), that are to be validated in ways determined (again usually implicitly) by the community of scientists within the discipline is the subject of vigorous current discussion (Rouse, 1987; McEvoy, 1988; Landan, 1984).

past three centuries. This does not mean that physicists accept (or reject) the specific content of classical mechanics but, rather, that it is the sort of theory they would most like to achieve. If we are to understand what scientists, including ourselves, are up to we need to employ something like Heidegger's "practical hermeneutics" to describe what is being done.

We believe that there has been a shift in what psychoanalysts hope to achieve through their investigations. Insufficient clarity about the nature of our psychoanalytic goals and ideals adds to the confusion of our discourse. Our community, like other communities involved in what may broadly be called the "sciences of man," is in the process of changing the meaning of the idea of a "good explanation" at all levels of discourse from the interpretation of individual acts to broad formulations of psychological function and development. It is our goal to chart certain aspects of this shift.

"Traditional" Psychoanalytic Thinking and the Mechanistic Worldview

Freud's biography and writings reveal the central role of his prepsychoanalytic studies of developmental neurobiology in the formulation of his metapsychology (Gill, 1976; Sulloway, 1979). Clarification of the place of this early study of the biological realm "beyond consciousness" (Freud, 1938) has fostered increased understanding of the distinction between Freud's avowed "scientific" worldview and his actual methods for studying meanings and intents through the psychoanalytic interview. His worldview sought to describe psychological function in terms of the mechanism of operation of a mental apparatus whose structure is determined by its embryonic and evolutionary development. This view applies the mechanistic biology program of the late 19th century to psychology. A second point of view, which Freud did not formally avow, approaches psychology in terms of the vicissitudes of meaning and the understanding of symbolic processes. Klein (1976) calls this Freud's clinical theory. In recent years, with an enlarged emphasis on psychoanalysis as a way to study the determinants of the meanings that people give experiences, there has been increased attention to problems posed and answered in terms of this second point of view.

Freud was dedicated to demonstrating the inadequacy of the notion that the determinants of attention were available to consciousness and to formulating the role of unconscious processes in governing attention and action. Thus, he attended little to the self from a conceptual point of view. In general, he equated the self with the person. Beginning in the

1950s with Hartmann's (1950) discussion of ego psychology and Jacobson's (1954, 1964) discussion of self and object development, psychoanalysts tried to formulate the organization of experience as a superordinate construct, to go beyond Hartmann's (1939a) idea of the "synthetic function of the ego." Winnicott's (1953) discussion of these matters was extended through the complementary theoretical and clinical studies of George Klein (1976) and Heinz Kohut (1977, 1984). Klein and Kohut both clarified Freud's assumptions about the understanding of wishes and intents. They distinguished between metapsychology and clinical theory and demonstrated the value of proximal, or "experience near," observation and investigation. Kohut's formulations continue to elicit intense controversy.[2]

At the same time that psychoanalysts were shifting their attention from mechanism to meaning, two other advances in the study of lives emerged in the work of developmental psychologists and were reflected in the work of some psychoanalysts. The role of continuity and change in lives over many decades, and a shift of emphasis within these life-course studies to the meanings people impart to changes in their lives, became a major topic of developmental research. An important focus of these studies is the ways people preserve a sense of coherence and integrity of their selves even in the face of unexpected adversity.

The study of life-course development, especially from direct infant observation, has led to new understandings of personality development. People turn out to be more adaptive and adaptable than was once believed. At life's beginning, infants have been shown to have marked competence, far beyond what earlier researches assumed. At the end of life the aged have been discovered to be involved in ongoing developmental processes, not the stagnation, fixedness, and deterioration assumed by earlier psychologists. Research shows that people are also less vulnerable than was once believed. For example, research on "sensitive" or "critical" periods in human learning shows essentially negative results; that is, no one epoch of life assumes primacy for determining the later course of life.

Influenced by this changing view of the course of life, develop-

---

[2]George Klein died in 1971 at a time when he was in the midst of work that poses a fundamental challenge to older ways of understanding psychoanalysis. We cannot know what Klein's later impact on the field would have been. Kohut developed his views over several decades, but his methodological contribution is so entwined with the controversy surrounding specific applications of his method that discussions of his work (including Kohut's own) almost invariably conflate his specific clinical and theoretical positions with his views of proper psychoanalytic investigative method.

mentalists have reconsidered the nature of evidence of the study of lives. In particular, there is a move away from positivism. The means to evaluate personality change over time have changed. Generally, a new view of what constitutes good explanations is emerging from the work of psychoanalysts, philosophers, and social scientists, namely, that exploration of the meaning of psychological phenomena, including the origin and course of personal coherence or integrity and the experience of self in relation to others, may be more important and interesting than reduction of personal understanding to mechanistically conceptualized functions of mind and physical mechanisms.

These changes in method of inquiry and evaluation of findings in the human sciences, together with reconsideration of fundamental issues of personality development and change over the course of life, point to the importance of reconsidering the psychoanalytic view of the course of development, including assumptions that link developmental processes to therapeutic interventions. Precisely because of its concern with the "experience near" study of wishes and intents, psychoanalysis has become of central importance in an emerging life-course human science. Over the past three decades, much of this inquiry has centered on the study of the self and its integrity and coherence over time. The initial recognition of the significance of self within psychoanalysis was founded in ego psychology, but ego psychology psychoanalysis was committed to a distal perspective and to explanations based on function and mechanism.

More recent work focuses explicitly on proximal developmental perspectives. In clinical theories as diverse as those of the British School of Object Relations (the Balints, Winnicott, Khan) and American approaches to the study of the self (G. Klein, Gedo, and Kohut and his associates), the view that personal integrity or self-coherence is the basis for interpreting the overall integration of the personality emerged. All these writers shift away from concepts of function and mechanism and emphasize experience, particularly experience in the psychoanalytic situation. Though there are important differences among them, these approaches, considered together, constitute enormous changes in the field. Even so, each of these views, to varying extents, implicitly continues to rely on Freud's neurobiological paradigm to describe the relationship of developmental processes and change in the sense of self over time.

Psychoanalysis and Psychology of the Self

The place of the self as an experience-near concept within an experience-distant theory[3] has been vigorously debated. The intensity of this discussion increased with Kohut's formulation of the psychology of the self. The work of Kohut and his associates departs significantly from other approaches to the self in psychoanalysis, but it shares their interest in rethinking the relationship between early personality development and mental health in later life. In particular, it explores the relationship between psychopathology that is believed to originate in psychological deficits experienced in early life and intervention to foster increased personal integrity by means of the psychoanalytic process. Such writers as Modell (1978, 1984), Settlage (1980), Gedo (1979, 1981), and Kohut and his associates recommend markedly varying interventions, but they share an interest in personality deficits arising in early life, the impact of such deficits on the experience of psychotherapeutic interventions, and the technical implications of this understanding.

In concert with these changing views of psychopathology, there was a shift in focus by researchers like Winnicott, André Green, Sander, Stechler, and Kaplan to the link between experienced aspects of caretaking and later variations in such attributes as creativity and capacity for enjoyment across many aspects of the personality. Similarly,

[3]Our use of the term "experience-distant" is not meant to imply that concepts such as "self" or "empathy" are any more a part of immediate experience than, say, "drive" or "ego." All these ideas arise from the interaction of existing theories (implicit or explicit) with the data of experience. We use the term "experience-distant" as a shorthand for theories that aim at explaining psychological phenomena in terms unrelated to subjective experience, that is, in terms unrelated to meanings and motives. The model for such theories is classical mechanics, in which concepts like "force," "mass," and "acceleration" are both defined and related purely in terms of their formal properties. "Experience-near" is used to refer to theories that attempt to explain psychological happenings in terms of meanings and motives. Freud's interpretations to Dora and the Rat Man are paradigmatic instances of "experience-near" understanding. It is a point of view whose rejection was essential to the scientific revolution of the 17th century, which rejected as unsatisfactory explanations of physical phenomena based on the wishes inanimate matter. The Aristotelian notion that "water seeks its own level" was rejected by 17th-century scientists not because ofits failure to predict experimental findings (which it does), but because explanations in terms of desire were deemed inappropriate in this context. Goldberg's (1988) discussion of these matters, which is explored more thoroughly later in this paper, focuses on the observation that analysis of the epistemological status of supposedly "experience-near" discourse reveals through discourse to be quite distant generalization and abstractions from the data of experience. In this, he is certainly correct. His is an analysis from the point of view of traditional philosophy of science. Our focus is on the ideal for explanation held (often implicitly) by those who approach matters from an "experience-near" point of view, which we believe is devoted to explaining and describing psychological events in terms that are "tasteable" and immediate to one's colleagues. Thus, insofar as "empathy" and "self" are generalizations from experience that lose the richness of experience, they become undesirable in experience-near conceptualizations; insofar as they point to that richness they are desirable. This is in sharp contrast to an "experience-distant" approach that values a concept precisely because of its wide applicability and gladly puts aside the details of experience in favor of broad explanatory power.

there was a dramatic shift in the accepted criteria for mental health, from experience-distant concepts of libidinal or drive satisfaction (Freud, 1950a; Hartmann, 1939b) to experience-near qualities, like sense of self-realization, creativity, capacity for self-comforting, and joyful spontaneity.

These new approaches have not been welcomed primarily for their intellectual merit but because, pragmatically, they provide a point of view more consistent with commonsense ideas of well-being and the good life and a framework for treatment of the many patients who fail to respond to conflict-oriented interventions. They have been applied to a wide variety of clinical situations, including "disorders of the self" with manifestations like hypochondriasis, a sense of personal depletion and low-level depressed mood, certain forms of delinquency and addiction, perversions, and difficulties with normative developmental crises. They provide frameworks for understanding important classes of transference (Kohut, 1971, 1977, 1984) and defense, such as disavowal (Basch, 1981a). They have informed psychotherapy, group therapy, and family therapy (Kohut, 1971; Kohut and Wolf, 1978; Galatzer-Levy, 1982; Cohen and Weissman, 1984; Elson, 1986; Muslin, 1984; Cohler and Galatzer-Levy, 1988). While the useful boundaries of this widening scope are not yet defined, there are reports of successful self-psychological approaches to borderline disorders (Tolpin, 1980), manic depressive illness (Galatzer-Levy, 1987), and other psychoses (Stolorow and Lachmann, 1980).

THE CONTROVERSY ABOUT SELF PSYCHOLOGY

Self psychology developed from the clinical situation; its clinical application remains its most significant accomplishment. Though many troubled people who were previously viewed as unanalyzable can now be treated using the psychoanalytic setup, there is continuing question whether this intervention is psychoanalysis or an ultimately less satisfying form of psychotherapy. The answer to such a question rests on the criteria employed in differentiating psychoanalysis and psychotherapy. If such characteristics as the analysis of resistance and analysis of oedipal transferences are explicitly included in making the distinction, then many of the activities of self psychologists are clearly not analysis. However, definitions of psychoanalysis that rest on the content of what is explored are unsound. These views imply that *by definition* the psychoanalytic method can never discover elements of the psyche that lie outside the boundaries imposed by these definitions, nor can psychoanalysis be used as a method to confirm or disconfirm these defining concepts. For instance, if psychoanalysis is "the science of human conflict" and (only properly) explores evidence for signs of conflict as the source of psychological phenomenon, it is logically impossible that one could ever discover nonconflictual determinants of behavior by way of psychoanalysis. More important, the distinction between psychoanalysis and psychoanalytic psychotherapy, based on the content of what is explored, is less clinically useful and also less clear in the daily analytic work than distinctions based on the manner in which transference is employed and the extent of working through.[4]

One useful way of distinguishing psychoanalysis from psychotherapy begins with the observation that in both the therapeutic relationship is central to change. In psychoanalysis, this relationship is permitted to evolve spontaneously, thereby facilitating the emergence of the patient's lifelong enactments within the therapeutic relationship. The analyst's central task is to bring them to the analysand's attention through interpretation. In psychotherapy, "useful" or positive transferences are promoted for therapeutic purposes. Other transferences are discouraged and defenses against them are supported. Psychoanalysis aims at interpretation of all transference enactments, facilitating their working through and permitting the analysand to engage in continuing self-analysis (Weiss, 1981). Galatzer-Levy (1988b) formulated a concept of working through as a central, normal aspect of psychological development whose interruption is characteristic of those disorders for which optimal treatment is analysis. The outcome of successful analysis is conceptualized as the stable resumption of this process.

Recognition that the ideal of thorough analysis of all major transference configurations is seldom attained led to a reconsideration of the goals of psychoanalysis that included such concepts as degree of analysis, analysis of specific sectors or aspects of personality, limitations based on attributes both of nature and of deficits in the analysand's development, and limitations of the psychoanalytic setting itself (G. Klein, 1976; Abend, Porder, and Willick, 1983; Winnicott, 1986). This broader, less puritanical, view supports analytic work with people previously precluded from analysis. Even Kohut's (1971) distinction between analyzable narcissistic personality disorders, in which the self is threatened, and fundamentally psychotic disorders, in which the self is severely

[4]Our views about the distinction between psychoanalysis and psychotherapy differ substantially from much of what has been written by self psychologists, as well as by more traditional theorists. Basch (1985) believes there is little value in distinguishing psychoanalysis from psychotherapy when considering disorders of the self, while Kohut (1984) disagrees with our position that self-analysis is an intrinsic component of a successful analytic outcome.

damaged or chronically fragmented, has not stood the test of time. The shift from a dichotomous position, analyzable versus unanalyzable, to a more complete description of the extent and nature of analyzability corresponds to the shift from a single-threaded, drive-based concept of developmental lines to one in which complex, interacting developmental lines influence and compensate for each other (A. Freud, 1965).

The abstract question of whether or not a treatment is psychoanalytic becomes most important pragmatically when nonanalytic intervention threatens the work that could be accomplished through analysis. The therapeutic applications of self psychology are controversial because they call into question the older psychoanalytic concept that the interpretation of conflict is mutative (Brenner, 1982; Curtis, 1985; Wallerstein, 1985) and thus may be seen avoiding vital psychoanalytic work.

Therapeutic efficacy is neither a test of conceptual validity nor an indication of a theory's place within a discipline. Psychoanalysis does not claim to be a panacea for psychological ills, only a means to understand wishes and intents. It could be argued that neither therapeutic efficacy nor broader conceptual range are relevant to whether self psychology is part of psychoanalysis. Wallerstein (1985) observes that the very efficacy of self psychology impedes consideration of the extent to which it is psychoanalytic. Self psychology perspectives can serve as resistance to other analytic positions. More important, since they deal with issues like the basis of psychoanalytic rapport, they may represent a point of view fundamentally extrinsic to psychoanalysis. Despite its therapeutic efficacy, psychopharmacology interventions are not psychoanalytic. Not only can the use of medication be used to avoid insight, but the methods and interests of psychopharmacology are not a part of psychoanalysis. Similarly, a cytologist whose research shifts to the optics of microscopes may be doing something worthwhile and his work may even ultimately lead to better understanding of cells, but it is no longer cytology.

The Concept of Self

Self psychology emerged in the context of widespread psychoanalytic *re*discovery of the concept of self. Freud's term "Ich" is better translated as "I" or "self" than "ego" (Hartmann, 1950; Laplanche and Pontalis, 1973; Gedo, 1979; Kernberg, 1982; Richards, 1982a; Meissner, 1986). The editors of the *Standard Edition* (Strachey et. al., 1923, 1961, pp. 7-8) note that they sometimes render *Ich* as "self" in an effort to distinguish Freud's different uses of the term. Kernberg claims that the Strachey translation is faithful to Freud's intent. However, Bettelheim (1983) notes that the inflected meaning of *Ich* is the reflective or introspective "I." Schafer's (1976, 1981, 1983) emphasis on the active self as central to psychoanalysis is probably more consistent with Freud's thinking than is evident to readers of the *Standard Edition*.

CONTRASTING PERSPECTIVES REGARDING THE SELF

The self is easily confused with psychosocial or interpersonal constructs. Differentiation between interpersonal and intrapsychic constructs was central to Hartmann's (1950) and Jacobson's (1954, 1964) efforts to clarify the concept. Together with Richards (1982), these authors view the self as including the ego, the sense of being the subject (vs. the object) of experience, the bodily self, and the sense of being a whole individual person. Even so, Meissner (1986) remains uneasy with Hartmann's equation of self and person. He views "person" as a social, not intrapsychologic, term. As both Gedo (1979, 1981) and Meissner (1986) note, Jacobson's (1964) view of the self concept fosters an inconsistent understanding of the self. Jacobson views the self as an intrapsychic function resulting from experiences or representation of others, as opposed to actual experiences with others (Sandler and Rosenblatt, 1962). It is both a structure in the ego, serving as the repository of the experience of an active sense of personal integration and coherence (G. Klein, 1976), and a structure containing the ego.

Kohut explicitly and actively avoided defining the self. His readers are expected to understand the term from its contexts and their experience. Partly as a result, an extensive literature has been devoted to explicating and exploring the meaning of the concept of self and its relation to the wide range of uses of the term both in and outside psychoanalysis (Jacobson, 1954; Balint, 1963; Lichtenstein, 1965; Levin, 1964; G. Lichtenberg, 1975; Klein, 1976; Schwaber, 1979; Alexander and Friedman, 1980; Treurniet, 1980, 1983; Basch, 1981, 1983a; Beres, 1981; Meyers, 1981; Spruiell, 1981; Stechler and Kaplan, 1981; Blum, 1982; Bollas, 1982; Kernberg, 1982; Mahler and McDevitt, 1982; Pine, 1982; Rangell, 1982; Richards, 1982a; Solnit, 1982; Grossman, 1982; Ticho, 1982; Chessick, 1983; Cassimatis, 1984). Much of this discussion centers on the relationship between mental representation and the represented object. Kohut sometimes refers to the self as agent and sometimes as a mental content. He implicitly indicates that adequate development of the self as an agent requires that the representation of self develop appropriately.

Several concepts are included in the term "self," reflecting different, but interrelated, developmental processes. Kohut (1977) describes three intertwined elements of the self: the grandiose pole, the ideal pole, and the area of talents and skills. The first component of the self refers to an experience, beginning in earliest infancy, of effectiveness, vitality, and vigor. The second element of the self refers to the sense of coherence and continuity in space and time and reflects a complex developmental line, beginning with the parent's image of the infant's physical and historical coherence and continuing in the infant's experience of ever more organized and differentiated positions in life, through the child's discovery of an essential psychological self that is associated with, but differentiated from, his body during the preschool years to a comprehension of one's personal integrity or coherence in ever wider contexts. Talents and skills have not been the object of systematic study by self psychologists.

Another psychoanalytic use of the term "self" refers to the experience of differentiation from others, which leads to psychological autonomy that is made possible through the use of talents and skills acquired through internalization of attributes of caretakers. (Stern, 1985). Kohut also assumes that children learn within a relationship, but self-psychology differs from other psychoanalytic perspectives on the self in assuming that others remain potentially available throughout life; consistent with common sense, but at odds with much ego psychology and Mahler's formulations (Mahler, Pine, and Bergman, 1975),[5] Kohut maintained that people *normally* continue experiencing others as sources of vitality and comfort throughout life.

Furthermore, in contrast to Mahler's view that infants move from an initial autistic unrelated state to form a confusional symbiosis in which baby and mother are experienced as one, Kohut maintains that, from the beginning caretaker actions are experienced by the baby as a function of the self (Cohler, 1980). From Kohut's perspective, only later, in the

[5]Stated in this way, Mahler's position is so counterintuitive that readers of earlier versions of this chapter protested that we had unfairly caricatured her formulation. Careful reading of her works and those of her followers (e.g., Settlage et al. 1988) consistently reveals that they view independence as the normal, if rarely achieved, goal of development. Though not based on Mahler's work, this point of view is seen in the ideals reflected in the collection of papers "Maintenance of the Psychoanalytic Identity and Functioning in a World in Flux" (Chasseguet-Smirgel, 1987). The authors in this work repeatedly set forth an ideal of mature psychological function that includes the capacity to remain independent of the most extreme social pressures. The essays focus on how as the Nazi experience demonstrates interdependence can go wrong. They then make that the capacity to deal with pathological interdependence the measure of full maturity. As Oliver Wendell Holmes observed, "Hard cases make bad law" (Dershowitz, 1988); so, too, extreme societal circumstances make poor general psychological theories. Separation-individuation theory has incorporated the moral values of American frontiersmanship and the tragic experiences of mid-century Europe into a view of normative psychology that is largely inaccurate in its emphasis.

second half of the first year, is there a dawning awareness that the caretaker's functions are performed by another, separate from the self. Both Kohut's and Mahler's views in these matters are based on reconstructions from the treatment and observation of older individuals, not from observations of babies at the time these states are supposedly in effect.

Stern did observe babies, and his discussion of this issue is particularly important. Stern (1985) shows that the capacity for discriminating self and other appears very early in life. The child's "subjective experience of the observable event" (p. 119) results from life experiences of each member of the dyad. Short-lived experiences of assistance with regulation and attunement start at birth; by the second half of the first year of the baby's life, caretaker and child gradually fashion a relationship that is based on reciprocally shared intentions and feelings and that permits the baby to match its own state with others' states. This forms the basis for the capacity to care for another (Sander, 1962, 1964, 1975).

Stern's perspective is consistent with Winnicott's (1953, 1960) view that children create an intermediate, transitional space between self and caretaker that, over time, increases the child's capacity for self-regulation. It is also consistent with the view of self psychology that infants experience their caretaker's regulation of their inner states in the same way they experience self-regulation. Stern describes a matrix of reciprocity that enhances self-regulation. His concern is not primarily with the child-caretaker relationship; he focuses on the child's *experience* of the relationship and its connection with the capacity for self-regulation, vitality, and creativity (Winnicott, 1953; Sander, 1962, 1964; G. Klein, 1976; Stechler and Kaplan, 1980).

Psychological autonomy is not a primary goal for a person of any age. People seek ties with others that provide solace in times of crisis and vitality in times of depletion. Kohut refer to these ties as "selfobject" relations, Stern (1985) uses the term "evoked companion," and Cohler and Galatzer-Levy (1988b) refer to "evoked other" to describe this continued psychological interdependence across the course of life. We currently favor the term "the essential other" (Galatzer-Levy and Cohler, 1990).[6]

From the perspective of psychology of the self, psychological health

[6]While there has been in the literature on life stress, coping, and mental health much discussion regarding the role of social supports as a "buffer" during times of adversity, to date there has been little discussion of how these supports function psychologically. Self psychology perspectives and concepts like the selfobject could provide a psychological understanding of "social support" and serve as an important link between psychoanalytic and social psychological studies.

does not mean giving up others as sources of solace and support. Psychopathology is reflected in the continuing use of others as archaic, urgently required selfobjects, in feelings of fragmentation when there is physical separation from the object, and in the compulsive need to seek recognition of others. These represent failures of normal selfobject function, less satisfactory attempts to meet these needs. It is the manner in which the needs are met, not the needs themselves, that is pathological. Systematic elaboration of the development of selfobjects over the course of life, as a phenomenon characteristic of all people, is the major task for developmental self psychology.

Developmental Theory and the Origins of the Self

Self psychology shares with other psychoanalytic approaches a dual focus on the phenomenology of the present *and* the genesis of present adjustment. Psychoanalysis was always a developmental psychology (Freud, 1913a; Hartmann and Kris, 1945; Cohler, 1986a). However, the use made of the developmental approach in more experience-distant psychoanalytic formulations poses problems in understanding the significance of the experience of a personal past (Cohler, 1986a; Cohler and Freeman, 1987).

We return to Freud, whose explicit ideals became the implicit models for psychoanalytic investigation. Beginning with his earliest studies in neurobiology, Freud explored how the evolutionary past is reflected in structure and function. Influenced by his reading of Darwin (1859) and Hackel (1868), the young Freud sought evidence, through detailed histological studies, of the ways "ontogeny recapitulates phylogeny" (Bernfeld, 1951; Gould, 1977; Sulloway, 1979). Many analysts regard Freud's extension of the program of developmental biology to psychology as a central dimension of his legacy. But this is not the point of view of many analysts, and Freud's most significant influence in the humanities and social sciences has been his clinical theory, including concepts of wish and intent delineated as multidetermined symbolic structures.[7] With regard to development, it is the meaning given to memories (whose content is, of course, influenced by that meaning) that is significant in

[7]Beginning with Lacan (1966, 1968, 1973), the intellectual significance of Freud's clinical method for understanding psychology and culture has gained appreciation by an ever-widening group of scholars, especially literary critics. This approach differs from the older "applied psychoanalysis," which was devoted to showing how Freud's biologically based theories explained cultural phenomena. It focuses instead on the operations by which meaning is disguised or transformed. (Bloom, 1976, 1982; Derrida, 1974).

understanding a person's present circumstances, not the events that the memories purport to recall. Both for theory and practice this position is distinct from an embryology of the mind.

Empathy

EMPATHY AS A RESEARCH TOOL.

Psychoanalysis is unique among the human sciences in emphasizing self-knowledge as a prerequisite to understanding others. It stresses that "tasting" others' experience is the foundation of psychological understanding (Fliess, 1942). Psychoanalysis focuses on the meaning of phenomena to the subject. It particularly explores how people make sense of their lives by building and maintaining life histories that furnish a sense of coherence, integrity, and goodness. For example, the repression of memories of infantile eroticism is an attempt to edit the life narrative to protect the person from feeling that he is bad. In fields as diverse as anthropology (Crapanzano, 1980) and literary criticism (Edel, 1984), psychoanalytic studies, based on introspective inquiry and focused on meaning, have had significant impact on contemporary thought.

We know much more about the internal states of others than can be accounted for by their words alone: we read people's feelings in a flash. Beebe and associates (1985) found that this assessment occurs in less than half a second and is based on posture, facial expression, and tone of voice. It employs information we ordinarily cannot begin to delineate. The assumption that others have motives like our own both facilitates and distorts an understanding of complex mental states. The ability to rapidly grasp complex psychological configurations in others, in ways that seem startling and magical when compared to the effort required to understand similarly complex physical phenomena, is not mysterious. A plausible argument for the biological value of this capacity was made by Darwin (1898) in terms of self-protection. This argument is properly extended to include an understanding of others' internal states of nondefensive purposes once we recognize the evolutionary value of cooperation (Axelrod, 1984).

Kohut differentiated experience-near, (empathic or proximal) observation both from intuition, which implies the undisciplined use of the "hunches" (Reik, 1952), and from natural science (distal) observation in which the experiential realm of the subject is not of central importance. The distinction between intuition and empathy is particularly important: confusion commonly arises in this area. In addition to being empathic, we also are expert, because of repeated experience, at predicting human behavior. Like a veteran cardiologist listening to a murmur, we can often translate from an observation—in this case, of human behavior—to its significance exceedingly rapidly. This is an example of expert functioning. It shares with empathy rapidity and lack of conscious awareness of its mechanism, but it is an entirely different mode of perception. Further confusion arises because, in the psychological field, the content of what is understood through expertise and through empathy may be similar. The distinction becomes clear in the difference between two hypothetical statements by an analyst: "being sure there was trouble in his toilet training" and "he feels that something ill defined and dreadful will happen if every detail of his life is not properly ordered." The former is an instance of expert knowledge, whereas the latter is a description of empathy.

The emphasis on the empathic method is consistent with the view that psychoanalysis is a human, not a natural, science whose proper focus is human experience. Empathic studies almost always use hermeneutic criteria, the coherence and internal organization of life (or analytic) histories, and the extent to which further and richer understanding is advanced as the appropriate ways to evaluate interpretation, in the consulting room and elsewhere (Ricoeur, 1970, 1977; Schafer, 1981a, 1983; Cohler and Freeman, 1987).

Empathy was long recognized as a *component* of analytic understanding, but Kohut was the first to make the controversial assertion that it is *the* essential element in the psychoanalytic approach (Kohut, 1974a, 1975, 1978; Muslin, 1984; Strozier, 1985). Kohut explored the use of empathy in psychoanalytically informed inquiry. For example, he criticizes Mahler's work on separation-individuation because it rests on observations whose psychological viewpoint is not centered on the subject's experience (Kohut, 1971). Sander's (1962) examination of the blissful back and forth play as mother and baby become partners in a reciprocal relationship or Kohut's (1974) recognition of the toddler's total sense of involvement the first time he hears his name called by his mother are examples of experience-near observation. Other examples of this method in developmental psychology, not specifically mentioned by Kohut, include Wolf's (1953) reports on personality development in the first two years of life, Murphy's (1962) studies of children's reactions in unfamiliar situations, and Jones' (1968) study of "the subjective curriculum" and the means by which elementary school students deal with social studies materials that arouse intense feelings.

The shift in emphasis from an experience-distant approach, with its ideal of explanations in terms of mechanism, to the experience-near approach has major implications for the theory and conceptualizing of therapy. The fact that metapsychology reflects Freud's worldview, not his empirical findings, supports the position that the theory most appropriate to psychoanalysis is based on the experience-near phenomena of the clinical encounter (G. Klein, 1976; Gill, 1976; P. Tolpin, 1986).[8] Ironically, there has been little systematic study of clinical phenomena although first steps have been taken by Luborsky (1967), Horowitz (1979), Gill (1982), and Weiss (Weiss and Sampson, 1986; Weiss, 1981). Even in these studies, which are based largely upon experience-distant coding of transcripts of psychoanalytic interviews, there has been little effort to include the therapist's "tasting" of the material.

We agree that empathy is the method of study in the human sciences that is most distinctly psychoanalytic. As the value of this approach is repeatedly demonstrated in studies ranging from infant observation to biographical study (Moraitis, 1987); it is increasingly appreciated. Like any investigative tool, its value is measured by the yield from employing it. Empathy is no less a systematic, scholarly approach than other complex observational methods. The effective use of a microscope requires familiarity with its practical operations, its limitations, the ability to interpret what is seen (and the likely errors in these matters). But the user's ignorance of the details of the microscope's optics, of the chemistry of staining solutions, or of the physiology of his own visual system does not invalidate his observations, though deeper knowledge of these matters may be desirable. The proper use of a microscope does require training and practice; so too empathy. The fact that we are only now becoming familiar with the details of its operations and development does not invalidate it as a observational method. In order to reach a level needed for research work, empathy requires training, practice, and systematic correction for error

EMPATHY AND THERAPEUTICS

Kohut's concept of empathy has major implications for understanding the therapeutic encounter. Though the need for the therapeutic alliance

[8]It is for this reason that Holzman (1985) is wrong in maintaining that the therapy in psychoanalysis will destroy the science. Indeed, the greater problem is that the concept of psychoanalysis as a natural science will obscure its significance for the human sciences. What Holzman misses is that there never was a science of psychoanalysis in the sense of a testable metapsychology. The paramount contribution of psychoanalytic thought to arts and letters, clinical practice, and understandings of man is its clinical theory, not metapsychology, and this is not because Freud's metapsychology needs updating but because the program of metapsychology is mistaken. Psychoanalytic metapsychology has only very rarely been successfully integrated with other natural science viewpoints and has certainly not contributed significantly to a natural science understanding of man.

has long been recognized (Zetzel, 1956; Stone, 1961; Greenson, 1967), Kohut's formulations about the therapeutic role of empathy make explicit sense for the first time of the position of the therapeutic alliance in therapeutic change. An empathic stance entails the therapist's attention to how patients experience the relationship and therapy. For example, while operating in this mode, the analyst remains aware that even a correct (in the sense of accurately describing the patient's psychology) interpretation can be disorganizing and that the patient's objection to such an interpretation is a valid protest—not merely resistance—against a situation that is damaging because it is overwhelming. This is not to say that Kohut invented tact or timing, but rather that he provided a conceptual framework that explains why they are so important in therapeutic work. Recognition of the place of the therapist's empathic response increases the range of interpretable therapeutic enactment and, consequently, widens possibilities for interpreting significant factors in psychological development, not only in infancy and early childhood, but throughout the course of life.

THE ANTIEMPATHIC POSITION

The analyst who works from the point of view of drives and defenses is inevitably ambivalent about empathy. For him all complex actions, including empathy, provide opportunities for distortions in the service of repression. Fenichel (1927), in his classic statement of analytic technique, says empathy is inappropriate to analytic work. He recommends that analysts imitate natural scientists (at least as he imagined them) dissecting and describing structures. Fenichel holds that others' subjective experience, accessible only by use of empathy, is an inadequate and confusing guide for analytic work and that the therapist should be unempathic. His job is to acquaint the patient with realities that the patient is reluctant to acknowledge. The analyst knows these realities from natural science investigation and has overcome his own fears of acknowledging them through his personal analysis. Fenichel recommends tact and the avoidance of trauma and unnecessary pain, but the therapist is always the scientist-detective-surgeon, uncovering an intentionally and deviously hidden mental content outside the realm of the patient's subjective awareness. Like the surgeon, he wishes to cause as little distress as possible, but his major goal must always be to drain the abscess even if this causes the patient much momentary discomfort.

Similarly, Hartmann's (1927) theory condemns empathy (as developed by Dilthey) as a mode of psychoanalytic comprehension. Hartmann asserts that it is precisely the abandonment of empathy for psychological research that makes psychoanalysis a scientific discipline. Thus, Kohut's (1959) assertion that empathy is the characteristic mode of psychoanalytic investigation is in direct contradiction to Hartmann's and Fenichel's positions.[9]

Some Consequences of the Mechanistic Worldview for Psychoanalytic Investigation

As Kohut (1984) notes, Freud's concept of reality testing as an ordinary psychological function is based on the same scientific ideals that shaped psychoanalytic theory. These ideals derive from the mechanistic science of the school of Helmholtz (Bernfeld, 1941). Extending this ideal, Freud held that adult function was normal and desirable in so far as it fostered increased rationality (Weber, 1905).

It is reasonable to question whether rationality, as characterized by the 19th-century scientific ideal (Sulloway, 1979), should be a defining characteristic of psychological health. And, indeed, self psychologists, among others, believe this criterion is no longer viable (Kohut, 1984). Such skepticism is consistent with many contemporary trends in exploring the value systems that underlie the so-called "scientific worldview." Contemporary thinkers question whether rationality as conceived in the 19th century is or should be a major criterion for the value of ideas even in the natural sciences (Kuhn, 1971, 1977; Gadamer, 1981; Bernstein, 1983). For example, the capacity to appreciate psychological experience can be seen as of greater importance to health than rationality. Freud's "truth morality" is now widely discarded.

Freud (1927a, 1927b) believed institutions function in the same way as neurotic symptoms, as compromises between drive satisfactions and the forces that oppose them. Ideally, Freud believed, these institutions should relinquish their nonrational, neurotic-like components. In contrast to this view, self psychology recognizes the psychological need of even the most psychologically mature person to participate in groups and institutions that meet not only material but also psychological needs. The clinical understanding of a profound commitment to institutions thus shifts, and the patient, who, for example, is committed to religious beliefs, can be understood as engaged in mature selfobject functioning, rather than

[9]Curiously, although virtually a response to Hartmann's paper (including use of Hartmann's language), Kohut's assertion is presented without reference to Hartmann's ideas about empathy and in a style that suggests he is summarizing and making explicit a widely accepted position in the field, rather than presenting a methodology that is radically at odds with the norm advocated in the standard psychoanalytic literature.

failed reality testing. From a self psychology perspective, there is no contradiction between personal maturity and participation in religion; participation fosters increased realization of important values and may further the welfare of the community as a whole (Bellah et al., 1985).

Psychoanalytic Explanations

Since Freud's metapsychology is inextricably tied to a late 19th-century mechanistic worldview, at the very least, it requires continual revision to keep pace with the natural sciences. But can any such revision encompass the meaning of wishes and intents that are the central concerns of psychoanalysis and seem to involve an entirely different kind of discourse? Extending G. Klein's (1976) observation that metapsychology is but a restatement of the 19th-century worldview, Cohler (1986a) concludes that the genetic viewpoint has little relevance for clinical psychoanalytic theory.[10] Clinical psychoanalytic theory, based on the study of wishes and intents rather than metapsychology, is Freud's enduring contribution to the study of lives. Clinical theory is certainly more relevant than metapsychology in understanding the origins, course, and treatment of psychopathology.

Freud's view of the continuing impact of unresolved conflicts derived from the infantile neurosis is the essential psychoanalytic paradigm for understanding later development in terms of earlier events. More recent psychoanalytic investigators have suggested that the nuclear neurosis is but one of several developmental tasks confronting children that, if inadequately resolved, contribute to adult psychopathology (Bibring, 1959; Gedo, 1979; Gedo and Goldberg, 1973).[11] Freud's concept of the

[10]The remaining four metapsychological viewpoints are likewise unacceptable as modern scientific constructs. However, they may serve as metaphors (although potentially confusing because of the reification) and summaries of clinical phenomena. Psychological forces, energies, and structures (in the psychoanalytic sense) simply do not exist as concrete entities. The adaptational point of view is of an epistemological class different from the other viewpoints.

[11]The problem of unacknowledged and unresolved wishes and concerns continues to be a difficult one for the psychoanalytic study of human development. Freud believed that the wishes of the family romance continue to generate conflict, even after their analysis (as evidenced by the continuation of dreaming), because the socially defined censorship of sexual wishes, including the incest taboo, is necessary for the family to fulfill its functions (Parsons, 1955). We disagree with the common analytic view that contrasts the psychology of mental conflict with that of archaic states and deficits on an "either/or" basis (e.g., Kohut, 1971; Gedo and Goldberg, 1973; Gedo, 1979, 1981; Schlessinger and Robbins, 1983). Just as everyone confronts the family romance, at least to some extent, everyone remains concerned with more archaic issues. Successful psychoanalytic intervention requires recognition of all these aspects of personality. To the extent that issues associated with the archaic states are the predominant cause of

nuclear neurosis, based on his intensive self-scrutiny (Sadow et al, 1968), is now supported by almost a century of clinical and normative investigation. At least in our culture, rivalries between children and their same-sex parents are decisive for subsequent self-experience and relations with others. Child observers (A. Freud, 1951; Roiphe and Galenson, 1981) find that triadic situations in the family produce specific developmentally important fantasies and fears in children. These concerns are readily recognized as a constellation of anxiety and defense, which Freud called the infantile neurosis (Bornstein, 1949; A. Freud, 1955; Nagera, 1975; Shapiro, 1977; Cohler, 1982, 1987; Panel, 1985).

Kohut's picture of infancy is less at odds with systematic infant observation than Freud's, but neither Kohut nor Freud evoked or needed to evoke the "clinical infant" (Stern, 1985) as a foundation for technique. Kohut's description of the baby, like Freud's, was composed of theoretical concepts and pieces of the thoughts, feelings, and actions of adult patients. This approach is epistemologically unsound. Concepts like "archaic disorders" may be acceptable as developmental metaphors, but they have no necessary relationship to specific developmental processes. In informal discussion, Kohut often uses the term "very early" when he means very important or central to the personality. Of course, some central and very important configurations are likely laid down early in development. But available evidence of *dis*continuity of development and of people's capacity to respond in adaptive, compensatory ways to difficulties and developmental failures implies that very important aspects of the personality need not result from early happenings.

The notion that the study of the past is important in understanding the present is not simply based on the demonstrated usefulness of this approach. Part of the fascination with the study of the personal past in psychoanalysis results from the culturally determined conviction that lives, like stories, have a beginning, middle, and end (Ricoeur, 1977). Psychological explanations are *expected* to show how earlier circumstances entail later outcomes: narratives of lives must have cohesive structure.

The emphasis on temporal unfolding and sequential plots first emerged during the Renaissance and achieved its full realization in the 18th century novel. Only with the Enlightenment did childhood events come to be viewed as determinants of adult psychological states (Rosseau, 1762). Childhood had no special, valued status until the 17th century (Aries, 1962; Shorter, 1975). The routine mistreatment (by our stan-

---

psychological distress, emphasis shifts from interpretation of the transference of conflict to such issues as disruptions of the therapeutic alliance, disavowed wishes connected with archaic states, and problems in the continued experience of coherence and vitality.

dards) of children reflected, among other things, the belief that such treatment did not damage the adult personality.[12] An increased concern both with origins and with beginnings and endings of stories and lives may be traced to what Polanyi (1944) termed the "Great Transformation," manifest in the development of the bourgeois capitalist ethos in the 18th century. The preoccupation of the social scientist with normative and deviant outcomes continues to reflect this widespread attempt to comprehend both social organizations and individual life histories.

While psychoanalytic metapsychology describes the nature of the problem to be studied, the clinical theory of personal meaning, pioneered in Freud's clinical reports, provides the method for understanding how, over time, people rework memories and create a coherent life-history in which the past is related to the present and the future in order to maintain a sense of personal integrity.

Thus, there are two very different but easily confused reasons for attending to history and development in psychoanalysis. The first, embodied in the genetic metaphysical point of view, explains how later states are mechanistically caused by earlier events that influence largely preprogrammed epigenetic unfolding. (The paradigmatic mechanistic model is the computation of the trajectory of a cannon ball, given its initial properties. The proximal representation of this paradigm was Roux's experiments in embryology.) The second reason for treating personal history as important is that it constitutes a central aspect of the way people understand their lives.

These two views imply different roles for history in clinical psychoanalysis. The first implies that the mechanism by which past events continue to have untoward effects requires alteration. The second implies that a reexamination of personal history will alter the present because the resulting change in the history's content and meaning will lead people to see themselves differently.

As the distinction between experience-distant and experience-near modes of observation and theorizing has become important in psychoanalysis, investigators have begun to explore more deeply the conceptual issues raised by this distinction. The idea that experience-near and experience-distant psychological thought can be separated leads to serious problems when examined from an epistemological standpoint. Goldberg (1988) notes that observation of any kind can only occur within a network

[12]Even today the child's development is regarded as important because of its effects on the mature personality. Parents considering treatment or educational alternatives for their children almost always focus on the outcome of development rather than on the child's current pleasure or suffering.

of meaning and (often implicit) theory. To describe or claim knowledge of any experience, and especially the experience of another, entails the assertion of very high order theoretical principles. This fact is often unrecognized because the theory is embedded in ordinary language or "common sense." The sources for such a theory are generalizations from experience, either of the individual or the community. (We would add innate dispositions in processing experience as another source of the theory.) Thus, Goldberg (1988) argues, experience-near observation is contingent on experience-distant theory and the idea of an experience-near approach to psychology ignores the central role of experience-distant ideas.[13] "...our field is composed of a network of essential experience-distant theories and concepts...this network allows us to make alive the experience-near data that occupy our lives in our practice" (p. 95).

Goldberg's cogent arguments attend insufficiently to the distinction we (and many students of the history of science) draw between the exploration of the formal theoretical structure of a group of ideas (including those theoretical elements that remain implicit) and the vaguer but, we believe, more important models of ideal scientific investigation shared by a community of scientists and embodied in their paradigms of scientific work. Thus, for example, a misquotation from Lord Kelvin inscribed on the facade of the University of Chicago Social Science Building, "[] 'When you cannot measure your knowledge is meager and unsatisfactory' Lord Kelvin," and the economist Jacob Viner's rejoinder, "When you can measure it, when you can express it in numbers, your knowledge is still of a meagre and unsatisfactory kind," reflect a debate over how scientific investigation should proceed that is not based on (even implicit) theoretical positions but rather on heuristic considerations and fuzzily conceptualized ideals little abstracted from the models these social scientists hoped, but failed, to emulate. (See Merton, Sills, and Stigler, 1984, for a delightful discussion of this particular quotation and McCloskey, 1983, for the role of this and similar catch phrases in the evolution of economics.)

The shift from experience-distant to experience-near positions is not,

[13]Goldberg also observes that, with clinical experience, terms that once seemed abstract and distant from experience frequently come to refer to experiential realities. An analyst who works with the idea of "drives" over time may be as confident and quick in his observation of them as a New Yorker in recognizing a taxicab. There may have been a time when he was learning specific manifestations of these things, but they are now immediately perceived in ordinary circumstances. The difficulty lies in the confusion that arises when terms are thought to refer to external world "facts" rather than experiences. Early in his career, the term "drive" indeed referred to a theoretical construct taught to the analyst; now it labels a group of his experiences. The two are historically interconnected in important ways but are not the same things.

we believe, based on philosophical concerns (although the particularly unsatisfactory epistemological status of many psychoanalytic concepts supports some kind of revision in analytic thinking), but rather on a shifting sense of what students of man want to know and on their notions of satisfactory explanation. Of the many possible "correct" answers to questions of why a person behaves as he does, some will strike us an important and interesting and others will leave us cold and unsatisfied. In psychoanalysis and the other sciences of man, we are in the process of shifting from a position in which satisfactory explanations take as a model classical physics (a discipline in which very general but operationally defined concepts yield equations that are applicable to particular situations) to a position where explicating meanings and motives of people in a way that seems comprehensible in terms of the observer's subjectivity is acceptable. Imagine a thought experiment in which a set of equations predicts behavior very accurately but makes no sense in terms of intention and motives. Most analyst would find such a set of equations thoroughly uninteresting.[14] It is important that analysts, like all scientists, be aware of the implicit assumptions underlying their endeavors and recognize the difficulties that result from those assumptions. The idea of athereotical investigation is clearly wrong. At the same time, the working scientist will be following a long and useful tradition of ignoring philosophical admonitions if he allows the fruits of an approach, rather than its philosophical status, to decide its usefulness. The "experience-near" approach (in the loose sense we are using the term, rather than the philosophically more precise sense used by Goldberg) has proved exceptionally fruitful in the psychoanalytic investigations of the past 20 years in a way that investigations employing concepts that appear more distant from experience have not. The tide may well turn, but, for the moment, this point of view, which represents a shift in the concept of ideal explanation, is gaining ascendancy among many investigators in the sciences of man.

Routes to Health and Illness

Standard psychoanalytic thinking views the "healthy development of vital pleasures" (Klein, 1976), defense, and psychological structures as largely inelastic. Again, basing his ideas on his study of embryology, Freud held

[14]The situation is not unique to analysts. Richard Feynman, who developed the theory of quantum electrodynamics, a theory that successfully encompasses all of physics above the intranuclear scale, observes that the lack of any intuitive interpretation of the theory and the impossibility of achieving any sense of why it works beyond the formal mathematics makes the theory fundamentally unsatisfactory (Feynmann, 1987).

that the major features of the mental apparatus, like those of a developing limb, unfold in a predetermined sequence, disturbed only by gross insults and that libidinal development (in Freud's view, the most "biological" aspect of the person) largely determines other developmental lines. In contrast, self psychology predicts less regular and more variable development. Self psychology claims that there may be several routes to psychological health, even when important elements of early experience are absent or unsatisfactory. Clinically, this implies that instead of needing to rework early experience to a point where it can serve as a foundation for further development, the task of psychoanalysis may often be to remove impediments to new development and to foster development in the absence of traumatic interference.

Psychological Development

When it comes to understanding human development, the worldview of self psychology entails different issues for study, different methods of study, and a wider arena for those studies than drive psychology, ego psychology, or separation-individuation theories. The advantage of this worldview is supported by empirical studies of development across the course of life. These studies, though often using a distal perspective, repeatedly demonstrate greater complexity and richness in developmental processes than are implied by other psychoanalytic points of view.

WHAT DIMENSIONS OF DEVELOPMENT REQUIRE STUDY?

Studies of young children show that matters not centrally related to infantile sexuality are important. Since the earliest psychoanalytic studies of development, it has been clear that there are other aspects of the personality that make the realization of satisfying relations with others and the maintenance of morale difficult. From Freud's (1905a) "Three Essays on a Theory of Sexuality" through the initial extensions of these formulations (Ferenczi 1913; Abraham 1921, 1924; Glover 1932a, 1932b; M. Balint 1935, 1937) to detailed direct observation of children (A. Freud, 1927, 1965; M. Klein, 1928, 1934, 1948,) and more recent clinical and developmental studies (Winnicott, 1953, 1960; Mahler, Pine, and Bergman 1975, Stern, 1985), there have been repeated demonstrations that variations in the child's experience of caretaking play a central role in determining adult adjustment.

In contrast with reconstruction from psychopathology, prospective studies repeatedly demonstrate that it is primarily the child's continuing experience of others over periods of months and years—and not an isolated event, no matter the magnitude—that affects a person's sense of others as sources of satisfaction, comfort, inspiration, and admiration. The child's experience of extended care provided by others is the foundation of self-regulation of tension states. This experience is actively constructed by the child as "good enough" caretaking (Winnicott, 1960). Differences in the caretaking experienced lead to differences in the extent to which others will be seen as sources of help in times of need and to varying degrees of deficit in the capacity to feel care and concern for others.

THE ROLE OF OTHERS THROUGH THE COURSE OF LIFE

The focus on others as a source of solace and comfort has important consequences for understanding development across the course of life. To date, psychoanalytically informed studies of adulthood have relied heavily on Mahler's separation-individuation paradigm to understand relations between self and others (Marcus, 1972; Settlage, 1980; Settlage et al, 1988). From this perspective, dependence on others is evidence of failure to attain psychological autonomy in early childhood (Goldfarb, 1970; Goldfarb, Goldfarb and Scholl, 1966). Settlage and his coworkers (1988) recently expressed this as follows:

> The attainment of a new function by the child requires a corresponding relinquishment by the child of the mother's no longer needed participation as an external auxiliary ego, and the relinquishment by the mother of the new function to the child. Such relinquishment is essential to the full internalization of functions in the progression toward integration and relative autonomy. Self regulation means that a function, although still related to its source, is operative without immediate external support. *Successful developmental process thus leads to a diminishing developmental need for the human object* ... [p. 353, italics added].

This formulation is inconsistent with numerous empirical studies of adult lives that show that interdependence, not autonomy or self-reliance, is most characteristic of satisfying adulthood (Cohler and Geyer, 1984; Cohler and Stott, 1986; Cohler and Galatzer-Levy, 1988b; Galatzer-Levy and Cohler, 1990).[15] Comfortable interdependence between adults

[15]Mahler's portrayal of psychological autonomy reflects cultural values of personal initiative and independence (Weber, 1905; Cohler, 1983; Cohler and Grunebaum, 1981; Cohler and Stott, 1986), rather than the reality of the interdependence of adult lives. Particularly during times of affliction, persons expect to be able to turn to others for help and assistance. The nature and degree of cultural dependence of this concept deserve extensive exploration. In the United States, a nation of immigrants, such heroes as the cowboy are often "loners," individuals detached from the social representations of

is a mark of psychological well-being. The healthy capacity to be alone includes the capacity to evoke others psychologically and to be comfortably alone because aloneness does not entail object loss (Winnicott, 1960).

Although self psychology provides a better means than separation-individuation theory for understanding adult lives, there are problems with all current psychoanalytic formulations of adult development. At least to some extent, confusion continues about the significance of actual others or their evoked memories for solace. What changes the psychological significance of others across the course of adult life? The detailed exploration of this important matter is just beginning. For example, Cohler and Galatzer-Levy (1988b) suggest that continuing social contact, in addition to psychological experiencing of others, may be more important in maintaining morale in the first than in the second half of life. Such questions can only be resolved through detailed, empathic psychoanalytic study across the course of life, based on the presumption that adult personality development is more than the playing out of early childhood experience.

BABIES

The description of the infant reconstructed from clinical psychoanalysis is two-dimensional compared to the description from detailed, direct observation. Reviewing the infant development literature, Stechler and Kaplan (1980), Basch (1983b), Emde and Source (1983), and Stern (1985) all note that, from the first months of life, infants are more attuned to others and more active in processing information than was previously realized. In spite of the problems in relating distal observation to subjective experience (Kohut, 1959, 1971; Cohler, 1986a), observation of caretaker–infant ties show that the infant has a greater sense of vitality (G. Klein, 1976) and is a richer being than has been reflected in reconstructive formulations.

In the first year the baby had innumerable opportunities to experience or match feelings with other people (Kaye, 1982; Stern, 1985). Developing intersubjectivity, a matching of his own and the caretaker's feelings, assists the child in learning self-regulation. These experiences, which Stern (1985) calls "Representations of Interactions that have been

---

selfobjects. The degree to which people of different cultures regard themselves as ideally separate from their origin and community varies greatly. Biblical Judaism, for example, espoused precisely the opposite ideal (Kaufmann, 1960), as does the modern Japanese business community (Ishinomori, 1988).

Generalized" (RIGs), teach children expectable outcomes in relations with caretakers and make major contributions to the sense of a "core self."

Momentary caretaker preoccupation, occasional incompatibility between parental responses and the child's state, and brief family crises generally lead to increased adaptive capacities in children. Parents need not be instantly empathic to every nuance of the baby's state. Rather, over periods of many months, the baby learns to expect particular responses from others. The "average expectable environment" (Hartmann, 1939b) or "ordinary devoted mothering" (Middlemore, 1941; Robertson, 1962) leads the child to expect that parents will respond appropriately to distress and to invitations to play, take care, and comfort. According to Kohut (1977), "transmitting internalization" results from *brief* lapses in the caretaker–offspring tie.

Most children are only affected by *sustained* adversity and continued failure to respond to their needs. Repeated and prolonged separation of caretaker and child or maternal emotional unavailability interferes with the child's nascent efforts towards self-regulation (Kinzie et al., 1986). Continuing inadequate care can deplete or lower vitality; over periods of months or years, this contributes to a disordered sense of self. Many problems in the caretaker–child relationship can lead to the child's failure to develop the capacity for self-regulation, but caretaker preoccupation with such concerns as career, marital conflict, or family problems commonly interferes with enthusiasm for the child's well-being (and well-dosed and timed comfort and solace).

When the mother is depressed or withdrawn, it is particularly hard for the baby to use her for comfort. Maternal depression appears to have a far greater impact on the child's development than schizophrenic disturbance (Stott et al., 1983; Klehr, Cohler, and Musick, 1983; Cohler and Grunebaum, 1985). Depressed states are probably transferred between generations, not primarily through the mechanism of specific identification proposed by Jacobson (1954), but by the depressed parent's unresponsiveness (secondary to depression), resulting in the typical affective reaction of a child to an unresponsive environment, a response that is itself depression (Tronick, Cohn, and Shea, 1986).

Little is known about infants' innate capacity for self-comfort, but temperament plays an important role. However, within limits, the match between the child's temperament and the caretaker's psychology is more important than a match of temperament per se (Thomas and Chess, 1977). Older children differ in their resilience to significant disruption in caretaking, for example, separations from parents prompted by birth of a sibling or hospitalization for psychiatric illness (Cohler, 1986b). Their ability to use comforting from others also varies markedly (Horton, Gewirtz, and Kreutter, 1988).

The idea of a "sensitive" or "critical" period for the development of self-regulation (and for other important aspects of personality), which some analysts have borrowed from studies of animals, has little relevance for humans (Cohler, 1980). The absence of particular responses at specific developmental points does not produce specific deficits. Children are very resilient and are generally able to recover after a period of disruption and maintain their relative place in the course of development (Kagan, 1980; Emde, 1981).

Many factors that influence development of the bipolar self are not ordered in a preset temporal sequence. As valuable as the idea of stages and phases of development has been, there is increasing evidence of multiple pathways to successful functioning, both in emotional and cognitive development (Kohut 1977, 1984; Levin, 1986). The content of experiences associated with realization of a vital and cohesive self is not constrained by vicissitudes of libidinal discharge or other highly specific phase-related needs. Furthermore, the two poles of the self can compensate for each other: successful development of either the grandiose or the idealizing self is essential to psychological well-being. Attainment of a sense of personal integration is possible without complete development of both aspects of the self.

Development of Self and the Theory of Technique

Much of the psychoanalytic theory of technique rests on the topographic model (Freud, 1900, 1915) and its implicit temporal organization of experience. Freud (1900, 1905b, 1915) described the analyst's function as similar to a dream's day residue: disguised, unconscious infantile wishes are transferred across the repression barrier onto the preconscious imago of the analyst (Kohut and Seitz, 1963). The transference neurosis is a transformed recreation of the infantile neurosis that initially determined the adult disorder. Interpretation of the underlying wish within the transference is more effective, and more useful, than explanation of the meaning of extra-analytic symptoms because both the wish and the defense against the wish are more immediate and visible to analyst and patient.

The Therapeutic Alliance and Facilitation of the Course of Analysis

Freud's structural model and concept of signal anxiety led to an increased understanding of resistance. The theory of technique came to include the value of interpreting resistance for recognition and resolution of the transference (A. Freud, 1936; Gill, 1982). But there was no increase in the understanding of the analyst's contribution to evoking and resolving the transference neurosis, and early discussions of technique ignored how analysands experienced aspects of the analytic situation *not* directly related to the transference neurosis.

Although Freud was sensitive to these issues (Freud, 1905b, 1909a; Lipton, 1977), his papers on technique make little reference to the analyst's contribution to the analytic situation (Stone, 1961). Concerns for the reputation of psychoanalysis partially determined Freud's reticence (Freud, 1914b; Jones, 1955). Because of the intimacy and isolation from ordinary social structures of the analytic situation, there was continuing danger that the analyst would misunderstand the analysand's confessions of love and respond with efforts to directly satisfy the analysand's wishes. Countertransference enactments interrupted the very first analysis, that of Anna O., and at one point threatened Jung's career (Carotenuto, 1984). Trying to counter this problem, Freud (1912) recommended that the analyst himself be analyzed and that he adopt a "surgeon's attitude," putting aside his personal feelings.

Freud's limited discussion of the therapeutic alliance reflects an additional dimension of his culturally shared scientific worldview, which resulted in a different relationship between physician and patient than exists today. Freud represented a new scientific medicine made possible, in part, by the studies in physiology pioneered by Helmholtz and his students, including Brucke, Freud's teacher. Freud and his patients endowed the scientifically trained physician with enormous prestige and authority. The acceptance of the physician's authority partially explains the therapeutic effects of suggestion by Freud: patients were expected to follow the doctor's orders. This "authoritarian alliance" of physician and patient has largely disappeared in the "postmodern" era of medicine (Shorter, 1985). It is less likely now than in Freud's time that therapist and patient will share an automatic, culturally syntonic alliance.

Freud's assumption of rapport between analyst and analysand (Lipton, 1977) was not examined until the mid-1950s, when the seminal papers by Zetzel (1956), Loewald (1960), Stone (1961), and Greenson (1965, 1967) appeared. This neglect partly resulted from apprehension that sympathetic interest might distort analytic neutrality or the analyst's role as transference-residue (Greenson, 1967).

Many of the patients Freud described to demonstrate the mechanisms of neurosis had troubles well beyond neurotic suffering. Anna O., Emma Ekstein, Dora, and the Wolfman became psychological invalids who needed treatment throughout life (Jones, 1955; Deutsch, 1957; Masson,

1984). Although each of these patients presented difficulties for the analyst, Freud devotes little discussion to the issue beyond noting the importance of maintaining a therapeutic alliance. This reflects Freud's intentions in writing the case studies, namely, to demonstrate that an epigenetic psychology could explain the origins and transformations of psychoneurotic symptoms. In part, the physician–patient relationship provided a matrix in which Freud's effort to understand incholate ideas was useful to the patient as an empathic response to psychological suffering. Insofar as the matrix functioned well, it was unnecessary to attend to it.

When Freud (1905a) first tried to understand perversions, he realized that not all psychological symptoms could be explained as compromises based on censored, unacceptable wishes. Between 1910 and 1915, Freud's concerns shifted from the control of consciousness to such clinical issues as identification of the childhood determinants of psychological disorders (Freud, 1911, 1915). He realized that perversions and psychoses require a different developmental understanding from neuroses. As early as 1909, Freud tried to understand the developmental progression from auto-erotism to narcissism to object love, which is a necessary prerequisite for the later emergence of the nuclear neurosis.

In response to Sadger's views about perversions, Freud observed that there are two sources of early satisfaction, mother and one's own person, and that an essential developmental task is overcoming overvaluation of either (Nunberg and Federn, 1967). Freud's 1914 essay "On Narcissism" differentiates narcissistic neuroses from object-related transference neuroses. This distinction parallels the difference between the infant's supposed preponderant interest in internal states and the older child's interest in external objects. Freud also recognized that narcisstic states affect object relations. A sense of satisfaction, based on a sense of integrity and coherence, is enhanced by including oneself in a social order. Freud (1914b) noted that the effort to obtain "respect for the ego (pp. 93–94)" is a critical factor in censoring infantile wishes. The child finds it unacceptable to view himself as aggressive, which fosters abandonment of the oedipal challenge, encourages infantile amnesia, and promotes the move to latency.

As psychoanalysis became a profession, the pioneer spirit of early psychoanalysis yielded to interpretive rules (Fenichel, 1927; Brenner, 1982). At the same time, therapeutic efficacy replaced theoretical cogency as the measure of the method. It thus became difficult to ignore the many afflictions that did not to yield to transference interpretations. Often problems that did not yield to the received interpretive stance were presumed to be beyond the scope of psychoanalytic work, and the unresponsive patient was pejoratively labeled unanalyzable.

Decades of analytic work showed that interpreting the transference neurosis was often therapeutically ineffective. But efforts to understand certain patients troubled by factors other than repressed memories by observing, in the psychoanalytic setting, the vicissitudes of their use of others to preserve a fragile sense of personal integrity are helpful. The situations usefully approached by these other sorts of therapeutic interventions, which Gedo (1979) terms "beyond interpretation," often appear as disruptions in the therapeutic alliance. To the extent that these disrupted states, later called "archaic states" (Gedo, 1977, 1981) or "primitive mental states" (Giovacchini, 1979), are more than regressions according to the topographic-structural model. Some analysts (Modell, 1978, 1984) suggest modifications in technique in the early phase of analysis to prepare certain patients to deal more effectively with analysis of the transference neurosis. This approach maintains the centrality of the transference neurosis in understanding and treating psychological illness. Conflict models are thus necessary, but insufficient, to understand the origins and course of psychopathology. Furthermore, consistent with the generalized developmental formulation of Gedo and Goldberg (1973), as Gedo (1979, 1981) has shown, archaic elements of the personality are commonly met in treating transference neuroses.

A shift from the psychology of the mechanistic, experience-distant, genetic point of view of metapsychology (Klein, 1976; Gill, 1976; Abrams, 1977; Cohler, 1987) to a psychology founded on empathic observation of development (Winnicott, 1953; Sander, 1962, 1969, 1975; Strechler and Kaplan, 1980; Emde and Source, 1983; Stern, 1985) fosters increased understanding of the origins of "archaic" states and points towards therapeutic interventions that facilitate their resolution. Despite efforts designed to preserve pure conflict explanations of such "preoedipal" phenomena as regression from oedipal situations (Brenner, 1982), it is now widely accepted that these problems require examination from other perspectives. However, it is less widely agreed that these forms of personal distress reflect analyzable psychopathology. For example, Arlow and Brenner (1964, 1969) and Wallerstein (1985) view the psychoses as reflecting psychic conflict in the same manner as the psychoneuroses, albeit in the context of a defective ego, and they regard such psychotic disorders as inaccessible to psychoanalytic intervention.

Other theorists of psychoanalytic technique believe that nonneurotic disorders might yield to psychoanalytic intervention but disagree on the extent to which such intervention should also focus on psychic conflict.

Winnicott, Modell, Green, Mahler, George Klein, and Kohut maintain either that analysis of the nuclear neurosis is not required or that it is only a part of the therapeutic task. Brenner (1982) and Abend, Porder, and Willick (1983) assert that analysis of oedipal conflicts should remain the central focus of psychoanalytic study, even for those patients with major structural deficits or preoedipal pathology.

Conclusion

Psychoanalysis, broadly conceived as the systematic study of action determined by wishes and intents, including both those socially prohibited or out of awareness and those inconsistent with a present sense of personal integrity, has provided a developmentally oriented study of the course of life and an approach to understanding and intervening in personal distress. Contributions by a large number of psychoanalytic theorists focusing on the study of the self and of the maintenance of personal integrity have enhanced our understanding of motivation and action by providing the outline of a more realistic understanding than drive psychology of the methods by which psychoanalytic investigation succeeds in promoting therapeutic change. Based on the study of how people experience or evoke a sense of the other in psychological life and emphasizing the significance of solace and psychological comfort in maintaining both personal integration and continued empathic understanding of others, the psychology of the self proposes a dramatic alternative to older approaches that center on the reduction of psychological phenomena to presumed biological constructs. Self psychology broadens the range of phenomena believed accessible to psychoanalytic intervention and understanding.

Thinking within psychoanalysis and other areas of study has converged within the disciplines of the human sciences. Recent psychoanalytic inquiry emphasizes the importance of studying persons over time from the point of view of their experiences, rather than in terms of functions and mechanisms that, in any event, are better understood within experimental psychology than by experience-near investigations. The equation of psychoanalysis with the study of such functions and mechanisms is an anachronistic scientism.

This scientistic approach is a continuation of Freud's wish to remain a scientist in the model of science he had learned during his formative training in the late 19th century. A quasi-religious devotion to this worldview was virtually ensured in the young Freud because of the spectacular scientific successes of the previous few decades that resulted from the shift from natural philosophy to disciplined observation and experimental inquiry in the biological sciences and because of the continued enthusiasm of those who had made these strides.[16] This worldview was equated with proper psychoanalytic inquiry for many years, and the resulting continued reliance upon metapsychology remained a major impediment to realization of the central goal of psychoanalytic investigation of studying persons' experience of self and others over the course of life.

Much of the present controversy regarding self approaches is related to current changes in the human sciences in general. These reflect a shift to a postmodern view of science, including employment of a distinctive empathic method to study people. Of course, there will be continued reformulations of the details of development of the self from earliest infancy to oldest age and increased understanding of the changes over time in how people maintain a sense of personal integrity. But the very widespread support for attention to understanding subjectivity in terms of meanings, as opposed to explanations based on mechanisms and functions, seems to have taken over most contemporary psychoanalytic discourse. This return of the study of subjectivity to the empathically informed investigator represents a reinvigoration of psychoanalysis as a discipline and promises both intellectual excitement and increased capacity to help the more troubled patient, using the methods of clinical psychoanalysis—interpretation of the repetition of lifelong means of responding to others within the psychoanalytic relationship itself.

We have tried to demonstrate that the movement from older psychoanalytic views to self psychology is, not merely a change in the content of psychoanalytic theory, but a shift in worldview from Freud's avowed scientific ideal of mechanistic reductionism to a view that makes empathic comprehension of meaning and motives the goal of investigation. We strongly believe that it is the latter view that holds the most promise for the study of man. We think that Freud's greatness does not result from his success in carrying out his avowed program but rather from his

---

[16]The situation is probably more complex and overdetermined. Freud's family had only recently left behind the cultural world of eastern European Jewish orthodoxy and Hasidism. Freud's wish to be modern was doubtless intense so that the scientific worldview held particular meaning for him. Freud's clinical method is intimately related to Jewish exegetical technique (Bakan, 1958; Handelman, 1982; Hartman and Budick, 1986), and his disavowal of religious Judaism is so intense that Bakan actually believed that Freud was conspiring to bring Hasidic thought to the Western world. In any case, Freud could never have avowed such an origin for many aspects of his thought, and his personal attachment to the rationalism of western science is almost certainly partly motivated by a wish to disavow the irrationality of his recent ancestors while at the same time employing their heritage.

explorations of the processes of meaning. Much of the controversy about self psychology does not concern particular theoretical formulations; it concerns the relative value of the different worldviews. Discussion between the proponents of these various positions will be facilitated by the recognition that they do not necessarily share common ground in their views on what needs explaining, what constitutes adequate explanation, or what constitutes adequate investigation.

References

Abend, S., Porder, M., Willick M. (1983), *Borderline Patients.* New York: International Universities Press.

Abraham, K. (1921), Contribution to a discussion on tic. In: *Selected Papers on Psychoanalysis.* New York: Basic Books, 1953, pp. 323-325.

——— (1924), A short study on the development of the libido, viewed in the light of mental disorders. In: *Selected Papers on Psychoanalysis.* New York: Basic Books, 1953, pp. 418-501.

Abrams, S. (1977), The genetic point of view: Antecedents and transformations. J. Amer. Psychoanal. Assn., 25:417-425.

Alexander, J. & Freidman, J. (1980), The question of the self and self esteem. *Internat. Rev. Psycho-Anal.,* 7:365-374.

Aries, P. (1962), *Centuries of Childhood.* trans. R. Baldrick. New York: Random House.

Arlow, J. A. & Brenner, C., (1964), *Psychoanalytic Concepts and the Structural Theory.* New York: International Universities Press.

——— (1969), The psychopathology of the psychoses: A proposed revision. *Internat. J. Psycho-Anal.,* 50:5-14.

Axelrod, R. (1984), *The Evolution of Cooperation.* New York: Basic Books.

Bakan, D. (1958), *Sigmund Freud and the Jewish Mystical Tradition.* Boston: Beacon, 1975.

Balint, E. (1963), On being empty of oneself. *Internat. J. Psycho-Anal.,* 44:470-480,

Balint, M. (1935), Pregenital organization of the libido. In: *Primary Love and Psychoanalytic Technique.* New York: Liveright, 1965.

——— (1937), Early developmental states of the ego. In: *Primary Love and Psychoanalytic Technique.* New York: Liveright, 1965.

——— (1951), On love and hate. In: *Primary Love and Psychoanalytic Technique.* New York: Liveright, 1965.

Basch, M. (1981a), Psychoanalytic interpretation and cognitive transformation. *Internat. J. Psycho-Anal.,* 62:151-75.

——— (1981b), Selfobject disorders & theory: A historical perspective. *J. Amer. Psychoanal. Assn.,* 29:337-352.

——— (1983a), The concept of "self": An operational definition. In: *Developmental Approaches to the Self,* ed. B. Lee & G. Noam. New York: Plenum, pp. 7-58.

——— (1983b), Empathic understanding: A review of the concept and some theoretical considerations. *J. Amer. Psychoanal. Assn.,* 31:101-125.

——— (1985), *Understanding Psychotherapy.* New York: Basic Books.

Beebe, B., Jaffe, J., Feldstein, S., Mays, K. & Alson, D. (1985), Interpersonal timing: The application of an adult dialogue model to mother-infant vocal and kinesic interactions. In: *Social Perception in Infants,* ed. T. Field & N. Fox. Norwood, NJ: Ablex, pp. 185-250.

Bellah, R., Madsen, R., Sullivan, W., Swindler, A. & Tipton, S. (1985), *Habits of the Heart*. Berkeley: University of California Press.

Beres, D. (1981), Self, identity, and narcissism. *Psychoanl. Quart.*, 50:515–534.

Bernfeld, S. (1941), Freud's earliest theories on the school of Helmholtz. *Psychoanal. Quart.*, 13:341–362.

——— (1951), Sigmund Freud, M.D., 1882–1885. *Internat. J. Psycho-Anal.*, 32:204–217.

Bernstein, R. (1983), *Beyond Objectivism and Relativism*. Philadelphia: University of Pennsylvania Press.

Bettelheim, B. (1983), *Freud and Man's Soul*. New York: Knopf.

Bibring, G. (1959), Some considerations of the psychological processes in pregnancy. *The Psychoanalytic Study of the Child*, 14:113–121. New York: International Universities Press.

Bloom, H. (1976), *Figures of a Capable Imagination*. New York: Seabury.

——— (1982), *Agon*. New York: Oxford University Press.

Blum, H. P. (1982), Theories of the self and psychoanalytic concepts: Discussion. *J. Amer. Psychoanal. Assn.*, 30:959–978.

Bollas, C. (1982), On the relation of the self as an object. *Psychoanal. Quart.*, 63:347–360.

Bornstein, S. (1949), The analysis of a phobic child. *The Psychoanalytic Study of the Child*, 3/4:131–226. New York: International Universities Press.

Brenner, C. (1982), *The Mind in Conflict*. New York: International Universities Press.

Butterfield, H. (1965), *The Origins of Modern Science, 1300–1800*, rev. ed. New York: Macmillan.

Carotenuto, A. (1975), *A Secret Sympathy*. New York: Pantheon.

Casper, R. (1983), On the emergence of bulimia nervosa as a syndrome. *Internat. J. Eating Disorders*, 2:3–16.

Cassimatis, E. G. (1984), "False self" existential and therapeutic issues. *Internat. Rev. Psycho-Anal.*, 11:69–78.

Chessick, R. D. (1980), The problematical self in Kant and Kohut. *Psychoanal. Quart.*, 49:456–473.

Chasseguet-Smirgell, J. ed. (1987), *Maintenance of the Psychoanalytic Identity and Functioning in a World in Flux*. London: International Psychoanalytical Association.

Cohen, R. & Weissman, S. (1984), The parenting alliance. In: *Parenthood*, ed. R. Cohen, B. Cohler & S. Weissman. New York: Guilford Press, pp. 33–49.

Cohler, B. (1980), Adult developmental psychology and reconstruction in psychoanalysis. In: *The Course of Life, Vol. 3*, ed. S. Greenspan & G. Pollock. Washington, DC: U.S. Gov. Printing Office, pp. 149–200.

——— (1982), Personal narrative and life course. In: *Life-Span Development and Behavior, Vol. 4*, ed. B. Baltes & O. G. Brim, Jr. New York: Academic Press, pp. 205–241.

——— (1983), Autonomy and interdependence in the family of adulthood. *Gerontologist*, 23:33–39.

——— (1986a), Approaches to the study of development in psychiatric education. In: *The Role of Psychoanalysis in Psychiatric Education*, ed. S. Weissman & R. Thurnblad. New York: International Universities Press, pp. 225–269.

——— (1986b), Adversity, resilience, and the study of lives. In: *The Invulnerable Child*, ed. E. J. Anthony & B. Cohler. New York: Guilford Press, pp. 363–424.

——— (1989), Psychoanalysis and education. III: Motive, meaning, and self. In: *From Motive to Meaning*, ed. K. Field, Be. Cohler & G. Wool. New York: International Universities Press, pp 11–83.

——— & Galatzer-Levy, R. (1988a), Self psychology and psychoanalytic psychotherapy. In: *New Concepts in Psychoanalytic Psychotherapy*, ed. J.M. Ross & W.A. Myers. Washington, DC: American Psychiatric Press, pp. 204–225.

_____ & _____ (1988b), Self, meaning and morale across the second half of life. In: *Psychoanalytic Perspectives on Age and Aging*, ed. P. Nemiroff & J. Calarusso. New York: Basic Books.

_____ & Geyer, S. (1984), Psychological autonomy and interdependence within the family. In: *Normal Family Process*, ed. F. Walsh. New York: Guilford Press, pp. 196–229.

_____ & Grunebaum, H. (1981), *Mothers and Grandmothers*. New York: Wiley.

_____ & _____ (1985), Development and mental health among offspring of parents with major mental disorder. Unpublished Manuscript, Committee on Human Development, University of Chicago.

_____ & Stott, F. (1986), Separation, interdependence and social relations across the second half of life. In: *The Psychology of Separation Through the Life-Cycle*, ed. J. Bloom-Feshbach & S. Bloom-Feshback. San Francisco: Jossey-Bass, pp.

Crapanzano, V. (1980), *Tuhami*. Chicago: University of Chicago Press.

Curtis, H. (1985), Clinical perspectives on self psychology. *Psychoanal. Quart.*, 54:339–378.

Darwin, C. (1859), *On the Origin of the Species by Means of Natural Selection or the Preservation of Favored Races in the Struggle for Life*. London: Murray.

_____ (1898), *The Expression of Emotion in Man and Animals*. New York: Appleton Century Croft.

Derrida, J. (1974), *Of Gramatology*. Baltimore, MD: Johns Hopkins University Press.

Dershowitz, A. (1988), *Taking Liberties*. Chicago: Contemporary Books.

Deutsch, F. (1957), A footnote to Freud's "Fragment of an analysis of a case of hysteria." *Psychoanal. Quart.*, 26:159–167.

Edel, L. (1984), *Writing Lives*. New York: Norton.

Elson, M. (1986), *Self Psychology and Clinical Social Work*. New York: Norton.

Emde, R. (1981), Changing the models of infancy and the nature of early development: Remodeling the Foundation. *J. Amer. Psychoanal. Assn.*, 29:179–219.

_____ & Source, J. (1983), The rewards of infancy: Emotional availability and maternal referencing. In: *Frontiers of Infant Psychiatry*, Vol. 1, ed. J. Call, E. Galenson, & R. Tyson. New York: Basic Books, pp. 17–30.

Fenichel, O. (1927), *Problems of Psychoanalytic Technique*. New York: Psychoanalytic Quarterly Press, 1941.

Ferenczi, S. (1913), Stages in the development of a sense of reality. In: *First Contributions to Psychoanalysis*. New York: Brunner/Mazel, 1980, pp. 213–239.

Feynman, R. (1987), *QED*. New York: Freeman.

Fliess, R. (1942), The metapsychology of the analyst. *Psychoanal. Quart.*, 11:211–227.

Freeman, M. (1984), History, narrative, and life-span developmental knowledge. *Human Dev.*, 27:1–19.

Freud, A. (1927), Four lectures on child analysis. In: *The Writings of Anna Freud, Vol. 1.* New York: International Universities Press, 1964, pp. 3–69.

_____ (1936), *The Ego and the Mechanism of Defense*. New York: International Universities Press, 1966.

_____ (1951), Observations on child development. *The Psychoanalytic Study of the Child*, 6:18–30. New York: International Universities Press.

_____ (1955), The concept of the rejecting mother. In: *The Writings of Anna Freud0, Vol. 4. New York: International Universities Press, 1968, pp. 586–602.*

_____ (1965), *Normality and Pathology in Childhood*. New York: International Universities Press.

Freud S. (1887-1902), *The Origins of Psychoanalysis: Letters to Wilhelm Fliess, Drafts and Notes (1887-1902)*. New York: Basic Books, 1954.

_____ (1900), The interpretation of dreams. *Standard Edition*, 4 & 5. London: Hogarth Press, 1953.
_____ (1905a), Three essays on the theory of sexuality. *Standard Edition*, 7:135–243. London: Hogarth Press, 1953.
_____ (1905b), Fragment of an analysis of a case of hysteria. *Standard Edition*, 7:7–122. London: Hogarth Press, 1953.
_____ (1909), Notes upon a case of obsessional neurosis. *Standard Edition*, 10:155–318. London: Hogarth Press, 1955.
_____ (1911), Formulations on the two principles of mental functioning. *Standard Edition*, 12:218–226. London: Hogarth Press, 1958.
_____ (1913a), Recommendations to physicians practising psychoanalysis. *Standard Edition*, 12:110–120. London: Hogarth Press, 1958.
_____ (1913b), On beginning the treatment. *Standard Edition*, 12:121–144. London: Hogarth Press, 1958.
_____ (1914a), Remembering, repeating and working through. *Standard Edition*, 12:145–156. London: Hogarth Press, 1958.
_____ (1914b), On narcissism: An introduction. *Standard Edition*, 14:73–102. London: Hogarth Press, 1957.
_____ (1915), Observations on transference love. *Standard Edition*, 12:157–168. London: Hogarth Press, 1958.
_____ (1916-1917), Introductory lectures on psycho-analysis. *Standard Edition*, 15 & 16. London: Hogarth Press, 1963.
_____ (1927), The future of an illusion. *Standard Edition*, 21:5–56. London: Hogarth Press, 1961.
_____ (1930), Civilization and its discontents. *Standard Edition*, 21:64–145. London: Hogarth Press, 1961.
_____ (1937), Constructions in analysis. *Standard Edition*, 23:255–269. London: Hogarth Press, 1964.
_____ (1939), Moses and monotheism. *Standard Edition*, 232:1–137. London: Hogarth Press, 1964.
_____ (1940), An outline of psycho-analysis. *Standard Edition*, 23:144–207. London: Hogarth Press, 1964.
Gadamer, H. (1981), *Reason in the Age of Science*. Cambridge, MA: M.I.T. Press.
Galatzer-Levy, R. (1982), The opening phase of psychotherapy of hypochondriasis. *Internat. J. Psychoanal. Psychother.*, 9:389–413.
_____ (1988), Manic-depressive illness: Analytic experience and a hypothesis. In: *Frontiers in self Psychology: Progress in self Psychology*, Vol. 3, ed. A. Goldberg. Hillsdale, NJ: The Analytic Press, pp. 87–103.
_____ (1988b), On working through: A model from artificial intelligence. *J. Amer.* 36:125–151. Psychoanal. Assn.
_____ & Cohler, B. (1990), *The Essential Other*. New York: Basic Books.
Gedo, J. (1977), Notes on the psychoanalytic management of archaic transferences. *J. Amer. Psychoanal. Assn.*, 25:787–803.
_____ (1979), *Beyond Interpretation*. New York: International Universities Press.
_____ (1981), *Advances in Clinical Psychoanalysis*. New York: International Universities Press.
_____ & Goldberg, A. (1973), *Models of the Mind*. Chicago: University of Chicago Press.
Gill, M. (1963), Topography and systems in psychoanalytic theory. *Psychological Issues*, Monog. 10. New York: International Universities Press.
_____ (1976), Metapsychology is not psychology. *Psychological Issues*, Monog. 26. New York: International Universities Press.

_____ (1977), Psychic energy reconsidered. *J. Amer. Psychoanal. Assn.*, 25:581–597.

_____ (1979), The analysis of the transference. *J. Amer. Psychoanal. Assn.*, 27:263–289.

_____ (1982), *Analysis of the Transference, Vol. 1*. New York: International Universities Press.

Gillispie, C. (1960), *The Edge of Objectivity*. Princeton, NJ: Princeton University Press.

Giovacchini, P. (1979), *Primitive Mental States*. New York: Aronson.

Glover, E. (1932a), A psychoanalytic approach to the classification of mental disorders. In: *On the Early Development of Mind*. New York: International Universities Press, 1956, pp. 161–186.

_____ (1932b), On the etiology of drug addiction. In: *On the Early Development of Mind*. New York: International Universities Press, 1956, pp. 187–215.

Goldberg, A. (1988), *A Fresh Look at Psychoanalysis*. Hillsdale, NJ: The Analytic Press.

Goldfarb, W. (1970), The clarifying experience in the psychotherapy of psychotic children. *Curr. Psychiat. Ther.*, 10:52–75.

_____ Goldfarb, N. & Scholl, H. (1966), The speech of mothers of schizophrenic children. *Amer. J. Psychiat.*, 122:1220–7.

Gould, S. J. (1977), *Ontogeny and Phylogeny*. Cambridge, MA: Harvard University Press.

Greenson, R. (1965), The working alliance and the transference neurosis. *Psychoanal. Quart.*, 34:155–181.

_____ (1967), *The Technique and Practice of Psychoanalysis*. New York: International Universities Press.

Grossman, W. I. (1982), The self as fantasy: Fantasy as theory. *J. Amer. Psychoanal. Assn.*, 30:919–938.

Hackel, E. (1868), *Naturaliche Schopfungsgesichte* (*Natural History of Creation*). Berlin: George Reimer.

Handelman, S. (1982), *The Slayers of Moses*. Albany: State University of New York Press.

Hanly, C. (1987), The vicissitudes of life which favour or threaten the maintenance of a psychoanalytic identity and functioning. In: *Maintenance of the Psychoanalytic Identity and Functioning in a World of Flux*, ed. J. Chasseguet-Smirgel. London: International Psychoanalytic Association, pp. 11–11.

Hartman, G. & Budick, S. (1986), *Midrash and Literature*. New Haven, CT: Yale University Press.

Hartmann, H. (1926), Understanding and explaining. In: *Essays in Ego Psychology*. New York: International Universities Press, 1964, pp. 369–404.

_____ (1939a), Psychoanalysis and the concept of health. In: *Essays in Ego Psychology*. New York: International Universities Press, 1964, pp. 3–18.

_____ (1939b), *Ego Psychology and the Problem of Adaptation*, trans. D. Rapaport. New York: International Universities Press, 1958.

_____ (1950), Comments on the psychoanalytic theory of the ego. In: *Essays on Ego Psychology*. New York: International Universities Press, 1964, pp. 113–141.

_____ & Kris, E. (1945), The genetic approach in psychoanalysis. *The Psychoanalytic Study of the Child*, 1:11–30. New Haven, CT: Yale University Press.

Holzman, P. (1985), Psychoanalysis: Is the therapy destroying the science. *J. Amer. Psychoanal. Assn.*, 33:725–770.

Horowitz, M. (1979), *States of Mind*. New York: Plenum.

Horton, P. (1981), *Solace: The Missing Dimension in Psychiatry*. Chicago: University of Chicago Press.

_____ & Gewirtz, H. & Kreutter, (1988), *The Solace Paradigm*. Madison, CT: International Universities Press.

Ishinomori, S. (1988), *Japan, Inc.* Berkeley: University of California Press.

Jacobson, E. (1954), The self and the object world. *The Psychoanalytic Study of the Child*,

9:75–127. New York: International Universities Press.
_____ (1964), *The Self and the Object World*. New York: International Universities Press.
Jones, E. (1955), *The Life and Work of Sigmund Freud, Vol. 2*. New York: Basic Books.
Jones, R. (1968), *Fantasy and Feeling in Education*. New York: New York University Press.
Kagan, J. (1980), Perspectives on continuity. In: *Constancy and Change in Human Development*, ed. O.G. Brim, Jr. & J. Kagan. Cambridge, MA: Harvard University Press, pp. 26–74.
Kaufman, Y. (1960), *The Religion of Israel from Its Beginnings to the Babylonian Exile*, trans. & abridged by M. Greenberg. Chicago: University of Chicago Press.
Kaye, K. (1982), *The Mental and Social Life of Babies*. Chicago: University of Chicago Press.
Kernberg, O. F. (1982), Self, ego, affects, and drives. *J. Amer. Psychoanal. Assn.*, 30:893–917.
Kinzie, D., Sack, H., Angell, R., Manson, S. et al. (1986), The psychiatric effects of massive trauma on Cambodian children. I: The children. *J. Amer. Acad. Child Psychiat.*, 25:370–376.
Klehr, K., Cohler, B. & Musick, J. (1983), Character and behavior in the mentally ill and well mother. *Inf. Mmental Health J.*, 4:25–27.
Klein, G. (1976), *Psychoanalytic Theory*, New York: International Universities Press.
Klein, M. (1928), *The Psychoanalysis of Children*. New York: Delacorte Press, 1976.
_____ (1934), *Contributions to Psychoanalysis: 1921-1945*. London: Hogarth Press, 1950.
_____ (1948), On the theory of anxiety and guilt. In: *Envy and Gratitude and Other Works, 1946-1963*, London: Hogarth Press, 1975, pp. 25–47.
Kohut, H. (1959), Introspection, empathy and psychoanalysis: An examination of the relationship between mode of observation and theory. In: *The Search for the Self*, ed. P. Ornstein. New York: International Universities Press, 1978, I:205–232.
_____ (1966), Forms and transformations of narcissism. In: *The Search for the Self*, ed. P. Ornstein. New York: International Universities Press, 1978, I:427–460.
_____ (1971), *The Analysis of the Self*. New York: International Universities Press.
_____ (1974), Remarks about the formation of the self—Letter to a student regarding some principles of psychoanalytic research In: *The Search for the Self*, ed. P. Ornstein. New York: International Universities Press, 1978, II:737–770.
_____ (1975), The psychoanalyst in the community of scholars. In: *The Search for the Self*, ed. P. Ornstein. New York: International Universities Press, 1978, II:685–724.
_____ (1978), Self psychology and the sciences of man. In: *Self Psychology and the Humanities*, ed. C. Strozier. New York: Norton, 1985, pp. 73–94.
_____ (1984), *How Does Psychoanalysis Cure?*, ed. A. Goldberg & P. Stepansky. Chicago: University of Chicago Press.
_____ & Seitz, P. (1963), Concepts and theories of psychoanalysis. In: *The Search for the Self*, ed. P. Ornstein. New York: International Universities Press, 1978, I:337–374.
_____ & Wolf, E. (1978), The disorders of the self and their treatment: An outline. *Internat. J. Psycho-anal.*, 59:413–425.
Kuhn, T. (1971), *The Structure of Scientific Revolutions*, 2nd ed. Chicago: University of Chicago Press.
_____ (1977), *The Essential Tension*. Chicago: University of Chicago Press.
Lacan, J. (1966), *Ecrits*, trans. A. Sheridan. New York: Norton, 1977.
_____ (1968), *The Language of the Self*, trans. A. Wilden. Baltimore: Johns Hopkins University Press.
_____ (1973), *The Four Fundamental Concepts of Psychoanalysis*. New York: Norton, 1978.
Landan, L. (1984), *Science and Values*. Berkeley: University of California Press.
La Planche, J. & Pontalis, J. B. (1973), *The Language of Psychoanalysis*. New York: Norton.

Levin, D. C. (1964), The self: a contribution to its place in theory and technique. *Internat. J. Psycho-Anal.*, 50:41–52.
Levin, I. ed. (1986), *Stage and Structure*. Norwood, NJ: Ablex.
Lichtenberg, J. D. (1975), The development of the sense of self. *J. Amer. Psychoanal. Assn.*, 23:453–484.
Lichtenstein, H. (1965), Towards a metapsychological definition of the concept of self. *Internat. J. Psycho-Anal.*, 46:117–128.
Lipton, S. D. (1977), Freud's technique as shown in his analysis of the "Rat Man." *Internat. J. Psycho-Anal.*, 58:255–274.
_____ (1979), Addendum: The advantages of Freud's technique. *Internat. J. Psycho-Anal.*, 60:215–216.
Loewald, H. (1960), On the therapeutic action of psychoanalysis, *Internat. J. Psycho-Anal.*, 41:16–33.
Luborsky, L. (1967), Momentary forgetting during psychotherapy and psychoanalysis: A theory and research method. In: *Motives and Thought*, ed. R.R. Hold. New York: International Universities Press, pp. 175–217.
McCloskey, D. (1983), The rhetoric of economics. *J. Economic Lit.*, 21:481–517.
McEvoy, J. (1988), Continuity and discontinuity in the chemical revolution. *Osiris*, 2nd series r:195–213.
Mahler, M. & McDevitt, B. (1982), Thoughts on the emergence of the sense of self, with particular emphasis on the body self. *J. Amer. Psychoanal. Assn.*, 30:827–848.
Mahler, M., Pine, F. & Bergman, A. (1975), *The Psychological Birth of the Human Infant*. New York: Basic Books.
Marcus, I. (1972), The experience of separation-individuation in infancy and its reverberations through the course of life: Maturity, senescence, and sociological implications. *J. Amer. Psychoanal. Assn.*, 21:633–645.
Masson, J. (1984), *The Assault on Truth*. New York: Farrar, Straus, & Giroux.
Meissner, W. (1981), Notes on the psychoanalytic psychology of the self. *Psychoanal. Contemp. Thought*, 1:233–248.
_____ (1986), Can Psychoanalysis find its self? *J. Amer. Psychoanal. Assn.*, 34:379–400.
Merton, R., Sills, D. & Stigler, S. (1984), The Kelvin dictum and social science: An excursion into the history of an idea. *J. Hist. Behav. Sci.*, 20:319–331.
Meyers, S. J. (1981), The bipolar self. *J. Amer. Psychoanal. Assn.*, 29:143–160.
Middlemore, M. (1941), *The Nursing Couple*. London: Hamish-Hamilton.
Modell, A. (1978), The conceptualization of the therapeutic action of psychoanalysis. *Bull. Menn. Clin.*, 42:493–504.
_____ (1984), *Psychoanalysis in a New Context*. New York: International Universities Press.
Moraitis, G. (1987), *Psychoanalytic Studies of Biography*. New York: International Universities Press.
Murphy, L. (1962), *The Widening World of Childhood*. New York: Basic Books.
Muslin, H. (1984), Empathy in the self/selfobject dyad. *Hillside J. Clin. Psychiat.*, 6:271–84.
Nagera, H. (1975), *Female Sexuality and the Oedipus Complex*. New York: Aronson.
Nunberg, H., Federn, E. (1967), *Minutes of the Vienna Psychoanalytic Society, Vol. 2, 1908-1910*. New York: International Universities Press.
Panel (1985), The Oedipus complex: A reevaluation. *J. Amer. Psychoanal. Assn.*, 33:201–216.
Parsons, T. (1955), Family structure and the socialization of the child. In: *Family, Socialization, and Interaction*, ed. T. Parsons & R.F. Bales. New York: The Free Press, pp. 35–131.
Pine, F. (1982), The experiences of self: Aspects of formation, expansion. *The Psychoan-*

alytic Study of The Child, 34:143–168. New Haven, CT: Yale University Press.

Polanyi, K. (1944), *The Great Transformation*. Boston: Beacon Press, 1957.

Rangell, L. (1982), The self in psychoanalytic theory. *J. Amer. Psychoanal. Assn.*, 30:863–891.

Reed, G. (1987), Scientific and polemical aspects of the term transference neurosis in psychoanalysis. *Psychoanal. Inq.*, 7:465–483.

Reik, T. (1952), *Listening with the Third Ear*. New York: Dutton.

Richards, A. D. (1982), The superordinate self in psychoanalytic theory and in the self psychologies. *J. Amer. Psychoanal. Assn.*, 30:939–957.

Ricoeur, P. (1970), *Freud and Philosophy*. New Haven,CT: Yale University Press.

_____ (1977), The question of proof in Freud's psychoanalytic writings. *J. Amer. Psychoanal. Assn.*, 25:835–872.

Robertson, J. (1962), Mothering as an influence on early development. *The Psychoanalytic Study of the Child*, 17:245–264. New York: International Universities Press.

Roiphe, H. & Galenson, E. (1981), *Infantile Origins of Sexual Identity*. New York: International Universities Press.

Rosseau, E. (1762), *Emile or On Education*, trans. A. Bloom. New York: Basic Books, 1979.

Rouse, J. (1987), *Knowledge and Power: Toward a Political Philosophy of Science*. Ithaca, NY: Cornell University Press.

Sadow, L., Gedo, J., Miller, J., Pollock, G., Sabshin, J. & Schlessinger, N. (1968), The process of hypothesis change in three early psychoanalytic concepts. *Psychological Issues*, 10 Monogr. 34 & 35.

Sander, L. (1962), Issues in early mother-child interaction, *J. Amer. Acad. Child Psychiatry*, 2:141–166.

_____ (1964), Adaptive relationships in early mother-child interaction. *J. Am. Acad. Child Psychiatry*, 3:221–263.

_____ (1969), Regulation and organization in the early infant caretaker system. In: *Brain and Early Behavior*, ed. R. Robertson. London: Academic Press, pp.

_____ (1975), Infant and caretaking environment: Investigation and conceptualization of adaptive behavior in a system of increasing complexity. In: *Explorations in Child Psychiatry*, ed. E.J. Anthony. New York: Plenum Press, pp. 129–166.

Sandler, J. & Rosenblatt, B. (1962), The concept of the representational world. *The Psychoanalytic Study of the Child*, 17:128–145. New York: International Universities Press.

Schafer, R. (1976), *A New Language for Psychoanalysis*. New Haven, CT: Yale University Press.

_____ (1978), *Language and insight*. New Haven,CT: Yale University Press.

_____ (1980), Narration in the psychoanalytic dialogue. *Critical Inquiry*, 7:29–53.

_____ (1981), *Narrative Actions in Psychoanalysis*. Worcester, MA: Clark University Press.

_____ (1983), *The Analytic Attitude*. New York: Basic Books.

Schlessinger, N. & Robbins, F. (1983), *A Developmental View of the Psychoanalytic Process*. New York: International Universities Press.

Schwaber, E. (1979), On the "self" within the matrix of analytic theory: Some clinical reflections and reconsiderations. *Internat. J. Psycho-Anal.*, 60:467–480.

Settlage, C. (1980), Psychoanalytic developmental thinking in current and historical perspective. *Psychoanal. Contemp. Thought*, 3:139–170.

_____ Curtis, J., Lozoff, M., Silberschatz, G. & Simburg, E. (1988), Conceptualizing adult development. *J. Amer. Psychoanal. Assn.*, 36:347–369.

Shapiro, T. (1977), Oedipal distortions in severe character pathologies: Developmental and theoretical considerations. *Psychoanal. Quart.*, 46:559–579.

Shorter, E. (1975), *The Making of the Modern Family*. New York: Basic Books.

______ (1985), *Bedside Manners*. New York: International Universities Press.

Solnit, A. J. (1982), Developmental perspectives on self and object constancy. *The Psychoanalytic Study of the Child*, 37:201–220. New Haven,CT: Yale University Press.

Spruiell, V. (1981), The self and the ego. *Psychoanal. Quart.*, 50:319–344.

Sroufe, A. (1979), The coherence of individual development: Early care, attachment, and subsequent developmental issues. *Am. Psychol.*, 34:834–841.

Stechler, G. & Kaplan, S. (1980), The development of the self, *The Psychoanalytic Study of the Child*, 35:85–105. New Haven, CT: Yale University Press.

Stern, D. (1977), *The First Relationship of Infant and Mother*. Cambridge, MA: Harvard University Press.

______ (1985), *The Interpersonal World of the Infant*. New York: Basic Books.

Stolorow, R. & Lachmann, F. (1980), *Psychoanalysis of Developmental Arrests: Theory and Treatment*. New York, International Universities Press.

Stone, L. (1961), *The Psychoanalytic Situation*. New York: International Universities Press.

Stott, F., Musick, J., Clark, R. & Cohler, B. Developmental patterns in infants and young children of mentally ill mothers. *Inf. Mental Health J.*, 4:212–235.

Strachey, J. (1957), Editor's note: An introduction to narcissism. *Standard Edition*, 14:69–71. London: Hogarth Press.

______ (1961), Editor's note: The ego and the id, *Standard Edition*, 19:3–11. London: Hogarth Press.

______ (1961b), Editor's annotation: Remarks on the theory and practice of dream interpretation. *Standard Edition*, 19:133. London: Hogarth Press.

______ (1961c). Editor's annotation: Civilization and its discontents. *Standard Edition*, 21:65–66. London: Hogarth Press.

Strozier, C., ed. (1985), *Self Psychology and the Humanities*. New York: Norton.

Sulloway, F. (1979), *Freud, Biologist of the Mind*. New York: Basic Books.

Thomas, A. & Chess, S. (1977), *Temperament and Development*. New York: Brunner-Mazel.

Ticho, E. A. (1982), The alternate schools and the self. *J. Amer. Psychoanal. Assn.*, 30:849–862.

Tolpin, M. (1971), On the beginnings of a cohesive self. *The Psychoanalytic Study of the Child*, 26:316–35l. New Haven, CT: Yale University Press.

Tolpin, P. (1980), The broderline personality: Its makeup and analyzability. In: *Advances in Self Psychology*, ed. A. Goldberg. New York: International Universities Press, pp. 299–316.

______ (1986), Psychoanalysis and the interpretation of dreams. Presidential address to the Chicago Psychoanalytic Society, June, 1986.

Treurniet, N. (1980), Concepts of self and ego in Kohut's psychology of the self. *Internat. J. Psycho-Anal.*, 61:325–334.

______ (1983), Psychoanalysis and self psychology: A metapsychological essay. *J. Amer. Psychoanal. Assn.*, 31:5–100.

Tronick, E., Cohn, J. & Shea, E. (1986), The transfer of affect between mothers and infants. In: *Affective Development in Infancy*, ed. T. Brazelton & M. Yogman. Norwood, NJ: Ablex.

Wallerstein, R. (1985), How does self psychology differ in practice? *Internat. J. Psycho-Anal.*, 66:391–404.

Weber, M. (1905-1906), *The Protestant Ethic and the Spirit of Capitalism*, trans. T. Parsons. New York: Scribner's.

Weiss, J. & Sampson, H. (1986), *The Psychoanalytic Process*. New York: Guilford Press.

Weiss, S. (1981), Reflections on the psychoanalytic process with special emphasis on child analysis and self analysis. *The Annual of Psychoanalysis*, 9:43-56, New York: International Universities Press.

Weissman, S. & Cohen, R. (1985), The parenting alliance and adolescence. *Adoles. Psychiatry*, 12:24–45.

Winnicott, D. W. (1953), Transitional objects and transitional phenomena. In: *Collected Papers: Through Pediatrics to Psychoanalysis*. New York: Basic Books, pp. 229–242.

_____ (1960), The theory of the parent–infant relationship. *Internat. J. Psycho-Anal.*, 41:585–595.

_____ (1986), *Holding and Interpretation: Fragment of an Analysis*. London: Hogarth Press, 1986.

Wolf, K. (1953), Observation of individual tendencies in the first year of life. In: *Proceedings of Conference on Infancy and Early Childhood*, ed. M. Senn. New York: Macy Foundation, pp. 97–139.

Zetzel, E. (1956), The concept of transference. In: *The Capacity for Emotional Growth*. New York: International Universities Press, 1970, 168–181.

Psychological Development and the Changing Organization of the Brain[1]

FRED M. LEVIN

Although few would argue that what is called psychological development occurs as a consequence of changes in the organization of the brain, there are differences of opinion within psychoanalysis regarding whether one needs to understand what these organizational changes consist of. Some believe that psychoanalysis can be practiced without any knowledge of mind/brain correlations whatsoever. However, a counterargument (Trevarthen, 1979; Levin, 1980; Joseph, 1983, personal communication; Levin and Vuckovich, 1983; Kandel, 1983; Reiser, 1984; Basch, 1979, 1985; Gunther, 1987; Levin and Vuckovich, 1987; Schwartz, 1987; Levin, 1988a; b) is that new knowledge of the brain, integrated into psychoanalytic theory, offers a special combination of insight and usefulness that enhances both psychoanalytic theory formation and clinical practice. The validation of scientific theories also requires that they be tested, at times by means of interdisciplinary research.

Development is difficult to comprehend because of its extraordinary complexity. There are many unanswered questions regarding how specific psychological milestones and the early development of the brain relate to each other and are integrated over time. In general, there are also major gaps in our knowledge regarding how basic subsystems of the brain correlate with psychological variables. Moreover, although there are psychoanalytic techniques for getting development "back on track",

[1]This chapter is dedicated to Dr. David Armstrong Breuckner, who pioneered in the area of interdisciplinary research. Earlier versions of this paper were presented on May 27, 1987, to the Chicago Psychoanalytic Society and on December 16, 1988, to the American Psychoanalytic Association.

the efficacy of such techniques will depend upon whether there is accurate knowledge regarding how these measures work. The central section of this paper, with its presentation of specific mind/brain developmental correlations, attempts to address some of the current gaps in our knowledge.

But there are other reasons why it seems especially timely to reevaluate psychological development. Questions about the viability of some psychoanalytic developmental theories have been raised by Demos (1985), Basch (1985), Stern (1985), and Gedo (1989), based upon infant observation studies. Lichtenberg (1983, 1988, 1989) has considered this field of infant observation research an extremely important subject for psychoanalysis. Gedo (1989) has recently presented a revision of his hierarchical model with Goldberg (Gedo and Goldberg, 1973), making the latest neuroscientific understanding of development a linchpin of his theorizing (Gedo, 1989; Levin, 1989a). In addition to these psychoanalytic efforts, Adams and Victor (1985) and Trevarthen (1979, 1985) have reviewed infant studies from a neuropsychological perspective, and Meyersberg and Post (1979) have tried to bridge neurology and psychoanalysis with a variety of complex considerations (e.g., by trying out analogies between such phenomena as "kindling", a neurological construct, and "fixation", a psychoanalytic conception). All of these efforts make valuable contributions.

Before we go further, some clarifications seem in order. First, it is most important at this stage of our theorizing to distinguish carefully between the various learning subsystems of the brain mentioned in this essay and the derivatives of such systems, such as self-conscious awareness. For example, no one knows when in life self-consciousness begins, and this paper cannot attempt to solve such a problem. It can consider, however, which learning systems of the brain might be necessary for the eventual experience of a core sense of self. This should become clearer as the discussion proceeds.

Secondly, Cartesian dualism is assumed to be disproven (see Basch, 1979, pp. 224–226); thus, all psychological variables are considered manifestations of known or at least potentially knowable brain processes, structure, chemistry, and so forth. In addition, in attempting to relate early psychological development to changes in the central nervous system (CNS), there is no attempt to be comprehensive; this would be impossible in a brief essay. Rather, the author's goal has been to select what appears most relevant from a very large body of neuropsychoanalytic research. In addition, because of the confusion that would otherwise result from correlating complex ideas across disciplines, an effort has been made, wherever possible, to differentiate facts from speculations.

Thirdly, this paper makes certain assumptions about memory and about development. Key parts of the brain are understood to carry essential memory trace circuits, that is, connections that seem necessary and sufficient for learning to occur. According to Thompson (1987), whose orientation is being followed here, the major problem in understanding learning has been in "localizing substrates of learning and memory" (p. 480). In the mammalian brain it appears that "the structures currently though to be most involved in memory trace formation are the cerebellum, hippocampus, amygdala, and the cerebral cortex" (p. 481). One should add here that the striatum is also important for a second major type of (habitual) learning and memory (Mishkin and Appenzeller, 1987).

The further assumption is made that some other parts of the brain, although not critical for long-term memory storage itself, are nevertheless part of the brain's system for creating and accessing memories. For example, there is evidence that together with the hippocampus, the Basal Nucleus of Meynert is important in enhancing "activation or consolidation" (as well as retrieval) of memories in the neocortex in response to novel visual stimuli that are judged important (Rolls, 1987, p. 531).[2]

As for development, it is assumed that the organizational changes of the brain occur stepwise, in genetically preprogrammed, environmentally released fashion. Scientists of many persuasions are in the process of specifying what these steps might be. There seems to be a consensus that memory divides functionally into two or more discrete forms, variously described as "semantic"/"episodic", "procedural"/"declarative", or "cognitive"/"habitual". It may help to describe or define these distinctions so that their psychoanalytic significance might better be appreciated. "Semantic"/"episodic" refers to the quality of memory that is either impersonal, left-hemispheric, and language-based (semantic) or personalized and related to the right hemisphere (episodic). "Procedural" and "declarative" are adjectives describing kinds of memories or knowledge, based upon their mode of retrieval. "Procedural" knowledge is elicited through "priming", that is, by action modes or sensory input experience (which, presumably, especially involves the vestibulocerebellar system). In contrast to this, "declarative" knowledge is recalled by direct, language-based requests for information (which appear to tap primarily the corticolimbic system). Finally, "cognitive"/"habitual" refers to specific

[2]Damage to this Basal Nucleus of Meynert, incidentally, appears to be a critical contributor to the memory deficit in Alzheimer's disease. Clearly, it is not possible to review comprehensively the subject of memory mechanisms within the space of this brief essay.

information-processing systems. Rapidly learned action patterns (habits) seem to involve the corticostriatal system in particular, and in the case of such learning, immature subjects do as well on tests as do adults. This is in contrast to complex, discriminative kinds of learning, which seem to involve the corticolimbic system. This kind of learning requires many repetitions, and adults generally do better than juveniles. Levin (1988a) might be consulted for a fuller discussion of some of these distinctions and their application and relevance to clinical psychoanalysis.

Finally, this paper implicitly follows the interdisciplinary model of the brain described by Ernest W. Kent (1981),[3] which derives from Ludwig von Bertalanffy's general systems theory. Kent's model is clearly an information-processing model. Basch (1975) has pointed out that Freud himself was extremely close to developing such a model in his "Project for a Scientific Psychology" (Freud, 1895) although he never published this during his lifetime, and in fact focused his theorizing instead on an explicit model based on the distribution of libidinal energy, rather than of information. Basch (1985), Rubinstein (1973), and many others have emphasized the current importance of the information-processing perspective for psychoanalytic theorizing. This perspective is employed in this paper as an intervening variable, that is, as a crucial step in the process of constructing a linkage between psychoanalytic and neuroscientific conceptions, to make the integration of concepts less of a speculative enterprise.[4]

[3]Kent (1981) approaches the brain from the points of view of artificial intelligence theory, psychology, and neurology more or less simultaneously. His model is at once hierarchical and parallel in organization (Kent, 1981, pp. 14–15). There are three major functional systems: input, goal direction, and output. Each of these three systems is represented hierarchically by low-, intermediate-, and high-level processors and interconnections with the other systems at each level. Data paths are multiple and parallel (often simultaneous). As one proceeds towards higher levels, one moves from large numbers of perceptual receptors and internal state indicators towards smaller networks of integrators and synthesizers. The output of the motor system is into the external world (which is also represented within the CNS), and the actual external world becomes a critical input to the sensory apparatus. The sensory analysis system (i.e., input system) and the motor (i.e., output) system are connected by the intermediate system, which measures internal states and determines which goals are to be targeted within an individual's goal hierarchy. The vast majority of decisions are assumed not to require conscious decision making and never reach higher levels of organization. A much smaller number of decisions are routed to the higher and highest levels of the goal selection system, where an extremely small number will actually enter consciousness. It should be clear that sensory analysis and coding of data play a critical role in coding for meaning, and possibly an additional role in establishing a kind of "machine language" that the brain can use to communicate with itself (see Levin, 1988b).

[4]An example of this approach is the author's analysis of connections between dream and sleep research which appears in the introduction to Stern's (1988) book *Repetition and Trauma* (see Levin, 1988a). In that project, sleep and dream research are each first

Because of time and space limitations, it will not be possible to review what is known generally about the development of the CNS per se. Those interested should consult Yakovlev and Lecours (1967), Adams and Victor (1985), or Gilles, Leviton, and Dooling (1983).

Specific Psychological, Developmental Steps: Their Sequence and Possible Neurological Correlates

In a series of research efforts, the author (Levin and Vuckovich 1983, 1987; Levin, 1989a, in press) has tried to build a case for combined neuropsychoanalytic models. In what follows, the focus will be on the evolution of learning-related subsystems of the brain that eventually become the basis for a core sense of self, for the cohesiveness of this sense of self, for certain psychological defenses (including the formation of a repression barrier), and for control over sexual and aggressive drives. These psychological developments are presumed to be the consequence of the following specific changes in brain organization:

(1) It is known that from the first days of life there is an actively functioning cerebellum, which will ultimately connect with the cortex via the upper brain stem and thalamic structures. Recent PET scanning research has shown (Chugani and Phelps, 1986) that from birth onwards the cerebellum (and also the thalamus) is extremely active metabolically and is therefore in a position to contribute decisively to "early" memory systems, subserving especially postural and coordinative motor control.[5] *It is worth speculating that this cerebellar (memory) system might serve as the basis for the first self-related experience, what might be called the core sense of self.* These archaic memories (chiefly of motor experience but possibly also involving other sensory modalities) in the newborn and young child would be loaded into the cerebellum (the most primitive motor-memory system that we know of) and potentially transferable later on in development to higher centers (e.g., in the brain stem, cerebral cortex, etc.) when these subsystems would become optimally functional. The result would be linkage and mutual enhancement of the various systems mentioned. Consistent with Piaget (Piaget and Inhelder, 1969) and the most recent theorizing of Daniel Stern (1985), this concept of the core self would thus

examined in terms of learning subsystems of the brain and then related (on this basis) to each other.

[5]According to Chugani and Phelps (1986, p. 841), the cerebellum is active at birth and even decreases in activity during the first year of life. Also, by the age of 3 or 4 months the parietal integration zone becomes especially active and, along with the cerebellar hemispheres, aids "visuomotor integration." The basal ganglia and limbic system mature at 3 months, the frontal and associative cortices at about 7.5 to 8 months.

be based on the earliest sensorimotor (cerebellar) memories, available from birth or very shortly thereafter, as a coordinating influence within the brain.

(2) It is known that the cerebellar memory system eventually becomes the vestibulocerebellar system (VCS), which unfolds as a bidirectional control loop (the VCS-cortical system), with consequences for the coordination of actions initiated at the cortical level (Levin and Vuckovich, 1987). *It is speculated that this coordination by the VCS-cortical system is an important step in the establishment of early physical self-cohesiveness.* See below regarding clarification of the word "cohesiveness" in the present context.) This "cohesiveness" would then improve and ultimately be expressed along with a variety of other self-related functions (agency, coordination, the early mapping of the sensory experience, awareness of body parts, their relationship to each other, and their position in space, etc.). But the increasing "cohesiveness" would be the result of the simultaneous activity of all self-related memory systems (cerebellar, striatal, cortical, limbic, etc.).

At this point it may help to define the word "cohesiveness" as used in this context. Usually this word refers psychoanalytically to "resistance to fragmentation", that is, the resistance against losing the sense of self-sameness, even in the face of significant emotional stress. In the present discussion of the word, the usual psychoanalytic meaning is still intended; however, a more strictly biological sense is included as well, namely, that property of memory that resists disruption so that what is learned can be retrieved in a timely manner (whether habit pattern or discriminative learning) and used for adaptive purposes. Clearly, the implication of using these two meanings together is that a relationship is postulated to exist between a psychological experience on one hand and a biological function on the other. Presumably this resistance to memory interference is experienced as an internal stability of self; moreover, any resistance to memory interference would be a consequence of the processing of critical, self-related long-term memories within multiple memory systems, each making its own contribution to the momentary sense of self and serving as a check on the possibility of failure of memory retrieval within any particular subsystem. Put another way, the multiplicity of functional biological systems for the processing of self-related information provides "backup" (i.e., reliability), much as does the redundancy built into certain strategically important physical systems (e.g., the computers on board a space shuttle).

(3) It is known that the central parietal cortex, which has unique abilities in the area of integrating experiences across the different sensory modalities, develops a map of the self in an absolute space, that is,

according to a coordinate system, (Kent, 1981). *It is speculated that this maturation of the central parietal cortex (and other crossed sensory integration zones) contributes, possibly decisively, to the "cohesiveness" of our early self-related memory systems.* This would be the functional or psychological significance of what Luria called the "tertiary cortical system".

At least two other structures also make important contributions to the mapping of the self in space, the first being the hippocampus (Rolls, 1987). "The hippocampus is ideally placed anatomically . . . in that it receives highly processed information from association areas such as the parietal cortex (conveying information about position in space), the inferior temporal visual cortex (conveying a visual specification of an object), and the superior temporal cortex (conveying an auditory specification of [the same] stimulus)" (Rolls, 1987, p. 526).

The second additional structure contributing to self-mapping is the amygdala, which specifically accomplishes this by means of rich sensory input. "It is possible that the amygdala not only enables sensory events to develop emotional associations but also enables emotion to shape perception and the storage [and retrieval] of memories" (Mishkin and Appenzeller, 1987, p. 88). The mechanism for the learning thus described apparently involves (as a necessary stage) the release of endorphins, opium-like neurotransmitters, which are present within the neuronic projections of the amygdala (p. 88).

Before we continue, it will help to consider briefly the function of crossed sensory integration, as is accomplished by such structures as the central parietal cortex, the amygdala, and, presumably, other brain structures as well. By whatever unknown mechanism this synthesis occurs, the result is that ongoing experience becomes coded independently of the original sensory mode(s) involved. Put another way, this step in information processing takes one from a sensory (or primary) stage of memory, in which various cortical and other (sensory) maps of experience are created, through a secondary or short-term stage, to a tertiary stage in which long-term memories have now formed. These are distributed in some unknown form, that is, the knowledge contained in the original experience is now coded in some "machine" language[6] of the

[6]An additional fascinating sidelight to this discussion, touching on the role of sensory experience, is the observation by the late David Marr (1978, p. 165) that when the brain processes a sensory modality, such as vision (and other modalities likely follow this pattern as well), and creates (a series of) internal visual maps, these maps become progressively refined (abstracted) and also more and more oriented towards the visual perspective of the experiencing subject. This suggests that the abstracting phase of long-term memory (LTM) is more individually variable than the sensory phase of memory. That is, as we process information and go from the sensory to the LTM storage stage, we make progressively more arbitrary choices about how to store particular knowledge. It is

brain; it is "abstract" (see Kent, 1981). Clearly, the unknown process involved in the tertiary stage is of fundamental importance for information processing and knowledge acquisition.

(4) *It is known* that over a period of years a system of two properly functioning cerebral hemispheres with a high level of interhemispheric (i.e., left-right and right-left) connectedness comes into being. *It is speculated that the resulting integrative tendency in cognitive/affective processing that results from the integration of the two cerebral hemispheres*[7] *makes a further contribution to cohesiveness and to the early formation of the repression barrier.*[8] As the cortical ramifications increase, involving complex interplays between the cortex and lower centers (striatum, thalamus, cerebellum, etc.), more subtle and still more abstracted self experiences become conceivable. As noted earlier, our actual sense of who we experience ourselves to be would seem to be a kind of derivative of all of the self-mapping, self-abstracting memory systems (central parietal, limbic/hippocampal/amygdalar, thalamic, striatal, cerebellar, etc.). The richness of the product would seem to flow from the multiplicity of specific memory systems involved and their unique contribution to the overarching system.

(5) *With the further refinement of the system of right cerebral hemisphere and limbic system* (which have intimate connection with each other [see Levin and Vuckovich, 1987]), it is known that affects are better regulated, and *it seems worth speculating that what psychoanalysts call the repression barrier further matures on this basis.*[9]

(6) *It is speculated that the remainder of the development of this defensive function, which Freud called the repression barrier, is accomplished by the increasing and*

---

possible that the meaning of all experience is more idiosyncratic than we might ever imagine. From this perspective it seems logical that the "filing" code of LTM is probably highly personal. Apparently, these biases show up as quickly as experience gets recorded.

[7]The subject of how the hemispheres are integrated is a complex, unanswered question, beyond the scope of the present discussion. That aspect of the subject regarding the defenses of repression and disavowal, and the cerebellum in particular, is discussed elsewhere (Levin and Vuckovich, 1983, 1987).

[8]A fuller discussion of the neurophysiology of "repression" by Hadley (1987, p. 3–4) points out that in addition to the more advanced form of (secondary) repression representing left-right interhemispheric blocking, there is probably a "primary repression" based upon the storage of engrams in basal areas and the cerebellum, memories that never reach consciousness (p. 4). She further refers to a kind of "passive repression" based on information storage in the right hemisphere, which needs left-hemisphere mediation to become accessible to consciousness; this latter information can, however, have access to "the motivational system through the basal ganglia and nucleus accumbens" (p. 4).

[9]Steps (4) and (5) depend upon the evolution and refinement of a large number of changes, including the establishment of specific psychological defenses, that the author believes involve specific neurophysiological mechanisms, as pointed out previously regarding the examples of "repression" and "disavowal" (see footnotes 7 and 8).

reversible dominance of the left over the right hemisphere, which is known to occur during brain maturation (Flor-Henry, 1983; personal communication, 1986). That is, the assumption of left-hemispheric dominance provides us with improved control over sexual and aggressive impulses (Flor-Henry, 1983; personal communication, 1986).

(7) If the preceding brain developments (together with other developments unknown or too complex to consider at present) eventually come together to form an overarching system with unique, "efficient" characteristics, then experience becomes possible at the end of the spectrum that has been called the "conflict-free sphere" or the area of "transformations of narcissism" (Levin, 1973).

The Contribution to Cohesiveness of the Vestibulocerebellar System

Recent research on autism is establishing that the cerebellum is indeed a crucial element in the learning process (Hadley, 1989, personal communication). In a paper on brain plasticity, learning, and psychoanalysis, Levin and Vuckovich (1987) bring together in one place a number of important observations that relate to the cerebellum and its role in our mental functioning. It is not possible to briefly summarize such a complex paper here, and in particular to indicate the substantial relevance of this area of general research to clinical psychoanalysis, but it is hoped that the reader will take the opportunity to review some of these references. This will make the conclusions in the following discussion seem much less speculative, especially regarding the possible contributions of the cerebellum to "cohesiveness", as defined above.

Whatever our sense of self is, it would seem to include as a necessary element the body/mind self, that is, some representation of the body parts and their relationships to each other, and some representation of the world of other people and of the inanimate world. In addition, all of these "things" eventually become organized by our brains within a coordinate system of absolute space. There are those (Kent, 1981) who feel that it is, in fact, the placement of our self-representation within such an absolute coordinate system that constitutes a decisive addition to the crystallization of self.

The self-definitional functions mentioned above are all properties of the vestibulocerebellar system (VCS). In addition, the VCS is active in coordinating the hemispheres before the corpus callosum becomes myelinated. It follows naturally that what psychoanalysts call the self, which involves self-definition, differentiation, and coordination (see

Gedo, 1989), in all likelihood requires an intact cerebellar data base. Whatever happens during psychosis or fragmentation states would seem to involve at least some perturbation in the availability of information from this cerebellar data base or within other core areas responsible for crossed sensory integration.[10]

But there is still another aspect of the cerebellum that suggests an important role in early self development. There is reason to believe that within the cerebellum we create a model of the self-in-the-world and that our manipulation of thoughts about ourselves and others (i.e., our thinking) at one time occurs by means of experimental manipulations or adjustments within this cerebellar model (Itoh, 1986). Without this cerebellar model to "play with", it is very likely that an individual would need to actually manipulate objects just to think about them! From this it follows that some individual psychopathology that appears overly instinctual and primitive in terms, for example, of the need to touch, mouth, and so forth, may actually be a reflection of an arrested psychological development that correlates best neurologically with the expression of an incomplete or primitive cerebellar system (model) for cognition, in the absence of any compensatory or more advanced system.[11]

To put these points somewhat differently, our ability to predict follows from the brain's ability to create internal models of sensory experience (Kohonen, 1983). To this end there exist multiple, organized, sensory maps within the brain, such as the somatosensory parietal map (see Lusek and Kaas, 1986, p. 83), tonotopic maps in the temporal cortex, and maps within the visual cortex, the cerebellum, thalamus, hippocampus, brain stem, and so forth. These feature maps are aspects of the self organization of the brain and lead to further abstractions about the self and the world we live in (Kent, 1981, p. 265). But they are maps without which there is no mapping; that is, they are part of the fundamental machinery necessary for information processing (and knowledge acquisition) itself.

---

[10]In this regard please see the discussion, p. 56, regarding Crow's work on schizophrenia and amygdalar malfunction.

[11]According to Hadley (1987), the Kluver-Bucy Syndrome (resulting from the removal of portions of both temporal lobes, including the amygdala on each side), which produces a condition in which the subject has an excessive need, among other things, to touch or to mouth objects, may well be "the operational equivalent of throwing the organism back from limbic or cortical control of behavior into 'cerebellar mode' " (p. 3). That is, in the early cerebellar mode, before we have created a self-in-the-world model, our learning/thinking requires that we touch everything in order to cognate. Since children are building on such a model, they generally need to touch and/or mouth everything; that is, such behavior is required for their internal model construction.

The Two Cerebral Hemispheres

To the extent that the two cerebral hemispheres represent processors of our ongoing experience, whose collaboration is required for the optimal learning subsystem of the brain to be brought to bear on a particular problem, the intact hemispheres working together by learned and hardwired means reflects a major quality of who we are. Our very identity is connected, much more than we realize, with the cognitive/affective style of this interhemispheric collaboration. The goals, qualities, and limitations of each hemisphere are unique. What may change during either analysis (or normal maturation) is the ability of the two hemispheres to complement each other. Creativity and self-reflection may also be consequences of more interactive use of the two cerebral hemispheres.

A final word about the hemispheres. There is reason for believing that there are many specific disconnection states wherein the hemispheres fail to adequately communicate, resulting in a self that is significantly divided. We have speculated that some of the so-called defenses, such as disavowal and repression, may be nothing more than the manifestation of disconnections in different directions (Levin and Vuckovich, 1983). Although we have implicated the VCS as a likely participant in such "disconnect" decision making, it should be obvious that much more needs to be done to understand psychological defenses in terms of brain physiology. Also, the implications for psychoanalysis of these mind/brain correlations are only just beginning to be appreciated (Levin, 1989b).

The Corticolimbic System

The corticolimbic system makes major contributions to the emerging and ongoing sense of self, as indicated in the preceding discussion. Pioneering work on the limbic part of this system by Dax, Brocca, Papez, MacLean, and Nauta has been reviewed by Nieuwenhuys (1985). Central to this work has been the "triune" brain theory of MacLean (MacLean, 1960, 1985; Moore, 1988). Of the three-brains-in-one, the first, or reptilian, brain subsumes programs for basic physiological need satisfaction; the third brain (the neocortex) receives sensory input about the external and internal worlds, from which it generates a composite image or "double exposure" (Moore, 1988, p. 6). The second, or lower mammalian, brain (which MacLean named the limbic system) plays a key role in social and emotional behavior, including language. It is through the limbic brain's contribution to successful bonding with the mother and others that the survival of the individual and the species is assured.

In humans and other mammals, the right hemisphere has a particularly close affiliation developmentally with the limbic system. Thus, the right hemisphere also plays a critical role in the identification of faces and the management of affect, two functions that therefore appear to be closely related.

MacLean's pioneering work, as noted previously, helped establish some of the particular mind/brain, developmental correlations that were presented earlier in this essay. Two additional areas of research on the corticolimbic system, however, have decisively influenced the author's thinking and will be noted briefly at this point.

T. J. Crow (1986a, b, 1986c; 1987, personal communication) has demonstrated that in right-handed identical twins, there is a clear concordance between schizophrenia and a defect in the amygdalar portion of the left temporal lobe, as demonstrated on CAT scanning. Reynolds (1987), working on autopsy material from the brains of the same patients, has shown that these damaged amygdalas contain abnormally high amounts of dopamine. The significance of these findings is that it is now possible to explain, in at least one class of schizophrenic patients, that the symptoms are due to damage to a single area of the brain subserving both affect and cognition. Put differently, on the basis of damage to part of the limbic system, the anhedonia and cognitive deficit of this disease become more readily understandable, and the critical role of the left amygdala in mental functioning becomes more obvious.

There is also evidence that the dominant hemisphere is essential not only for the control over the motor system, but also, for most of us (Flor-Henry, 1983), for a left over right hemispheric control of affects as well. This relates particularly to major affects that are of interest to psychoanalysis, namely, sexual and aggressive drives, which Flor-Henry connects principally with the right hemisphere. Flor-Henry (1986) has collected evidence from male exhibitionists, for example, that identifies a defect in part of the left temporal pole (identical in all patients thus far studied), as seen on computerized EEG recordings. From this and other evidence he has concluded that the loss of control of these individuals seems best explained, physiologically, as a failure of the left to "police" the right hemisphere.

Hadley (1985) has also stated, regarding the amygdalar and hippocampal systems for information processing (the systems disturbed in both Crow's and Flor-Henry's patients), that psychological hatching is likely "a behavioral correlate of the maturational coordination of multiple sensory, motor, attentional and affective processes" such as is contributed to by the amygdala in particular (p. 536; also see pp. 537–41). Clearly, one can investigate such processes from either an ontogenetic or phylogenetic perspective. The former perspective represents psychoanalysis; the latter, the biological perspective. This paper has attempted to relate the two by means of a developmental series with mind/brain correlations.

Comments about the Overall System

As discussed by Levin and Vuckovich (1987), the overall (and oversimplified) system of right hemisphere/limbic system, left hemisphere/motor system, together with critical brain stem nuclei and the vestibular cerebellar system, comes together to form a unique brain both in mammals generally and in *Homo sapiens* in particular, with very special learning capabilities. The human brain, under optimal organization, is capable of being self-reflective, coherent, and cohesive under a vast array of stresses; it also appears to be self-organizing as a fundamental property. Moreover, our brains are particularly capable of learning within a relationship with the brain of another member of our species in a one-to-one relationship, whether it be parent/child, teacher/student, therapist/patient, or friend/friend. Whether we are correct or not in our ascription to the cerebellum of many roles, including an important function in learning, this observation about learning in dyads would still appear to need an explanation.

In trying to better understand development this paper has focused on research that offers the possibility of dividing the brain into parsimonious functional units. Some will differ over what these units should be; of course, to some extent this decision is arbitrary. Those interested in more of the relevant neuroscientific research might wish to consult Nieuwenhuys (1985), Kety (1982), Shashoua (1982), Reinis and Goldman (1982), and Agranoff (1978). Obviously, the brain's considerable complexity continues to create problems for all of us in attempting to fathom how best to bridge psychoanalytic psychology and neuroscience.

Summary

Eventually we will know both the psychologically relevant parts of the brain and their schedule for development. In this paper the following correlations and sequence of development have been presented (as a speculative enterprise):

1. immediate postpartum availability of the cerebellum (VCS) as a critical contributor to the formation of archaic, self-related memories (making possible, eventually, the beginning of a core sense of self);

2. establishment of VCS/cortical system as a bidirectional control loop providing tentative "cohesiveness" for this ancient memory system;

3. maturation of the central parietal cortical system (as well as the hippocampus and amygdala bilaterally), adding polymodal and self-mapping potential and thus decisively augmenting "cohesion";

4. development of two properly functioning hemispheres, their connectedness and coordination, resulting in further solidity to the self-related memory systems, and early formation of the repression barrier (based upon functional interhemispheric blocking as early psychological "defense");

5. preferential connection between the right cerebral hemisphere and the limbic system, with resultant improved regulation of affects and a strengthening of the repression barrier;

6. the establishment of dominance of the left (or language-related hemisphere) over the right hemisphere, with a resulting consolidation of the repression barrier and more effective control over the "drives".

The system presented in roughly tripartite terms (see Levin and Vuckovich, 1983, 1987) coincides well with the analysis of a number of other theoreticians, for example, the system described by Mesulam (1981, p. 314), wherein an interacting sensory component (i.e., posterior parietal cortex), exploratory/motor component system (i.e., frontal cortex), and motivational map (i.e., the cingulate cortex) feed into and are feed by a system for arousal, attention, and vigilance (the reticular structures, such as limbic connections, nucleus locus coeruleus, and brain stem raphe nuclei). In addition, Mesulam's views are clearly compatible with Kent's model as described earlier in this paper. The point here is that there is sufficient agreement among scholars that it is time to consider in more detail a bridging of psychoanalytic psychology and neurology. We know that the sensory input into our brains relays to unimodal and eventually polymodal areas of the cortex (see Levin, 1980) and that various abstractions that psychoanalysis is concerned with then become possible. These would include the very sense of self at the core of our being, our sense of self-cohesiveness, our psychological defenses, our repression barrier, and our control over sexual and aggressive drives. To change this core, to understand how and why our psychoanalytic technique works, we might at least not exclude a priori detailed knowledge of the brain; and neuroscientists would do well not to ignore the insights of psychoanalysis.

REFERENCES

Adams, R. B. & Victor, M. (1985), Normal development and deviations of the nervous system. In: *Principles of Neurology* (3rd ed.), ed. R. B. Adams & M. Victor. New York: McGraw-Hill, pp. 419–448.

Agranoff, B. W. (1978), Biochemical events mediating the formation of short-term memory. In: *Neurological Basis of Learning and Memory,* ed. Y. Tsukuda & B. W. Agranoff. Chichester: Wiley, pp. 135–147.

Basch, M. F. (1975), Perception, consciousness, and Freud's "Project." *The Annual of Psychoanalysis,* 3:3–20. New York: International Universities Press.

_____ (1985), Development and defense in psychotherapeutic interventions in adolescence. Presented to the American Society of Adolescent Psychiatry, Dallas, TX, May 17 (Tapes #1, 204-1A,B,C available through Infomedix, Garden City, CA 92643).

Chugani, H. T. & Phelps, M. E. (1986), Maturational changes in cerebral function in infants determined by FDG positron emission tomography. *Science,* 231:840–43.

Crow, T. J. (1986a), Left brain, retrotransposons, and schizophrenia. *Brit. Med. J.,* 293:3–4.

_____ (1986b), Secular changes in affective disorders and variations in the psychosis gene. *Arch. Gen. Psychiat.,* 43:1012–14.

_____ (1986c), The continuum of psychosis and its implications for the structure of the gene. *Brit. J. Psychiat.,* 149:419–29.

Demos, V. (1985), The revolution in infancy research: Its implication for the modification of developmental theory. Presented to the American Society of Adolescent Psychiatry, Dallas, TX, May 17 (Tapes #1, 204-1A,B,C available through Infomedix, Garden City, CA 92643).

Flor-Henry, P. (1983), *Cerebral Basis of Psychopathology.* Littleton, MA: Wright-PSG.

Freud, S. (1985), Project for a scientific psychology. *Standard Edition,* 1:295–397. London: Hogarth Press, 1966.

Gedo, J. (1989), Psychoanalytic theory and Occam's Razor. Presented to the Chicago Psychoanalytic Society, February 28, 1989.

_____ & Goldberg, A. (1973), *Models of the Mind.* Chicago: University of Chicago Press.

Gilles, F. H., Leviton, A. & Dooling, E. C., eds. (1983), *The Developing Human Brain.* Littleton, MA: Wright-PSG.

Gunther, M. (1987), Discussion of earlier version, this paper. Presented to the Chicago Psychoanalytic Society, May 27, 1987.

Hadley, J. L. (1985), Attention, affect, and attachment. *Psychoanal. Contemp. Thought,* 8:529–550.

_____ (1987), Discussion of earlier version, this paper. Presented to the Chicago Psychoanalytic Society, May 27, 1987.

Itoh, M. (1986), *The Cerebellum and Neural Control.* New York: Raven Press.

Kandel, E. (1983), From metapsychology to molecular biology: Exploration into the nature of anxiety. *Amer. J. Psychiat.,* 140:1277–93.

Kent, E. W. (1981), *The Brains of Men and Machines.* Peterborough, NH: BYTE/McGraw Hill.

Kety, S. (1982), The evolution of concepts of memory. In: *The Neural Basis of Behavior,* ed. A. L. Beckman. Jamaica, NY: Spectrum, pp. 95–101.Kohonen, T. (1983), Representation of information in spatial maps which are produced by self organization. In: *Synergetics of the Brain,* eds. E. Basar, H. Flohr, H. Haken & A. J. Mandell. New

York: Springer Verlag, pp. 264–273.

Kohonen, T. (1983), Representation of information in spatial maps which are produced by self organization. In: *Synergetics of the Brain,* ed. E. Basar, H. Flohr, H. Haken & A. J. Mandell. Berlin: Springer Verlag, pp. 264–273.

Levin, F. M. (1973), Pleasure: A hierarchical, developmental model. Unpublished manuscript.

_____ (1980), Metaphor, affect and arousal: How interpretations might work. *The Annual of Psychoanalysis,* 8:231–248. New York: International Universities Press.

_____ (1988a), Introduction to *Repetition and Trauma,* by Max Stern. Hillsdale, NJ: The Analytic Press, pp. 1-34.

_____ (1988b), New developments in the integration of brain and behavior. Presented at the 44th Annual Midwest Clinical Conference of the Chicago Medical Society, March 4, 1988.

_____ (1989a), Discussion of John Gedo's paper, "Psychoanalytic Theory and Occam's Razor." Presented to the Chicago Psychoanalytic Society, February 28.

_____ (in press), Psychoanalysis and the brain. In: *Psychoanalysis: The Major Concepts,* ed. B. E. Moore B. D. Fine. New Haven, CT: Yale University Press.

_____ Vuckovich, D. M. (1983), Psychoanalysis and the two cerebral hemispheres. *The Annual of Psychoanalysis,* 11:171–197. New York: International Universities Press.

Levin, F. M. & Vuckovich, D. M. (1987), Brain plasticity, learning and psychoanalysis. *The Annual of Psychoanalysis,* 15:49–96. New York: International Universities Press.

Lichtenberg, J. (1983), *Psychoanalysis and Infant Research.* Hillsdale, NJ: The Analytic Press.

_____ (1988), A theory of motivational-functional systems as psychic structures. *J. Amer. Psychoanal. Assn.,* 36:57–72.

_____ (1989), *A Psychoanalytic Theory of Motivation.* Hillsdale, NJ: The Analytic Press (in press).

Lusek, C. G. & Kaas, J. H. (1986), Interhemispheric connections of cortical sensory and motor representations in primates. In: *Two Hemispheres—One Brain: Functions of the Corpus Callosum,* eds. F. Llepore, N. Ptito & H. H. Jasper. New York: A. R. Liss, pp. 85–102.

MacLean, P. D. (1960), Psychosomatics. In: *Neurophysiology, Vol. 3,* ed. J. Field. Washington, DC: American Physiological Society, pp. 1723–44.

_____ (1985), Stepwise brain evolution with respect to socialization and speech. Presented to the American Society of Adolescent Psychiatry, Dallas, TX, May 17. (Tapes #1, 204-1A,B,C available through Infomedix, Garden City, CA 92643.)

Marr, D. C. (1978), Representing visual information. In: *Theoretical Approaches to Neurobiology,* eds. W. E. Reichhardt & T. Poggio. Cambridge, MA: The MIT Press.

Mesulam, M. A. (1981), A cortical network for directed attention and unilateral neglect. *Arch. Neurol.,* 10:304–25.

Meyersberg, H. A. & Post, R. M. (1979), An holistic developmental view of neural and psychological processes: A neurobiologic-psychoanalytic integration. *Brit. J. Psychiat.,* 135:139–55.

Mishkin, M. & Appenzeller, T. (1987), The anatomy of memory. *Scientific American,* June, pp. 80–89.

Moore, B. E. (1988), On affects: Some biological and developmental perspectives. Unpublished essay.

Nieuwenhuys, R. (1985), *Chemoarchitecture of the Brain.* New York: Springer Verlag.

Piaget, J. & Inhelder, B. (1969), *The Psychology of the Child.* New York: Basic Books.

Reinis, S. & Goldman, J. M. (1982), *The Chemistry of Behavior: Molecular Approaches to Neural Plasticity.* New York: Plenum Press.

Reiser, M. F. (1984), *Mind, Brain, Body.* New York: Basic Books.

Reynolds, G. P. (1987), Dopamine receptor asymmetry in schizophrenia. *Lancet,* April 25, p. 979.

Rolls, E. T. (1987), Information, representation, processing and storage in the brain. In: *The Neural and Molecular Bases of Learning,* eds. J.-P. Changeux & M. Konishi. New York: Wiley, pp. 503–540.

Rubinstein, B. B. (1973), *Psychoanalysis and Contemporary Science: An Annual of Integrative and Interdisciplinary Studies, Vol. 2.* New York: Macmillan.

Schwartz, A. (1987), Drives, affects, behavior and learning: Approaches to a psychobiology of emotion and to an integration of psychoanalytic and neurobiologic thought. *J. Amer. Psychoanal. Assn.,* 35:467–506.

Shashoua, D. N. (1982), Biochemical changes in the CNS during learning. In: *The Neural Basis of Behavior,* ed. A. L. Beckman. Jamaica, NY: Spectrum, pp. 139–164.

Stern, D. N. (1985), *The Interpersonal World of the Infant.* New York: Basic Books.

Stern, M. M. (1988), *Repetition and Trauma.,* ed. L. B. Stern. Hillsdale, NJ: The Analytic Press.

Thompson, R. F. (1987), Activity-dependence of network properties. In: *The Neural and Molecular Bases of Learning,* eds. J.-P. Changeux & M. Konishi. New York: Wiley, pp. 473–502.

Trevarthen, C. (1979), The tasks of consciousness: How could the brain do them? *Brain and Mind.* North Holland: Excerpta Medica (CIBA Foundation series 69, New Series), pp. 187–253.

——— (1985), Facial expressions of emotion in mother-infant interaction. *Hum. Neurobiol.,* 4:21–32.

Yakovlev, P. I. & Lecours, A. R. (1967), The myelogenetic cycles of regional maturation of the brain. In: *Regional Development of the Brain in Early Life,* ed. A. Minkowski. Oxford: Blackwell, pp. 30–70.

II

CLINICAL STUDIES

Notes on Stalemate: A Particular Negative Reaction Affecting Therapeutic Outcome

J.G. MAGUIRE

Even more ambiguous in the psychoanalytic literature than the status of the negative therapeutic reaction is that of the therapeutic stalemate. Attesting to its uncertain position in our inventory of clinical concepts is its absence in the major psychoanalytic indexes. Frequently identified with the negative therapeutic reaction, therapeutic stalemate has shared with it the categorization of superego resistance (e.g., Glover, 1955; Panel, 1970). Alternatively, and most apocryphally, it has been attributed to a countertransferential blind spot or deficiency in the analyst. This latter perspective has often carried the implication that steady, tactful management of the analysand's unsettling aggressions, be they directed toward the analyst or himself, will carry the day in most instances. Although, to be sure, "even simple masochism . . . is a tax on our powers" (Freud, 1937, p. 243), improved technical responses to the "masochistic trend in the ego" (Freud, 1920, p. 14) have greatly facilitated the successful working through of these burdensome clinical problems (Brenner, 1959; Asch, 1976). But significant questions remain: Is stalemate invariably reducible to issues of self-analysis or reanalysis or to the need for better conceptual and technical tools? That is, must the analyst invariably assume the burden for the analysand's intransigence? In assuming this responsibility, must he invariably give priority to countertransferential issues, be they derived from his ignorance, psychology, or therapeutic weariness (Novick, 1980)?

Although I believe that the spectrum of negative reactions to the therapeutic process implicates a plethora of factors, I wish to argue for one genre of therapeutic stalemate that presupposes a negative answer to the foregoing questions. I refer to stalemate as an inescapable fate of those analyses in which the analysand's intuitive perception of the analytic task ahead generates such incalculable tensions, and consequently such intractable resistances, as to preclude the regressive mobilization of the transference neurosis. In fact, it is frequently this vaguely anticipated regressive odyssey that militates against further progression in the therapeutic process. Contra Freud's (1912) vision of the role of the positive transference, the failure to libidinize or alternately to sustain a libidinal investment in the therapeutic process itself undermines its continuing vitality and dynamism. This explanation, which surely does not account for all varieties of stalemate, does take stalemate to be a discrete entity in need of specification. Before I proceed further, let me briefly consider what I mean by therapeutic stalemate.

Let us note at the outset that the many negative vectors arising in the therapeutic process may have an indistinguishable manifest content or descriptive dimension, at least initially. In addition, any genre of negative reaction in the exercise inevitably proceeds from resistance, be it in the analysand or the analyst. These caveats notwithstanding, we may identify three distinct categories of negative reaction that enter into analysis and analytic therapy: (1) resistance, an integral element of the therapeutic process that, even in its most severe forms, may remain amenable over time to interpretative intervention; (2) the negative therapeutic reaction, a paradoxical phenomenon not infrequently associated with the apprehended development of the transference neurosis, which arises out of the treatment process and yet rapidly becomes extraneous to, and subversive of, this process; and (3) therapeutic stalemate, a species of negative reaction that must be distinguished from both resistance and the negative therapeutic reaction according to various phenomenological and dynamic criteria set forth in the following paragraphs.

Originally defined by Freud (1923) in an unfortuntely placed addendum to his structural model of mentation, the descriptive phrase "negative therapeutic reaction" pertained to a distinctive oppositional response of the analysand to the analyst's interpretation, a response that usually led to a paradoxical worsening of the analysand's symptoms and overall clinical condition. Beginning with Freud's own explanations of the negative therapeutic reaction as unconscious superego-generated guilt (Freud, 1923, 1926) and aggressive instinctuality associated with the death instinct (Freud, 1920, 1923, 1924, 1937; cf. Loewald, 1972), the analytic literature has offered divergent and frequently competing explanations for this opposition to both interpretation and the therapeutic enterprise itself. In Freud as well, we can see a failure to distinguish adequately over time between the negative therapeutic reaction as a specific response to interpretation (Freud, 1923) and a more general adverse phenomenon affecting the entire course of the analytic procedure (Freud, 1916–17, 1918, 1937). On the other hand, given his grounding of resistance, the negative therapeutic reaction, and stalemate within a common explanatory framework implicating aggression and the regulatory principle of the death instinct, a plausible inference might be that Freud (1937) did not assign any merit to a slavish adherence to such distinctions.

I will not attempt a review of analytic opinion with respect to negative therapeutic reaction subsequent to Freud, given that Limentani (1981), Resenfeld (1987), and especially Finell (1987) have provided helpful expositions of the literature on this topic. Here I call attention only to pregenital explanations cast in terms of primitive aggression and envy (e.g., Horney, 1936; Riviere, 1936; M. Klein, 1957), the vicissitudes of narcissism intertwined with those of aggression, envy, or shame (e.g., Nacht, 1957; Grunberger, 1971; McDougall, 1980; Limentani, 1981; Rothstein, 1984), primitive defenses against regression to an identification with primary objects (A. Freud, 1952) or against oral incorporation and engulfment (Lewin, 1950; Sterba, 1957), and primitive modes of object relatedness (e.g., Bion, 1962; Olinick, 1964; Guntrip, 1969, Fine, 1971; Kernberg, 1975; Asch, 1976; Robbins, 1988) or defenses against such relatedness (e.g., Modell, 1971) as influential alternative accounts. Of particular relevance for my thesis is the matter of narcissistic resistance, to whose analytic specificity Abraham (1919) first alerted us. More recently, Rosenfeld (1987) has denoted the motivational complexity underlying such a clinical phenomenon by persuasively demonstrating the interdigitation of grandiosity and aggression mobilized as a defensive configuration against an apprehended state of vulnerability occasioned by the intimacy of the therapeutic entente. In a similar vein, Robbins (1988), citing an urge to mastery that counters the patient's apprehended state of disorganization, argues in behalf of the adaptive value of the more troubled analysand's negative attitudinal responses to object engagement and treatment. Despite a strong trend in the literature to remain faithful to Freud's understanding of these negative vectors in terms of a defused aggressive instinct, a descriptive and explanatory vagueness remains regarding the distinctions between resistance, the negative therapeutic reaction, and stalemate. A preliminary remedy to this state of affairs must establish, it seems to me, some descriptive criteria that may serve to distinguish these different clinical events. It is to this task that I now turn.

Following Brenner (cf. Panel, 1970, p. 661), I subscribe to the original Freudian descriptive constraints that would restrict the status of the negative therapeutic reaction to a specific and implicitly time-delimited response to interpretation; conversely, I assign a negative attitudinal reaction to the analytic procedure to some condition of stalemate, especially if such a reaction constitutes a sustained disruption of the analytic process that affects outcome and transcends a simple untoward reception of an interpretation or series of interpretations dealing with a particular conflictual issue. Lacking the relatively precise definitional criterion by which we identify a negative therapeutic reaction, therapeutic stalemate is associated with certain presumptive characteristics. I say presumptive because many of the features I describe here may initially herald a negative therapeutic reaction or a severe, but tractable, mode of resistance. In general, however, a condition of stalemate tends to be a much more insidious affair that is often recognized only retrospectively. The first portent of stalemate may be the analysand's initial failure to engage the therapeutic process affectively. Alternatively, stalemate may be heralded by the analysand's gradual and insidious withdrawal of affective investment from the process once engaged, what I like to refer to as the devitalization of the analytic compact and situation. Before diagnosis of a stalemate is established, the analyst must evaluate the status of the analysand's resistances, given that very intense resistances and stalemate are easily mistaken for one another. Resistance, even powerful and pervasive resistance, is part of the fabric of the therapeutic process. As such it, like transference (Freud, 1914, p. 2) is amenable to the employment of the psychoanalytic method. Unlike powerful resistance, which, if tractable, inevitably gives way to interpretation, even if at a frustratingly imperceptible pace, true stalemate is frequently overcome only by "parameters" (Eissler, 1953), including consultation or transfer.

Descriptively, a stalemated analysis is betrayed not only by the lack of vitality that betokens the analysand's (and analyst's) withdrawal from the process, but through other presumptive signs as well. In particular, the therapeutic structure becomes a target for the analysand's unremitting disenchantment, with persistent tardiness or absences that remain inaccessible to salubrious intervention. To be sure, it is often this inaccessibility to intervention and the analyst's response to his own impotence that provides the clue. Conversely, stalemate occasionally assumes the guise of a slavish devotion to attendance, easily confused with the obsessional ritualization of the process as a part of the resistance, which has the analysand, as part of a parody of treatment, likewise identifying with a ritualized schedule rather than with the objectives of the therapeutic process. The distinction to be made in such a circumstance is derived from an assessment of the analysand's engagement in the process, a telltale sign of which is his invariant attempts to recruit the analyst into his obsessional schemes and enactments in the case of resistance. Such an attempt at conscription of the analyst does not, in my experience, occur in stalemate; the behavior merely takes on, in epicyclic fashion, a life of its own.

Along with the analysand's (and sometimes the analyst's) affective disengagement, we note the immutability of the analysand's resistances and defensive organization. With the enshrinement of his "personal myth" (Kris, 1956), there is a cessation of the usually paced ebb and flow that typifies the recurrent sequence of engagement, revelation, and resolution in the therapeutic process. Discourse becomes an endless and circular series of emotionally arid monologues that are meant to distance and obscure. The entire process is intellectualized, and an intractable recycling of old issues, interpretations, and "insights" substitutes for the engagement of new issues and developmental crises. Alternately, the analysand lapses into progressively longer periods of silence, which places him beyond the perimeter of the analyst's technical competence. Not infrequently the analysand regresses to a fixed state of hostile dependency, challenging the analyst's competence and good will by evincing a defensive demandingness that preempts further engagement. Using depressive affect as a weapon for purposes of vengeful distancing, the analysand oscillates between unremitting recriminations about the process and a general state of lethargy; the result is termination, consultation, or transfer to another analyst.

The genre of therapeutic stalemate illustrated in the following paragraphs evinced some of the foregoing descriptive and motivational characteristics. At the same time, my clinical narrative points to the fact that certain types of stalemate cannot be adequately delineated if we restrict ourselves to issues of description and a circumscribed vision of motivation. As useful as they are in accounting for certain aspects of these untoward events in treatment, issues of guilt, aggression, and masochism, collectively exemplifying superego influence, are not always sufficiently explanatory if they are not reconciled with other dimensions of the therapeutic process and clinical theory. The same can be said of the countertransference, which, in the realm of negative reactions and therapeutic stalemate, may be not only a primary etiologic agent but, alternately, a secondary response to dispiriting developments. Both sets of factors, to be sure, must always be considered in the estimation of a stalemate; it goes without saying that the analyst's limitations, especially as they impair effective resonance with the analysand, may be just as decisive a determinant of stalemate as analysand limitations that abort an unfolding analytic process.

A qualification is in order here that will help to place in sharp relief the central issue that I believe is involved in many, though assuredly not all, instances of stalemate. Specifically, I refer to my analytic experience that suggests a uniformly pessimistic outlook on the part of the analyst to be unwarranted. Some genuine conditions of stalemate that are not severe but are imperceptibly tractable resistances have demonstrated congenial outcomes on occasion. The ingredients in those stalemated analyses that have had a more favorable outcome were twofold: (1) an early recognition on the part of the analyst of a condition of stalemate before the underlying credibility of the analysis became irreparably damaged and an acceptance by the analyst of the analysand's negative perception of the process as both psychologically and realistically valid, and (2) the presence of a minimal amount of good will on the part of the analysand that could be mobilized to counter the narcissistic resistances containing the paranoidal anxieties evoked by the therapeutic collaboration. In both cases the basis for the requisite resonance lies in the deceptively simply nostrum implied in Freud's (1912) positive transference. While further discourse on the matter of tractable conditions of stalemate must await another occasion, the subject does highlight the centrality of the fate of the transference, "the hardest part of the analysis" (Bird, 1972), in the outcome of a stalemated treatment.

In the narrative to follow, stalemate proceeded from the analysand's failure to shift from the "defense transference" (Fenichel, 1945, p. 524) to the transference neurosis proper (Freud, 1914, 1920). And this failure, in turn, was the legacy of a successful childhood defense through which the analysand coped, more or less adaptively, with the unremitting traumatization of her early family milieu. Carried forward into adulthood, her solution became an aspect of her "personal myth" (Kris, 1956), which gained expression in both her character and her resistance (Boesky, 1983a). Carried into the analytic situation, this personal myth, which was tantamount to a mode of "being-in-the-world," prevented the analysand from libidinizing the therapeutic process to a degree that would have permitted the engaging and sustaining of the transference neurosis. The transference neurosis, which, following Freud (e.g., 1914, 1916–17, 1920) and Bird (1972), I differentiate from transference as manifestation, is the sine qua non of an analytic process: it is that uniquely regressive, restorative, and recreative (Loewald, 1971) reaction to the application of the psychoanalytic method that makes successful analysis possible.

The difference between transference as manifestation and transference neurosis both parallels and relies on the difference between an external object and an internal object. Following Boesky's (1983b) distinction between object representation as subjective experience and as an internalized psychic structure, I differentiate between external and internal objects as follows: An external object is an experiential content of the ego lodged primarily in the preconscious. It is essentially a phenomenal entity. An internal object, on the other hand, is a part of psychic structure intimately associated with components of the superego; we may conceptualize it as occupying the border between clinical theory and metatheory. It is essentially an inference, a mental construct not directly experienced. Lacking the specifically archaic and recreative character of the transference neurosis, transference as manifestation represents a combination of the external world (as mediated through perception) and actual characteristics of the external object, to which unconscious determinants can also be imputed by way of attaching further latent meaning to the experience. In short, we may say that transference as manifestation is a repetitive and idiosyncratic reaction to the external object to whose internalized structures access is sharply limited by virtue of its nature as an experience as well as by the conditions of representability (e.g., Freud, 1900, p.) that govern its sensate expression. The transference neurosis, by contrast, takes its specific character from the analysand's internal object, the principal referent of which is an unconscious fantasy derived from the complex interplay of such inferred structures as instinct, ego, and archaic imago. It is the yield of this interplay that is internalized as a superego structure (Freud, 1923) and that provides the basis for the specific configuration of the transference neurosis.

In the clinical narrative to follow, the analysand had abundant transference manifestations, largely in the guise of her defense transference, that is, the therapeutic enactment of her personal myth. But she could not engage a transference neurosis proper, for the latter pointed to a threatening regression from which there would be no return. Understood thusly, her intractable resistance derived in large measure from the familiar need for mastery (Freud, 1920, 1926), which, for analysands who exist in a chronic state of apprehended trauma, is forever challenged by the proffered intimacy and assistance of the analytic situation.

A Clinical Illustration

The patient, a 39-year-old attorney, presented herself at the initial consultation in a dysarthric, ataxic, and moderately intoxicated state. She immediately acknowledged having ingested 1200 mg of sodium amobarbital that day, a predilection that had become increasingly severe in the past year. She now believed her addiction to be uncontrollable, and she feared for her safety. Despite signs of intoxication, the patient managed to provide me with a coherent narrative of her present difficulties as well as the history of her previous treatment.

Her life was now in crisis, she averred, with her professional career in particular in a shambles. Lacking friends, she found herself progressively isolated and in a state of profound despair that included suicidal ruminations. Relying on drugs instead of people, she said, had characterized her entire adulthood; it was only in the present, however, without a group through which to feel connected, that she was confronted with the enormity of her evasion and the illusoriness of her solutions to life issues. Two events, she thought, might have exacerbated her downhill course. The first was a gynecological procedure she had undergone some 15 months previously for a suspected Stein-Leventhal syndrome, an intervention that evoked certain reflections on the emptiness of her life in addition to the age-related ebbing of her generativity. Seven months previously she had been dismissed from her position at a prominent law firm following a confrontation with the managing partner, whom she described as an autocratic and sadistic bully.

Of her psychological treatment, she said she had had some psychotherapy during law school that stabilized her as she prepared to establish herself in the professional world. Upon relocation a decade ago she began analysis but abandoned this enterprise some 18 months before seeking treatment with me, declaring her analyst bankrupt of insight and inspiration. A subsequent psychotherapy with an analyst she liked had also failed because of his insistence that she renounce drugs or be hospitalized. At this point she quickly reminded me that there was no law against addiction that could force her hospitalization; she also disavowed any suicidal preoccupation should I attempt to use that disclosure as a basis for her involuntary admission. To her, hospital admission represented psychological catastrophe from which she would never recover. On the other hand, if I were willing to treat her within these contraints and in ignorance of what she expected from treatment, she would be inclined to return for another interview. I silently marveled at the imperious dignity of this bright woman who dictated these terms of my engagement in her treatment. Without any further data and intrigued by a defiance that spoke of tenacity and smoldering vitality, I agreed to see this soft-spoken "iron lady" again, never specifying any condition. In so doing, and without an attitude of masochistic resignation, I may have communicated to her a sense of helplessness over the clinical situation she presented that was similar to the helplessness she felt with respect both to her life and her psychology—yet I, like her, seemed willing to persist despite this feeling.

Arriving on time the next day—and I thought, perhaps wishfully, in a state of milder intoxication—true to her bargain, she forthrightly began a narrative of her background. She was the second of four children whose immigrant European parents had somehow lost their way after a successful intergenerational leap into a professional middle-class milieu. The father's initial success in law proved ephemeral, since his fate neurosis conspired to thwart his original promise. Rejecting many promising opportunities, he settled into what the patient called a dispiriting practice responding to the banalities of the uninformed, lower middle-class bourgeoisie. Coincident with this retreat, the father sought solace in alcohol at night, an addiction that became steadily worse and whose complications eventually killed him. With four children arriving in rapid succession, his shrewd yet infantile wife resented his withdrawal, seeing her only avenue to a fulfilling life gradually evaporate. In her primitive despondency, the mother became more querulous, provoking arguments with the father as the only way of making contact with him. By the time the patient was six years old, the parental discord had reached daily proportions, with the mother trading allegations of infidelity for her husband's physical abuse. By the time the patient was ten, the infidelities were no longer a fiction but a regular occurrence as the father absented himself continually from the home. She actually was aware at this time of the father's philandering. A particularly telling moment in early adolescence had the patient looking out a shop window near her father's office one day and seeing him in late afternoon with a rosy glow on his face, as she described it, obviously after seeing his paramour. The patient's rage, one might think, was due to the father's so unhesitatingly allowing himself this caprice; in point of fact, the rage was a response not to oedipal stirrings but to the care of a mother who was becoming increasingly mentally disabled and who had been made the patient's de facto burden. In other words, I took her rage to signify a partial but disavowed identification with this irresponsible father. Here she was, left with the burden of the mother by a father who had no compunction about shirking all family responsibility.

But her burden, she recounted, had begun long before adolescence. She recalled a particularly harrowing epidode as a prepubescent girl when the mother guided the four children to the river that coursed through the center of the city. Coming to the bridge, the mother began removing her own clothes in preparation for jumping into the ice-covered water below. The cries of the children attracted passersby, who restrained the mother and called the authorities. The recollection of such exhibitions, as I suspected, served the function of screen memories that concealed the hostile depression and psychotic excesses of earlier years through which the mother exacted vengeance for the way her life had turned out.

As this story of pathos and chaos unfolded, the personalities of the parental imagos became more discernible. The father, an only son of an immigrant family, had been spared the vagaries of life by a doting mother, who vicariously saw her life fulfilled by his achievements. The paternal grandfather, an honest but unimaginative man, could not be relied on to yield the satisfactions his wife felt to be her due. Not being able to call his life his own, the patient's father proceeded to build a life wherein initial and partial success gave way to failure and disappointment, particularly where women were concerned. Being quite intelligent, he was able to accomplish a great deal with little effort. However, having never been encouraged to engage in life's struggles and possessing the sense of entitlement conferred on him by his mother, he evaded every appropriate life crisis. As the children grew older, he turned to them for support and at times even guidance. From adolescence the patient worked in his office, trying to keep him out of difficulty, which included liaisons with female clients, as best she could. The patient's mother, on the other hand, saw in her marriage to an aspiring young attorney an opportunity to improve dramatically on the humble circumstances into which she had been born. The mother's personality, however, had a particularly vicious side to it that not only perpetrated horrors like the bridge incident but had her use her affective states as weapons with which to romp destructively through her children's psyches. The eldest child, a son, somehow escaped psychologically although, taking a leaf out of the father's book, he too abandoned his family in early middle life.

In the first seven months of treatment, as the status of both her family and treatment emerged, the patient gradually appeared less toxic. By the seventh month, she announced one day that she had withdrawn herself completely from barbiturates, albeit without renouncing her right to resort to them again if she wished. During this opening phase of treatment, when the patient wanted nothing from me other than emotional congruence, I was forced into an analytic, as opposed to an actively psychotherapeutic, stance, whether I wanted to assume it or not. During this period of time my interventions, or so I thought, were very modest; I confined myself to clarifications (Stone, 1984) that attested to my appreciation of the patient's isolation, helplessness, and despair. Her isolation, I felt, was linked to her narcissistic vulnerability, a phenomenon, given its significant defensive function, I treated with considerable caution in my interventions. I attempted to establish an emotional resonance that would support the analytic task. I hoped that such congruence would leave her with the sense that she was not alone in her misery. Typical of my interventions during this period of treatment was a comment in response to her observations that the aging clientele she had taken with her on her departure from the firm had apparently not noticed her diminished vigor and ability, or, having noticed it, had said nothing lest they offend her. I remarked that in telling me about these helpless clients she was telling me something about herself, namely, her own experience of being without hope, helpless, and limited to what she could obtain from this therapeutic situation. I was cast, I averred, in the role of the devalued counterpart, a counterpart who, in being perceived by her as being devalued, tended to reduce the disparity she felt existed between the two of us. Such clarifications, with their unstated genetic implications, she accepted without comment. Other interventions, seemingly more benign in appealing to her aspirations, produced violent upheavals, often leading temporarily to renewed addictive behavior. Remaining uncertain about their genetic basis at the time, I classified such events as negative therapeutic reactions. For example, after many sessions, indeed many months, of hearing her talk about her lost opportunities to have a baby, a preoccupation that typically did not include any mention of a man, I suggested to her that she was communicating to me her despair at ever being able to create a new life for herself. To be sure, I saw her as a depressed, overburdened child, with her preoccupations about a baby representing both the latent, deeply buried hope for a new beginning as well as the means for vicariously experiencing a childhood she never had. I also told her that such despair enabled her to evade any hopefulness that her life could be any different. It was this type of intervention, an interpretation rather than a clarification, that usually produced a negative therapeutic reaction. However, without knowing the full significance that my comments on this matter had for her, I then postulated that such negative reactions had less to do with guilt than with the destabilizing disruption of her psychological balance that followed the emotional disjunction created by these interventions. As we concluded what I retrospectively saw as the opening phase, the patient's depression began to emerge; seldom did a session go by without a stream of tears accompanying her narrative, usually about a baby. Concurrently, she spontaneously began to use the couch.

A much more dramatic reaction to my interpretative interventions occurred nearly a year and a half later. After spending months talking to me about her lost opportunity with a man named Joseph, a narrative that chronicled every detail of the only sustained relationship outside the family she had ever experienced, she reintroduced the theme of her overburdened childhood. Specifically, she complained anew of her father's delinquencies, which often left her saddled with both the mother and the father's own maudlin tale of misfortune, which was somehow supposed to justify his behavior. She described the diligence with which she attended the organization of his office during high school and college, often working for him without compensation and at the expense of extracurricular activities that would have given her some life outside the family. An intercurrent event evoked further memories of her mother's coercive, cacophonous, and intrusive behavior. One day she reported a family event attended by her mother and siblings. The mother, apparently feeling neglected, proceeded to trip over a scatter rug, falling to the floor with considerable noise and drama. The brother, correctly estimating the mother's motives (she had not been paid enough attention), was provoked into an outburst that culminated in a fierce, sadomasochistic exchange with the mother bordering on physical violence.

While recounting these events the next day, she produced a photograph taken of the mother and three of her four children. I confess I have never seen such a sourpuss; I could not imagine anything but imprecations and fulminations emanating from that embittered facies. It certainly clarified my own assessment of the patient's identifications, for she too had a pained, forbidding scowl for anyone who would dare attempt to engage her. By way of contrast, on two occasions in the entire eight years of our collaboration, I briefly noted a smile that betrayed a warmth and sensuality that I could never mobilize in a transference. There was just no manifest libido.

As this event with her mother passed without further comment, the patient resumed her litany of complaints about her persecutors, both past and present. As I continued listening, however, I thought I detected the first stirrings of a transference neurosis among these remonstrations; I began to plot an interpretative strategy wherein I could prepare the patient for an intervention that would show her that I too, like the parental imago before me, had placed a burden on her in this analysis. The aims of this strategy I saw as the following: to deal with her avoidance of the inner needs contained in her memories, needs that often were threatened with revival by object contact; to reach the child in her and set her ontogenetic program in motion again by bringing her needs for response and nurturance into the analysis once again by means of the transference; to have the experience of the analysis and the understanding analyst provide a sense of nurturance in order to launch a process of mourning; and to offer a way to heal the narcissistic wounding that had simultaneously contributed to both her depression and her defensive organization.

I chose a moment wherein I not only offered a comment about her repetitive pursuit of burdensome experience but included as well the suggestion that she needed to experience the analysis as burdensome rather than potentially liberating, that this was a means of maintaining her attachment to old ghosts as testimony to her entitlement to feel loved by her father. I deliberately chose the father because of the material presented to me by the patient; I also felt that inferring an attachment to an archaic maternal imago would have been premature, lacking in resonance, and even dangerous by virtue of the further regression it might provoke. Nevertheless, this intervention seemed to hit a nerve as none had before. What I had unfortunately exposed without adequate preparation was the personal myth (Kris, 1956) that had partially nourished this empty woman for many years and had made it possible for her to stay alive.[1] The next day she arrived for her 9 AM hour dressed in an expensive, décolleté, black cocktail dress and a diamond necklace and diamond earrings. She remained mute on the couch, with her hands folded just above her abdomen. After ten minutes of silence, I intervened with a rhetorical question, since the significance of her enactment seemed obvious to me: "When do you plan to kill yourself?" My recognition of her enactment of how she would look in her coffin broke the ice. I requested that she sit up so that we could discuss the matter more completely. What emerged for a brief time, and then never again, was her pathetic belief that her only worth lay in being useful to someone else. By commenting on her motivations for experiencing the world in such a burdensome way, I had undermined the last shred of purpose that she felt for living. To experience any pleasure or joy in one's accomplishments was totally irrelevant for her.

After this disquieting epidode, which proceeded without further turbulence, the patient settled very gradually into an inaccessible state. To be sure, the complaints and the tears, as well as my interpretations of her resistances, resurfaced, but largely as a weary, passionless exercise with little to commend it. The dramatic event that preceded this gradually developing stalemate was inaccessible to analytic scrutiny; the lesson of the analysis to date, namely, that issues could be dealt with only to the extent that the patient elected to put them on the table, precluded a forced inquiry into the event. Another year and a half would pass before I declared the analysis stalemated and deemed a consultation in order. During this time, changes did occur both in the patient's observable behavior and in my own reflections on the progress of the analysis.

---

[1]I had been reading at the time a recent paper by Valenstein (1973), who discussed the propensity of certain patients to remain attached to painful affects.

The patient, to be sure, did not cease her interminable complaints; nor did my interpretations, that the form of her discourse as opposed to any specific content seemed to suggest a way of dealing with her inner and outer world, achieve any success. My own reflections naturally made me wonder about my conduct of the treatment. In particular, I wondered about my possible failure to interpret specific narcissistic resistances, an issue to which Abraham (1919) called attention long ago. I did not communicate to the patient, probably because of narcissistic sensibilities evoked by the patient, my own sense of helplessness over the psychological gridlock she had created. I did wonder if I had sufficiently addressed the meaning of treatment to her, her thoughts about whose success a successful treatment would be, and her fantasies about my need to help or "cure her." Rather than belabor this manifestation of my countertransferential response to her, I suggested a consultation as a potential means of breaking the impasse. Surprisingly, she accepted with little hesitation; she did reveal her motivation after the consultation took place, to wit, the old resistance of seeing other people as impotent and lacking efficacy. In this instance, the exposure of my limitations to another analyst served to justify the patient in her logical system organized around "an illusion of self-sufficiency" (Modell, 1976). As it turned out, the consultant merely commiserated with me, adding that the patient was still alive. While not being optimistic about a traditional outcome, he suggested that a stable stalemate in her case might be an acceptable conclusion to the venture.

In the next year another fortuitous event took place. Encountering an old acquaintance and colleague on the street one day, the patient was informed of a newly created position at another law firm that might make use of her skills and special interests. Perhaps the analytic work had tamed her narcissistic and aggressive proclivities to a certain extent, for she did pursue the matter. Her application was accepted with the stipulation that she formalize her expertise with the academic credential she had failed to obtain a number of years previously. Until she acquired this credential—and she was given two years to do so—she would be on probation. I was surprised when she announced her intention of pursuing both the position and the credential, since she had long reveled in her reputation of being "difficult." As she liked to put it, "Nobody tells Miss A what to do." During this period, which turned out to be the denouement of the analysis, her professional activities increased, and her isolation diminished proportionally. The narcissistic rewards she obtained from her job and the revival of her practice had a reciprocal effect on her productivity. She dressed more brightly, although she had always, even in her darkest moments, been very stylishly attired. Without ever acknowledging it, her need for me became progressively less intense until one day she declared that our venture would conclude at the end of the month.

I heard nothing from her subsequent to the treatment. I met a colleague some six years later who told me that two years after terminating with me the patient had resumed psychotherapy on a twice-weekly basis for a year and a half, the only appreciable gain from which, he felt, was that she had begun "to tolerate fools a little more gladly."

Some Reflections

In the first instance, of course, is the obvious matter of analyzability and the extensive use of a parameter in the prolonged opening phase of the analysis resulting from my decision to acquiesce in the patient's tacit demands that I clarify rather than interpret for prolonged periods, a posture that allowed her resistances to go largely unchallenged. A corollary to these matters is the nature of the treatment: Was this a psychoanalytic psychotherapy that allowed a less hazardous maladaptive response to existential exigencies to be substituted for a more hazardous and imminently self-destructive one? My answer, of course, is that my initiative was an attempt to apply the analytic method, with all the causal properties inhering in the acts of psychoanalytic observation, free association, and evenly suspended attention. That the patient, as part of her resistances, did not permit the full elaboration of method, which would have included interpretation especially of the transference neurosis, does not disqualify my initiative as an analyst. Rather, the treatment was a genuine attempt at analysis, albeit one that succeeded only in keeping a self-destructive patient alive; by conventional therapeutic criteria, it must be adjudged a failed analysis. Consonant with the verdict that my effort was analytic is my belief that the psychoanalytic method does not and should not entail a result or even a specific clinical course; it stands independent of the consequences of its application and utilization.

Another important consideration in this report of a stalemated treatment is the role of countertransference. I do not dismiss the possibility that an unrecognized countertransference to the analysand and her transference manifestations may have operated from the outset; nor do I believe that such a countertransference could be reduced quite simply to my concerns for the survival of this precariously balanced woman. I could, for example, postulate certain reaction formations on my part that attenuated my assertive engagement of her arrogantly manifested resistances. But this retrospective estimation, however plausible, must remain speculative, since to this day I can only recall my preoccupations with keeping her alive. Any latent displeasure or narcissistic rage on my part would have been threatening to me, given this patient's very real and ever-present self-destructive threats.

Focusing on the descriptive aspects of this treatment, we may first of all address the question of diagnosis, even though nosological considerations are often inadequate to the task of determining the nature of the patient's dynamic issues, therapeutic requirements, and even prognosis. There is enough presumptive evidence to label this woman a depressed hysteric whose character structure represents the maladaptive outcome of a tension that exists between her contradictory identifications, namely, the clearly inadequate "second chance" offered by her irresponsibile, self-indulgent, yet partially successful, professional father on the one hand and her negative identification with a repudiated sense of femininity derived from her perception of an extremely hostile, destructive, and disillusioning maternal imago. This oedipal tension, it may be argued, was merely a cover for more profound fixations that involved issues of self-esteem and nurturance, issues that always threatened a regressive state of helplessness and passive engulfment in uncongenial affective experience. The patient's omnipotent defensive organization could be understood as a conflict between her ego ideal on one hand and her regressive libidinal desires on the other, that is, her desire and need for a nurturing experience and responsive object.

Proceeding further with descriptive considerations, we must note the two kinds of negative reactions that occurred in the treatment. Sharing the spotlight with the condition of stalemate that eventually became entrenched in the process and around which the analysand paradoxically organized and stabilized herself were a number of circumscribed negative reactions that fulfill the narrow criteria of a negative therapeutic reaction. Consider the dramatic episode in which the patient enacted her own wake; this event surely qualifies as a specific untoward reaction proceeding from my attempt at a mutative interpretation of the narcissistic motive behind her masochistic resistance. Can we say, though, that other aspects of the traditional definition of the negative therapeutic reaction obtain here, namely, an unconscious sense of guilt derived from the vagaries of the oedipal drama? Further, can we state that the oedipal configuration is mainly the vehicle for narcissistic issues that derive primarily from the ego ideal and determine the analysand's internal balance? To the first question, I would answer that undoubtedly oedipal factors, including unconscious guilt, played a part in the clinical picture; however, the major threat was the loss of a narcissistically prized object, that is, the loss of a much-needed external object that was a source of psychological nourishment in her masochistic fantasy, the loss of an object that protected her from regression and all its proclivities, anxieties, and conflicts. To be sure, one can argue that the patient was enacting structural conflicts involving the ego ideal and its anthropomorphized target, the ego/self. But compelling evidence for such an assertion is lacking because of the obfuscations created by the analysand's pervasive and immutable resistances. Given that these resistances were grounded in a fear of passivity and helplessness, I believe we must conclude that she was dealing with the threatened emergence of more primitive issues of a basically regulatory nature, issues that threatened to overwhelm her and induce a traumatic state. In sum, then, the brief manifestations of a negative therapeutic reaction that occurred when the analysand yielded in her otherwise intractable resistances of omnipotence suggest the presence of some relatively superficial structural conflicts; the engagement of those structural conflicts, on the other hand, seemed to evoke such depressive anxiety and an apprehended state of being overwhelmed with her memories and archaic needs that she was unable to take the additional and formally regressive initiative of locating these feelings in a transference neurosis. What she intuitively anticipated, I believe, was not the engagement of a transference neurosis but the experience of a transference neurosis from which she could not recover (cf. Kohut, 1977, p. 24). As a consequence, her initial attempt at engagement rapidly gave way to the reemergence of a familiar defensive posture in the form of the personal myth that had served as the basis for a ubiquitous defense transference. As her father had needed her, so, in her mind, I needed her as my patient, that is, as the one who validated my clinical competence and professional self-worth. Mine was the neediness; hers the burdensome responsibility of caring for others. On descriptive grounds alone we may argue that the aborted progression of the analysis from defense transference to the stage of the transference neurosis proceeded from a psychologically induced inability to sustain a process that would cause the unremitting trauma and reaction to unmet need to recur without any hope that things would now be different. Quite simply, either she had lost the ability to mourn, or her losses exceeded her capacity to mourn them. The inability to invest in the therapeutic process and the person of the analyst also reflected this inability to mourn. Unable to mourn, she could not hope, either for herself or the outcome of the process. Just to hope would induce a state of profound regression and mourning. Stalemate and an incomplete analysis were her only psychological options.

Proceeding from the purely phenomenological ground to more dynamic considerations, let us carry our inferences about this material further. Her behavior toward me did have the quality of a relationship. But, like all her other relationships, it had a constraint built into it that prevented her from mobilizing a sense of confidence that she could rely on another person to help her deal with her psychological needs and developmental imperatives. We may say that she did make use of me, albeit in a circumspect and distancing manner. Any attempt on my part to interpret the nature and motive of her masochistic resistance was ignored or denigrated, save for one instance in which she underwent the alarming regression. To be sure, she weaned herself from drugs and even remained alive as she reflected on the very painful lessons of a misspent youth. Yet, at the moment of truth, when the therapeutic process invited her to embark upon a regressive odyssey that would engage her deeper psychological structures, she could not adequately invest in the analyst without concomitantly rendering herself extremely vulnerable to the affective legacy of her chaotic upbringing. Not being able to hope without suffering an overwhelming negative backlash as a consequence of her deprivation and disillusionment, she could hardly engage a transference neurosis that left her vulnerable to an internal object that either threatened to destroy her or that she needed to destroy in order to survive.

It was this interplay between external and internal objects that I believe determined the fate of the transference and ultimately that of the analysis as well. When we talk of these objects, as I indicated earlier, we are specifying two different categories of conceptualization and two different inferences to be applied to the analysand's report. In this treatment the analysis proceeded largely on the basis of her very qualified attachment to me as an external object, the consciously remembered paternal imago, whose only task was to approve her masochistic enactments and not challenge her customary ways of dealing with her inner and outer worlds. I was the substitute for the addicting substance that provided her with some relief from her inner torments, especially those that derived from aloneness and loneliness. When I became anything more than a basis for transference manifestations and threatened to become the piece of psychic structure that contained the representations of the internal object, that is, the maternal imago, with all the threats of psychological annihilation that went along with such an eventuality, severe turbulence ensued. Here we may recall Asch's (1976) expanded definition of the negative therapeutic reaction that ultimately implicated the affective concomitants of separation issues in the genesis of the negative therapeutic reaction. While appreciative of the applicability of Asch's perspective to my experience, I find it difficult to treat the phenomena I encountered in just this conceptual manner. I tend to agree with the psychoanalytic opinion that would see the Mahlerian perspective in social rather than depth-psychological forms. Focusing on the transactions that obtain in a two-body system (cf. Balint, 1950), Asch's Mahlerian vision of individuation does not, in my view, accommodate such notions as the internal object and the transference neurosis; nor does it accommodate the structural interplay between the object referents of the superego and the ego/self. And it is just these internal representations that are crucial referents for an understanding of the pregenital caste of the transference neurosis, an understanding in which the interplay can be reformulated in terms of the primitive transactions that object between internal object and ego/self, where the internal object has achieved the status of a not yet completely internalized introject (cf. Meissner, 1981). I will not address the relation between the ego/self and the structural ego here (cf. Spruiell, 1981).

In this analysis, which I view as a qualified social success and an analytic failure, we can see the ability of the analysand to use the analyst within the constraints of her maladaptive capabilities. What emerged as a successful childhood solution to unbearable trauma, disillusionment, and despair proved to be an inappropriate and inadequate set of measures for coping with adult imperatives. One might say that the patient brought her defense transferences into the analysis but could not use them to establish a libidinal investment in either the process or the analyst to the degree required for the engagement of the next stage of the endeavor, namely, the establishment of the transference neurosis. In looking at the material in this fashion, I have used the condition of stalemate not only as a point of differentiation from the negative therapeutic reaction, but as the heuristic basis for an inquiry into other distinctions involving our conceptualizations of transference and the intrapsychic functions of external and internal objects alike.

REFERENCES

Abraham, K. (1919), A particular form of neurotic resistance against the psycho-analytic method. In: *Selected Papers of Karl Abraham.* London: Hogarth Press, 1927, pp. 303–311.

Asch, S. (1976), Varieties of negative therapeutic reaction and problems of technique. *J. Amer. Psychoanal. Assn.,* 24:383–407.

Balint, M. (1950), Early developmental states of the ego: Primary object love. *Internat. J. Psycho-Anal.,* 30:265–281.

Bion, W.R. (1962), A theory of thinking. *Internat. J. Psycho-Anal.,* 43:306.

Bird, B. (1972), Notes on transference: Universal phenomenon and hardest part of analysis. *J. Amer. Psychoanal. Assn.,* 34:275–288.

Boesky, D. (1983a), Resistance and character theory: A reconsideration of the concept of character resistance. *J. Amer. Psychoanal. Assn.,* 31s:227–246.

——— (1983b), The problem of mental representation in self and object theory. *Psychoanal. Quart.*, 52:564–583.

Brenner, C. (1959), The masochistic character: Genesis and treatment. *J. Amer. Psychoanal. Assn.*, 7:197–226.

Eissler, K.R. (1953), The effect of the structures of the ego in psychoanalytic technique. *J. Amer. Psychoanal. Assn.*, 1:104–143.

Fenichel, O. (1945), *The Psychoanalytic Theory of Neurosis.* New York: Norton.

Fine, R. (1971), *The Healing of the Mind.* New York: David McKay.

Finell, J.S. (1987), A challenge to psychoanalysis: A review of the negative therapeutic reaction. *Psychoanal. Rev.*, 74(4).

Freud, A. (1952), A connection between the states of negativism and emotional surrender. *Internat. J. Psycho-Anal.*, 33:265.

Freud, S. (1900), The interpretation of dreams. *Standard Edition,* 4 & 5. London: Hogarth Press, 1953.

——— (1912), The dynamics of transference. *Standard Edition,* 12:97–108. London: Hogarth Press, 1958.

——— (1914), Remembering, repeating and working-through. *Standard Edition,* 12:145–156. London: Hogarth Press, 1958.

——— (1916–17), Introductory lectures on psycho-analysis. *Standard Edition,* 15 & 16. London: Hogarth Press, 1963.

——— (1918), From the history of an infantile neurosis. *Standard Edition,* 17:7–122. London: Hogarth Press, 1955.

——— (1920), Beyond the pleasure principle. *Standard Edition,* 18:7–64. London: Hogarth Press, 1955.

——— (1923), the ego and the id. *Standard Edition,* 19:12–59. London: Hogarth Press, 1961.

——— (1924), The economic problem of masochism. *Standard Edition,* 19:159–170. London: Hogarth Press, 1961.

——— (1926), Inhibitions, symptoms and anxiety. *Standard Edition,* 20:87–172. London: Hogarth Press, 1959.

——— (1937), Analysis terminable and interminable. *Standard Edition,* 23:216–253. London: Hogarth Press, 1964.

Glover, E. (1955), *The Technique of Psycho Analysis.* New York: International Universities Press.

Grunberger, B. (1971), *Narcissism.* New York: International Universities Press, 1979.

Guntrip, H. (1969), *Schizoid Phenomena, Object Relations and the Self.* New York: International Universities Press.

Horney, K. (1936), The problem of the negative therapeutic reaction. *Psychoanal. Quart.*, 5:29–44.

Kernberg, O. (1975), *Borderline Conditions and Pathological Narcissism.* New York: Aronson.

Klein, M. (1957), Envy and gratitude. In: *Envy and Gratitude and Other Works, 1946–1973.* London: Hogarth Press, 1975.

Kohut, H. (1977), *The Restoration of the Self.* New York: International Universities Press.

Kris, E. (1956), The personal myth. *J. Amer. Psychoanal. Assn.*, 4:653.

Lewin, B.D. (1950), *The Psychoanalysis of Elation.* New York: Norton.

Limentani, A. (1981), On some positive aspects of the negative therapeutic reaction. *Internat. J. Psycho-Anal.*, 62:379.

Loewald, H. (1972), Freud's conception of the negative therapeutic reaction, with comments on instinct theory. *J. Amer. Psychoanal. Assn.*, 20:235–245.

McDougall, J. (1980), *Plea for a Measure of Abnormality.* New York: International Universities Press.

Meissner, W.W. (1981), Internalization in psychoanalysis. *Psychological Issues, Monogr. 50.* New York: International Universities Press.
Modell, A.H. (1971), The origin of certain forms of pre-oedipal guilt and the implications for a psychoanalytic theory of affects. *Internat. J. Psycho-Anal.*, 52:337.
Nacht, S. (1957), Technical remarks on the handling of the transference neurosis. *Internat. J. Psycho-Anal.*, 38:196.
Novick, J. (1980), Negative therapeutic motivation and negative therapeutic alliance. *The Psychoanalytic Study of the Child,* 35:299–320. New Haven, CT: Yale University Press.
Olinick, S.L. (1964), The negative therapeutic reaction. *Internat. J. Psycho-Anal.*, 45:540.
Panel (1970), Negative therapeutic reaction, S.L. Olinick, reporter. *J. Amer. Psychoanal. Assn.*, 18:655–672.
Riviere, J. (1936), A contribution to the analysis of the negative therapeutic reaction. *Internat. J. Psycho-Anal.*, 17:304.
Robbins, M. (1988), The adaptive significance of destructiveness in primitive personalities. *J. Amer. Psychoanal. Assn.*, 36:627–652.
Rosenfeld,H. (1987), *Impasse and Interpretation,* ed. D. Tuckett. London: Tavistock.
Rothstein, A. (1984), Fear of humiliation. *J. Amer. Psychoanal. Assn.*, 32:99–116.
Spruiell, V. (1981), The self and the ego. *Psychoanal. Quart.*, 50:319–344.
Sterba, R. (1957), Oral invasion and self-defense. *Internat. J. Psycho-Anal.*, 38:204.
Stone, L. (1984), Notes on the noninterpretive elements in the psychoanalytic situation and process. In: *Transference and Its Context.* New York: Aronson.
Valenstein, A. (1973), On attachment to painful feelings and the negative therapeutic reaction. *The Psychoanalytic Study of the Child,* 28:365-392. New Haven, CT: Yale University Press.

A Few Comments on Psychoanalytic Stalemate

JEROME A. WINER

Dr. Maguire has tackled one of the most difficult topics in our clinical experience: transference stalemate. Specifically, he has selected to investigate the phenomenon in which the analysand fails to effect a transition from the defense transference to the transference neurosis proper. He believes this situation proceeds from the analysand's inability to abandon a successful childhood defense against unremitting traumatization—one that is often quite an appropriate adaptation during childhood. Mindful of the function of fantasy in development, he does not fall into the trap of accepting the analysand's narrative as historical truth. The stalemate proceeds from the analysand's inability to libidinize the therapeutic process sufficiently. To such patients the proffered intimacy of the situation means more opportunity for hurt. Consequently, no transference neurosis develops.

In his technique paper "On Beginning Treatment" Freud (1913), compared analysis to chess. There are standard openings and endgames, but the midphases are all different. I presume the term "stalemate" comes from the fact that it is one well-known type of ending. Dr. Maguire gives us an operational definition of stalemate that carefully differentiates it from a state of exceptionally intense resistance. In stalemate the therapeutic structure itself becomes a target, with the analysand's persistent tardiness or absence remaining inaccessible to intervention. Or, by contrast, ritualized attendance may occur, yet the analyst's presence as an interpretive catalyst is excluded. There is a cessation in the usual ebb and flow of analytic discourse; the analysand removes his affective presence. An intractable recycling of old issues substitutes for the engagement of new issues. The analysand engages in unremitting recriminations that alternate with a de-energized state. Silence can grow until it casts a pall of despair over both parties. Maguire does not forget the possible contribution of limitations of the analyst, but that is not the issue here. To Maguire, stalemate lies in the patient's pathology; it is like a chess game in which one player won't play. With intense resistance there is a game, but the analysand is a master opponent.

Recently Merton Gill shared a favorite joke of David Rapaport's. A Hungarian physics student came to his final exam, an exam that would consist of only one question. The frightened young man was asked, "What is kinetic energy?" Completely blank, the student importuned the examiner for another chance. Disregarding the rules, the examiner mercifully asked, "What is static energy?" After another significant mute period, the miserable student begged for yet another chance. Grimly the examiner replied, "Okay then. What is the difference between static and kinetic energy?" Gill used this joke to illustrate the weakness of discussions about the differences between psychoanalysis and psychotherapy when neither have been well defined.

Unlike the Hungarian physics student, Maguire also carefully distinguishes between stalemate and negative therapeutic reaction, which is intimately associated with the transference neurosis. In stalemate there is no transference neurosis; the analysand will not allow the activation of internal objects because of excessive childhood traumatization. Even when the analyst's technique is unimpeachable, the defense transference stands unbreachable and the patient remains unreachable.

Let us now turn to Dr. Maguire's clinical material. He reports on the treatment of a drug-abusing attorney who had eight years of previous analysis and years of other psychotherapy and who was left with a sense that the therapists had nothing to give her. Her father was alcoholic, abusive, and unfaithful, leaving the patient with the burden of care of a hostile and psychotically depressed mother. When Dr. Maguire maintained a stance of clarification, conveying that he knew what the patient was going through, things remained stable and she gave up barbiturates. Once he felt the first glimmering of a transference neurosis and interpreted the patient's need to experience the analysis as a burden, just as the relationship with her parents had been, she arrived for the next session in a black cocktail dress, dressed for her funeral. What emerged was her belief that her only value lay in her usefulness to someone else and that this had been challenged. Dr. Maguire feels that his intervention exposed the last shred of purpose she felt for living. The patient settled into an inaccessible state. After a year and a half he declared the treatment a stalemate and a consultation in order. He did not communicate to his patient explicitly his sense of helplessness. She accepted the consultation with little hesitation, largely motivated by the wish to reveal to the consulted analyst the inability of anyone to help her, thereby justifying her illusion of self-sufficiency. She stayed on for two more years and left after a job change, only to reenter psychotherapy with yet another analyst for very modest gain. Maguire believes that the patient knew she could not recover from a transference neurosis and that she employed her personal myth to reinforce the defense transference. She could neither mourn nor hope; stalemate was her only option. She could not activate internal objects that either threatened to destroy her or that she needed to destroy in order to survive. While Maguire remained an external object, the consciously remembered paternal imago, he remained the substitute for the addicting substance from which she was able to withdraw herself. When he threatened to become the piece of psychic structure that contained the representation of the internal object, severe turbulence ensued. Recall that Maguire defines the internal object in terms of the unconscious fantasy derived from the complex interplay of instinct, ego, and archaic imago—the same complex factors that govern the formation of the superego.

Dr. Maguire's attempt to apply the analytic method to patients who have no other hope is seen by many as an occurrence that will become far more common in the near future. Stalemates too will then become more common. We have become increasingly aware of stalemates that are caused by a real similarity between the analyst and the negative transference object; Maguire's case is not of that type.

Racker (1968) has discussed stalemates that are brought about by a complementary identification of the analyst with the internal archaic object of the patient and that go unrecognized. Here lies more fertile ground. Kenneth Newman (1988) elaborates on this concept and feels that "many patients develop a sense of experience near conviction of their inner world *only after* the stimulating effect of the analyst's countertransference enactments and selfobject failures" (p. 252). When the analyst's failures parallel those of the parents, the analytic process freezes. The analyst remains unusable unless he or she can not only recognize the pattern and interpret it, but also supply "a missing function for the patient, that of being an advocate for his needs and supporting the legitimacy of his affect states" (p. 264).

Dr. Maguire has presented his views largely in terms of a more traditional metapsychological understanding. I would like to hear more examples of his interventions and the patients' responses to them before the dramatic shift into stalemate. Could it be that his early stance was more definitive than he realized in that he was an advocate for her needs and supported the legitimacy of her affect states? In trying to establish and analyze a transference neurosis with such patients, are we setting up a situation in which the operation will be a success but the patient gets no better unless one systematically interprets countertransference enactments and selfobject failures? With stalemate, of course, such questions are easy to raise. Answers come more slowly.

I thank Dr. Maguire for extending our knowledge in one of the most troublesome areas of both our clinical work and theory by doing what we as psychoanalysts so infrequently do—present a case where our labor was great and the yield was meager.

REFERENCES

Freud, S. (1913), On beginning treatment. *Standard Edition,* 12:121–144. London: Hogarth Press, 1958.

Newman, K. (1988), Countertransference: Its role in facilitating the use of the object. *The Annual of Psychoanalysis,* 16:251–285. New York: International Universities Press.

Racker, H. (1968), *Transference and Countertransference.* New York: International Universities Press.

The Dream Screen Transference

DAVID R. EDELSTEIN

An unusual type of transference is based on the dream screen. This type of transference appears as a long-lived, durable intrapsychic mise-en-scène, analagous to a dream screen, upon which other transferences are visualized and experienced. The manifest content of the intrapsychic mise-en-scène is drawn from aspects of the analyst or his surround while the latent content is based on a soothing preoedipal relationship. After reviewing Lewin's ideas on dreaming and the dream screen, I will describe a clinical case that demonstrates this type of transference and will then discuss it from several theoretical perspectives.

Lewin (1955) compares the analytic session to the dream. The manifest dream content matches the session content, and the day residue corresponds to the preceding analytic session residue. In both, a latent content is to be deciphered. The good analytic session resembles the successfully interpreted dream, since in each the latent content surfaces in a discussible way. Both occur in a recumbent pose with limited attention to outside stimulation. One gauge of the depth of the analysand's regression is his closeness to a sleeping state. Lewin (1954) has suggested that a result, and possibly a motive, of interest in ego psychology has been to rouse the analysand, nipping off the more regressive and primary process mental life of sleep in favor of the more clearly ordered secondary process focus of the awakened analysand.

Lewin stresses the importance of the deeply regressive aspects of the dream and of the analytic session. He cites Freud's (1900) remark that dreaming is motivated by the wish to sleep as leading to Freud's (1915)

The author wishes to thank Drs. Robert Koff and Barbara Rocah for their helpful discussion of this material.

later formulations about the wish to regain a narcissistic state in sleep. Lewin emphasizes that sleep is a regressive return to narcissistic and oral gratification with the preoedipal parent and that this regressive state is characterized by hazy boundaries, affects difficult to describe, and a loss of the crisply defined sense of self in favor of the oceanic self experience.

As part of his interest in the deeply regressive aspects of sleep, Lewin elaborated the concept of the dream screen. He defines the dream screen as "the surface on to which a dream appears to be projected. It is the blank background, present in the dream though not necessarily seen, and the visually perceived action in ordinary manifest dream contents takes place on it or before it" (Lewin, 1946, p. 420). Lewin also notes that "in the practical business of dream interpretation, the analyst is not concerned with it" (p. 420). He sees the dream screen as representing the wish for the breast and for sleep, which is opposed by the push toward wakefulness by the dream's visual contents. Lewin sees the blank dream as a clinical example of the dream screen. The blank dream represents the infantile oral experience of satiation at the mother's breast followed by visually blank sleep. Lewin (1955) notes that "the analyst is not a unitary element that can be directly mapped to a unitary spot in the diagram of the psychic apparatus and into the psychology of sleep and the dream" (p. 192) and points out that the analyst or the analytic setting may represent more advanced analytic transferences as well as the blank dream background, the dream screen, onto which these more advanced analytic transferences are projected. The analyst can, in other words, appear in a dream as "a soothing atmosphere and the homologue of the breast or dream screen" (p. 196), as well as the symbolic representation of more advanced strivings.

In the case I will describe—Mrs. A—there was a viable and long-lived dream screen structure in the transference. She could use the analyst and his life setting like a long-term blank dream, a dream screen, on which to project a host of other transference fantasies. This intense transference experience permitted Mrs. A an extensive look into her unconscious functioning and was, like Lewin's dream screen, rooted in her preoedipal experience.

Case Description

Mrs. A came to analysis in her early 20s, complaining of chronic depression and self-doubt. She was a teacher of social sciences and had a special interest in nonverbal communication. This interest grew out of her natural capacity and orientation towards perception in a visual mode.

Mrs. A's family consisted of mother, father, and two older sisters. Father was verbally abusive to mother and was seductive with his daughters, often talking in detail of sexual matters and physically exposing himself through seeming inadvertence. Mother was chronically depressed with low energy and few interests. Mrs. A desperately attempted to nurture and enliven her mother.

Mrs. A was very close to a nanny, a woman of few words whose affection for Mrs. A came across in her caring gaze and who lived with the family until Mrs. A was 16. As an older child, Mrs. A tried consciously to make a visual memory recording of events in her life for later integration and in hopes of finding more meaning in her past experiences. At 16, after her nanny left, she had a brief period of anorexia. She recovered spontaneously, without treatment, but continued to have a persistent uncertainty about her body image. After high school, she successfully left home for a distant college, where she had sustaining relationships with female friends and an active social life. Mrs. A continued to have painful underlying self-doubt, focused internally now on her feelings and relationships and less on her body image. After college, she married a man whose level-headed practicality provided a method for managing self-doubts. Her dissatisfaction with this marital solution was a factor in her seeking analysis.

Early in the analysis, Mrs. A had many erotized dreams and daydreams about me. These erotized dreams initially dealt with the theme of my comforting Mrs. A for some loss or injury. For example, before we were due to miss a session because of a holiday, Mrs. A dreamed that she cried in a session and held out her hand to me and that I then sat on the couch next to her and kissed her. She associated to a visit by a friend who broke the rules of the friendship by complaining too much, as if Mrs. A were her psychiatrist. I interpreted that she felt anxious about the missed session, feared she would demand too much, and in her dream transformed this into breaking the rules by seducing me, with the hope that I would prefer her sexual offering. We understood that she dealt with her anxiety and her rage around separation by erotizing her feelings. Mrs. A continued to have erotized dreams and daydreams, and her transference shifted to her excitement and anxiety that I might be aroused by her seductiveness and might behave as a dominant and sexually intrusive man. We learned that she had often stepped in to shield mother from father's verbal abuse, with both the unconscious feeling of being victorious over mother in getting father's attention and the unconscious fear of being raped. This led her to a phallic counterattack against me, with angry depreciation of all men, and then later to longings for my protection in the mother transference. She wanted to view me as a close female friend who could share all her feelings. She elaborated more historical material about her mother, sisters, and aunts and became more open about her deeper maternal longings.

At this time, 15 months into the analysis, Mrs. A learned by chance that I lived three blocks from her home. Mrs. A then constructed, using the raw material drawn from her observations of the three-block area near our homes, a mise-en-scène, a stage setting, on which unfolded an array of transference fantasies. From this time, 15 months into the analysis, and to a gradually diminishing extent over about the next year and a half, she reported that, aside from her time at work, she spent most of her waking hours intensely imagining an array of fantasied interactions between us, enacted in her mind on this mise-en-scène. She walked past my home several times per week hoping for a view of my family. During these walks, she was almost in a fugue state, walking within a world of fantasy, only partially mindful of reality. These half-awake daydreams often flowed into her night dreams. My purpose is not to highlight any one specific transference fantasy but to underline Mrs. A's use of this mise-en-scène as a setting on which to project many intense transference fantasies.

For example, Mrs. A had strong sibling rivalry conflicts. She repeatedly visualized, in a way that was almost physically palpable to me, helplessly watching as I neglected my youngest child and favored the older children as we walked near our home. She was able to maintain a split while transference issues, such as being a valued child, envy, guilt at her longings, and rage at her own past experiences of neglect, were interpreted and discussed. The focus of her analytic work was centered around the visualized mise-en-scène. Another example of Mrs. A's extremely intense fantasizing, projected onto this mise-en-scène, was her imagining me having automobile trouble in front of her home, leading to a variety of interactions. The variations on this fantasy included themes of tenderness, sexual contact, and dominance. These fantasies engrossed Mrs. A for hours at a time and often blended into sleeping dreams at night. These prolonged fantasies flooded her mind; the mise-en-scène seemed to contain and organize this intensely affective experience.

As the analysis progressed over these one and a half years, new genetic material emerged about the nanny. Mrs. A described how she had felt soothed by her nanny, a reliable watchful presence, through difficulties with her mother and father. Also, she and her nanny often looked at things together, and she felt a deep sense of shared interest and mutual participation at those times. In a similar way, she felt an underlying sense of trust in me as she depicted the fantasies she imagined on the mise-en-scène. Over this year and a half, the exquisite focus on fantasied transference interactions on this stage-like setting gradually diminished. As the extremely intense visual mode of experiencing faded, she began to speak more directly about her feelings and her introspective efforts were now focused in the analytic room. The mise-en-scène gradually became less prominent in her associations. It was not mourned; it seemed it had served its purpose and could be discarded as no longer necessary.

Discussion

From a traditional psychoanalytic viewpoint, Mrs. A's intense fantasies about the analyst and his surround would be described as a transference neurosis. The interplay of wish and defense, as infantile conflicts are reexperienced with the analyst in the transference neurosis, can be seen in Mrs. A's intense fantasies on the mise-en-scène. For example, her focus on the visual interaction with me was a repetition of the erotic visual interaction with father. In this father transference Mrs. A sought gratification of regressive voyeuristic and exhibitionistic wishes while defensively making me an ever-present intrusive father to be avoided. She was able to express revenge on her intrusive father by watching me and by attempting to keep me wondering where she might pop up. Keeping the interaction in a visual mode on the mise-en-scène was a transference resistance to speaking directly about her feelings. Another aspect of her transference neurosis was her intense wish to gain maternal love and her guilt and anxiety about this wish. Her wish for maternal love was gratified because we were seen as always close together in the same area; at the same time her guilt was expressed in masochistic dramatizations in which I was in the warmth of my family while she was the excluded child out in the cold, three blocks away. Her rage at being excluded by her depressed mother was expressed in her hovering intrusiveness and yet defended by being kept secret. Another aspect of Mrs. A's transference neurosis was her wish to undo the traumatic experience of being out of control. In her fantasies on the mise-en-scène, she felt out of control and excluded while at the same time she could, in her fantasies, manipulate me at will. Playing out her fantasies on the mise-en-scène was also a resistance in that it gave her more control than she would have had by directly confronting them in the analytic room.

Mrs. A had a hysterical personality structure. Another, and broader, view of Mrs. A's fantasizing would be that it was an extensive daydream, consistent with a hysterical defensive retreat from true feelings to discharge in conscious and unconscious daydreams. Such daydreams are distorted renditions of the underlying conflicts, their distortion being the result of regression to earlier fixation points, of defensive pressures, and of the aim of achieving a substitute discharge. In this way, Mrs. A's fantasizing would be seen from a traditional analytic viewpoint as a defensive daydream guarding against a more direct awareness of her true feelings and allowing some discharge through distorted daydream fantasies. These fantasies could also be understood as related to infantile masturbation, making the mise-en-scène a vehicle for a masturbatory type of discharge.

From a traditional viewpoint then, Mrs. A used the analyst's life setting to express her transference neurosis and to subject it to a regressive daydream distortion consistent with analytic process with a hysterical character. From this viewpoint, her mise-en-scène was an aspect of her transference neurosis that developed after considerable analytic work, when her transference neurosis had grown more intense, and that gradually faded over one and a half years as her defensive daydream distortions were analyzed and as she worked through more of her true feelings.

The traditional viewpoint addresses Mrs. A's intense fantasizing, but it points only to resistance as the explanation for her exclusive focus on the mise-en-scène. I believe that the mise-en-scène also served a developmental function for Mrs. A. As a child she had not been able to experience a reliable and soothing interaction, except with her nanny. Her mother had been quite depressed, and her father had been unreliable because of his abusiveness and inappropriate sexuality. Mrs. A had been overstimulated with her parents' needs, without the internal capacity to handle this stimulation and with insufficient outside help. She was traumatized and had intense and unintegrated conflicts. Her description of having made mental videotapes as a child for the purpose of later integration reflected her preconscious awareness of her lack of integration and self-definition, as did her later difficulty with body image. The early analytic work led not only to the emergence of an intense transference neurosis, but also to a deepening of Mrs. A's capacity to bring up her previously unintegrated feelings and traumas in order to master them and to better define herself. She was increasingly able to use the analyst and his life setting as a screen on which to project intense affects and conflicts. As her nanny transference deepened, she could, like Lewin's sleeping infant secure at the breast, use the analysis like a dream. Her ability to so vividly reanimate childhood wishes and anxieties through dreamlike immersion in her fantasies was a new step for her. It was an accomplishment for her to be able to lose herself in expressing and exploring feelings and fantasies on the mise-en-scène.

The visual form of Mrs. A's mise-en-scène was influenced by her strong innate visual capacities, the visually erotized atmosphere of her parents' home, and her past conscious efforts to create visual memories. But the most important determinant of the visual form of Mrs. A's deeply trusting bond with the analyst was her preoedipal relationship with her nanny, whose soothing had been in a visual mode. Mrs. A used the analyst, as she had her watchful nanny, to hold her intense feelings. She was able to tolerate this painful view because she felt soothed in using the analyst as a dream screen. This deep preoedipal relationship, upon which the more advanced transferences of the infantile neurosis were projected, could be called the "dream screen transference."

In Lewin's work, the dream screen is described in terms of fixation at, or regression to, a primitive oral level. Lewin, (1961) explained the dynamics of mania, centered around the oral triad, as exemplary of fixation at this level. The dream screen transference, however, should be viewed from a progressive, rather than a regressive, standpoint. It facilitated Mrs. A's integration and mastery of infantile conflict and trauma so that she could move ahead developmentally.

This developmental function was addressed by Lewin (1968) in his later work when he speculated that ancient man lived in a way that felt oceanic, not as sharply conscious as modern man. He felt that there had been a gradual development towards a fuller consciousness and a more objective sense of mental contents. Lewin based this conclusion on his study of cave drawings at Lascaux, in which he included the cave as well as the drawings in his considerations. The cave, to him, was the head image in which the drawings, the mental contents, could be integrated. Just as Mrs. A had struggled with her body image during her brief adolescent anorexic episode, she struggled in analysis to define her head image, her mental contents. The mise-en-scène, on which Mrs. A could fantasize freely, was the cave in which she could draw herself. Through the dream screen transference she could experience and define her wishes and her anxieties, working them through in her transference neurosis so that she could progress developmentally. As the analysis proceeded and Mrs. A showed increasing integration and ego expansion, the mise-en-scène fell away. She had been able to define herself and master her anxieties sufficiently so that she no longer required the safety of the dream screen transference. She became increasingly able to identify her own dynamics, to soothe herself, and to have analytic discussions with herself.

Other clinical and theoretical observations are helpful in understanding the dream screen transference. Winnicott (1953) described the transitional phenomenon as located between reality and fantasy and as a creative act to gain self-definition. Mrs. A's dream screen transference drew on the external three-block reality setting as well as on her internal fantasies. And the dream screen transference was the vehicle for Mrs. A to gain self-definition. It provided an opportunity for a literal internal sighting of affect and fantasy on the mise-en-scène and served as a visually oriented transitional phenomenon. The dream screen transference, like the transitional phenomenon, was not itself mourned. As Winnicott (1953) stated, the transitional phenomenon "is not forgotten and it is not mourned. It loses meaning" (p. 91).

Self-psychological studies have also addressed these issues. Tolpin (1971) sees the transmuting internalization of selfobject functions in the interaction between the child and the "good enough" mother as enabling the child to develop the capacity to master affect through the use of fantasy. Tolpin equates this gradual, bit by bit, accretion of the capacity for fantasy with the transitional experience. From a self-psychological model, the dream screen transference was employed by Mrs. A to contain and calm her intense affects until she could slowly build stronger psychological structure with which to handle these affects. This structure included the ability to better use verbalization, anticipation, and fantasy. Lewin's later work, Winnicott's ideas on the transitional phenomena, and self psychology are all useful in explaining the dream screen transference.

Another perspective on the dream screen transference is offered by the work of Gedo and Goldberg (1973). They describe the developmental unfolding of types of mental functioning. Mode 2, prior to the attainment of self-cohesion, is understood from the clinical perspective of fragmentation of the self into discrete self nuclei. Mrs. A's dream screen transference could be seen as reflective of Mode 2 functioning. In other words, it could be viewed as an attempt to remain cohesive in the face of a partial fragmentation of the self undertaken for the purpose of conflict resolution and reintegration. In this view, the dream screen transference helped Mrs. A to achieve self-unification by drawing the self nuclei, the discrete and intensely affective versions of self and other in interaction, together on the mise-en-scène. She was able to contain, to use Winnicott's term, several different self-concepts on the mise-en-scène so that understanding could be gained and integration could occur. Her overall functioning, however, was simultaneously in both Mode 2 and in a more advanced mode, characterized by the representation of unconscious material in symbolic language, namely, the mode of the fully differentiated psyche operating by the topographic model, Mode 5. Gedo and Goldberg note that the combination of Modes 2 and 5 is the state of the typical dreamer (p. 121). From this perspective, Mrs. A experienced a waking dream, which helped her in the task of self-unification.

Lewin described the dream screen as transient, existing only for the duration of the dream, but Mrs. A's analysis shows that dream screen-like experiences can be more long-lived. Gedo (1988) has discussed waking dreams, in the form of enactments rather than visualized fantasies, in a recent work. And Kepecs (1952) observed a long-standing "waking screen" in one of his patients.

It is important to differentiate the dream screen transference, with its fuguelike involvement with the analyst and his home setting, from delusional or psychotic transference. Several authors have discussed psychotic transference (Reider, 1957; Bychowski, 1966; Weinshel, 1966; Frosch, 1970; Kernberg, 1975; Rosenfeld, 1978, 1979). It occurs in patients who, unlike Mrs. A, diagnostically have a borderline or psychotic character disorder. The psychotic transference consists of a specific primitive object relationship and is unlike Mrs. A's dream screen transference, which facilitated the introduction of a great number of dynamic issues. With psychotic transference, the analytic split is lost and the ego is overwhelmed. The dream screen transference formed a secure basis on which Mrs. A could experience distressing affects without being overwhelmed; she maintained a therapeutic split throughout the analysis. The psychotic transference lasts from one session to, at most, a few months, while the dream screen transference persisted for about one and a half years. Mrs. A's dream screen transference was an ongoing transference foundation for analyzable illusion, rather than an abrupt ego collapse into a barely discussible transference delusion. The dream screen transference allowed Mrs. A, as a new experience, to visualize her unconscious over a prolonged period and achieve mastery and integration of her needs and her self-image. Her feelings needed to come vividly alive to be worked on analytically and the dream screen transference was the setting for their long-lived resuscitation.

Conclusion

I have described an analytic situation in which the analysand created an intrapsychic mise-en-scène, a stage composed of elements of the analyst's personal surround, on which to experience and explore very intense transference issues. This mise-en-scène was analogous to a dream screen, was a durable and adaptable structure, and can be called a dream screen transference. The dream screen transference served an important growth function, similar to a transitional phenomenon, and was the background upon which the more advanced transference neurosis was projected.

The concept of the dream screen transference may provide an additional framework with which to examine clinical issues. Just as the dream screen is generally unnoticed when the analyst attends to the dream contents, the dream screen transference may also be generally present, though unnoticed, in analyses. If so, it would offer a way to look at the analytic alliance in terms of dream psychology. It could also account for the sensory texture of an analytic experience. For Mrs. A it had a strong visual emphasis, largely a result of her relationship with her nanny. For others the preoedipal dream screen transference could involve other sensory modalities. The concept of the dream screen transference may also help to explain the gradual progress toward insight in analysis. For Mrs. A insight developed from a literal visual sighting of conflict and affect on an intrapsychic mise-en-scène. This transitional type of experience then led to insights that could be more readily verbalized. The concept of the dream screen transference may broaden the way in which the dream can be a useful metaphor for clinical psychoanalysis.

REFERENCES

Bychowski, G. (1966), Psychosis precipitated by psychoanalysis. *Psychoanal. Quart.*, 35:327–339.

Freud, S. (1900), The interpretation of dreams. *Standard Edition,* 4 & 5. London: Hogarth Press, 1953.

_____ (1915), A metapsychological supplement to the theory of dreams. *Standard Edition,* 14:222–235. London: Hogarth Press, 1957.

Frosch, J. (1970), Psychoanalytic considerations of the psychotic character. *J. Amer. Psychoanal. Assn.*, 18:24–50.

Gedo, J. (1988), *The Mind in Disorder.* Hillsdale, NJ: The Analytic Press.

_____ & Goldberg, A. (1973), *Models of the Mind.* Chicago: University of Chicago Press.

Kepecs, J. G. (1952), A waking screen analogous to the dream screen. *Psychoanal. Quart.*, 21:167–171.

Kernberg, O. (1975), *Borderline Conditions and Pathological Narcissism.* New York: Aronson.

Lewin, B. D. (1946), Sleep, the mouth, and the dream screen. *Psychoanal. Quart.*, 15:419–434.

_____ (1954), Sleep, narcissistic neurosis, and the analytic situation. *Psychoanal. Quart.*, 23:487–510.

_____ (1955), Dream psychology and the analytic situation. *Psychoanal. Quart.*, 24:169–199.

_____ (1961), *The Psychoanalysis of Elation.* New York: Psychoanalytic Quarterly.

_____ (1968), *The Image and the Past.* New York: International Universities Press.

Reider, N. (1957), Transference psychosis. *J. Hillside Hosp.*, 6:131–149.

Rosenfeld, M. (1978), Notes on the psychopathology and psychoanalytic treatment of some borderline patients. *Internat. J. Psycho-Anal.*, 59:215–221.

_____ (1979), Transference psychosis in the borderline patient. In: *Advances in Psychotherapy of the Borderline Patient,* ed. J. LeBoit & A. Cappone. New York: Aronson, pp. 485–510.

Tolpin, M. (1971), On the beginnings of a cohesive self. *The Psychoanalytic Study of the Child,* 26:316–352. New Haven, CT: Yale Universities Press.

Weinshel, E. M. (1966), Symposium on severe regressive states during analysis. *J. Amer. Psychoanal. Assn.*, 14:538–568.

Winnicott, D. W. (1953), Transitional objects and transitional phenomena. *Internat. J. Psycho-Anal.*, 34:89–97.

Varieties of Therapeutic Alliance

BERNARD BRANDCHAFT
ROBERT D. STOLOROW

Few would dispute that the establishment of a bond between analyst and patient that permits the work of analysis to unfold is a sine qua non of our work. Yet serious differences exist regarding the essential nature of this bond, and the clinical implications of these differences are profound. The problem of resistances has thwarted psychoanalysts in their efforts to bring about more predictable structural change, leading to criteria for analyzability that increasingly exclude large numbers of persons seeking analysis. (Waelder, 1960; Greenson, 1967). Freud's (1937) final work, "Analysis Terminable and Interminable," reflected his preoccupation with the severe limitations posed by resistances on the therapeutic efficacy of psychoanalysis. In this summary he held a large number of factors, all intrapsychic, to account. If Freud's conclusions were to be accepted as final, psychoanalysts were faced with either an analytic procedure severely restricted in its scope or with the necessity of having to alter significantly the basic principles and techniques of psychoanalysis in the hope of increasing its therapeutic effectiveness. This dilemma provided a powerful stimulus for the reexamination of the nature of the therapeutic bond. And so the concept of a therapeutic alliance, already implicit in much of Freud's writings, became the focus of great interest in the 1950s.

In retrospect, it is clear that in the United States the interest in the therapeutic alliance, a particular object relationship between patient and analyst (Sterba, 1934; Bibring, 1937; Fenichel, 1941; Greenson, 1954; Zetzel, 1956; Stone, 1961), was stimulated by the development of ego psychology and paralleled the burgeoning interest in the more general subject of object relations in Great Britain, as exemplified in the work of Klein, as well as that of Winnicott, Balint, and Fairbairn. Both developments were rooted in the recognition that breakdowns of the therapeutic process came about because of disruptions within the analytic dyad, and so it was to these subjects that analysts turned their attention in attempts to extend the scope of analytic influence.

The ego psychologists, focusing on the central role of the ego in development and pathogenesis, visualized the analytic relationship as having two dimensions. One was rooted in the patient's identification with the analyst and especially with his understanding of the patient's unconscious. This, they held, was the basis for the therapeutic alliance. The other part of the patient's ego was engaged in resistance to the unfolding of the unconscious regressive instinctual forces and the structural conflicts that constituted the pathogenic oedipal complex of the transference neurosis. The maintenance of the therapeutic alliance was dependent on bringing about a split between an experiencing ego and a more reasonable, detached, and observing ego (Zetzel, 1956; Greenson, 1967) in order to deal with the resistance. This was to be facilitated by the patient's rational wish to cooperate with the analyst in order to overcome his suffering and by "his ability to follow the instructions and insights of the analyst" (Greenson, 1967, p. 192). Greenson (1967) emphasized the patient's identification with the analyst's interpretive approach as the specific goal of the therapeutic alliance. He took a step away from the traditional view when he considered the establishment of this relationship between patient and analyst, the "ingredient which is vital for the success or failure of psychoanalytic treatment," as "relatively nonneurotic, rational"—in other words, *nontransference* (Greenson, 1967, p. 46).

It is to be emphasized that in describing the establishment of a therapeutic alliance the ego psychologists were not only claiming that the patient must identify with the analyst's basic investigative methods and with such general principles as transference, resistance, and unconscious forces shaping subjective experience. The process of identification also had to include the analyst's theory-rooted assumptions about the patient's basic motivations and about the contents of the patient's mind. Thus, if the patient rejected or failed to recognize the correctness of the analyst's view that drive-related conflicts, particularly the oedipal conflict, were central in his symptoms and in his development, this continued to be regarded as the ultimate expression of the rivalry belonging to the very oedipal complex that the analyst had been seeking to uncover, now inevitably working its way into the transference (Abraham, 1919).

Understanding the resistance as deriving from conflicts arising solely from within the patient, the ego psychologists also required the patient to identify with the analyst's view of himself as essentially neutral in relation to the patient's conflicts, a blank screen upon which these were played out. Accordingly, transference was to be seen as the result of the patient's displacements or distortions, except where it might be influenced by those countertransference intrusions that the analyst was able to recognize. Chronic and intractable resistances were believed to be signs of negative therapeutic reactions or unanalyzability and were ascribed to ego weakness or a masochistic need to fail.

The dominant school of object relations in Great Britain, that of Melanie Klein, on the other hand, held that the therapeutic alliance was embedded in the transference, which itself was a complex object relation. The attachment of a "normal" dependent part of the self to a "good" part-object, the breast, was revived in the analysis, and the identification with it formed the nucleus of the therapeutic alliance. Disruptions in this bond were attributed to the operation of primitive defensive measures of the ego, which shaped and distorted the patient's perception of "real objects," including the analyst, and resulted in pathogenic introjections of cruel objects or objects damaged in omnipotent fantasy by the patient's destructiveness. The reestablishment of the therapeutic bond, and with it a secure tie with good, protecting, and protected internal objects, was thought to be the foundation of growth and creativity. This was brought about by the interpretation of the unconscious archaic defense mechanisms, by the working through of the infantile conflicts of ambivalence and pathological envy that the patient was defending against, and by the patient's developing trust in the analyst and his explanations of the nature of the patient's subjective experience, anxieties, and depressive feelings.

Klein (1950), unlike the ego psychologists, believed that the functioning of the ego was at all times determined by its relationships to its external and internal objects. Archaic ties between the ego and primitive objects or part-objects existed from the beginning, she insisted, and thus the history of any individual's development could be found in the record of the complex relationship between ego and objects. As a consequence of this view, the scope of psychoanalysis was for her automatically extended. The constitutional strengths or adaptability of the patient's ego were not stressed as a prerequisite, and consequently, children and psychotics were accepted, in principle, as being suitable for analysis. This remained a point of contention between the two schools.

Strachey's (1934) conceptualization of the "mutative interpretation" illustrates the Kleinian view of the therapeutic process. Strachey believed, as did the ego psychologists, that identification with the analyst occupied a central role. For him the operative mechanism was that of introjection, whereby the analyst's interpretations enabled him to be installed as a less severe and more benign influence than the patient's existing internal objects or superego. However, in Strachey's formulation the mutative value of the object relation to the analyst lay not only in an analytic attitude or stance that might open the possibility of a transforming introjection. It was essential that the identificatory process extend to the analyst's interpretations of the impulses and defenses that characterize the paranoid-schizoid and depressive positions postulated by Klein, since these were assumed to reappear in the transference. These "mutative interpretations" would have to be accepted as "true," so that the patient's view of himself and his history would come to conform to what the analyst had reflected to him.

Klein's followers adhered to a stance whose basic principles she (1961) described as follows:

> The psychoanalytic procedure consists in selecting the most urgent aspects of the material and interpreting them with precision. *The patient's reactions and subsequent associations amount to further material which has to be analyzed in the same way* . . . I was determined not to modify my technique and to interpret in the usual way even deep anxiety situations as they came up and the corresponding defenses [pp. 12–13; emphasis added].

The interpretive principles derive from Klein's view of the central importance of primitive defense mechanisms, especially splitting and projective identification, directed against internal instinctual forces or internal objects distorted by projected contents. Within this system intense and prolonged resistances leading to negative therapeutic reactions were and continue to be ascribed to the workings of pathological destructive envy, a vicissitude of the death instinct (Klein, 1957; Joseph, 1982; Rosenfeld, 1987). This clinical formulation is hardly surprising in view of the primary etiologic role Klein's metapsychology attributed to the innate conflict between life and death instincts. Here also, as in the case of the ego psychologists, the unsuccessful therapeutic result was assumed to demonstrate the correctness of the theory no less than the successful one. Despite their profound differences, in this crucial aspect these two divergent theoretical schools were in accord. The therapeutic alliance and the success of the analysis were held to depend on the ability of the patient ultimately to see the events of the analysis according to the basic concepts that organized and informed the analyst's observations and interpretations. This is a requirement with which patients often felt compelled to comply, as the price for maintaining the vitally needed tie to the analyst.

We have chosen to discuss the concepts and practices of these two dominant schools not only because of their leading position and continuing influence on psychoanalytic thought, but also because, in their approach to a therapeutic bond, they illustrate a basic and largely unchallenged philosophical assumption that has pervaded psychoanalytic thought since its inception, namely, the existence of an "objective reality" that is known by the analyst and distorted by the patient (Atwood and Stolorow, 1984; Stolorow, Brandchaft, and Atwood, 1987). This assumption lies at the heart of the traditional view of transference and its insistence on the dichotomy between the patient's experience of the analyst as distortion and the analyst's experience of himself as real. This dichotomy is one of the foundation stones on which the more elaborate and experience-distant theoretical scaffoldings of the two divergent psychoanalytic schools have been built. It is not the philosophical assumption with which we are here concerned, but the serious and insufficiently acknowledged consequences of its clinical application.

In agreement with Schwaber (1983), we contend that the only reality relevant and accessible to psychoanalytic inquiry (that is, to empathy and introspection) is *subjective reality*—that of the patient, that of the analyst, and the psychological field created by the interplay between the two. The belief that one's personal reality is objective is an instance of the psychological process of "concretization," the symbolic transformation of *configurations of subjective experience* into events and entities that are believed to be *objectively* perceived and known (Atwood and Stolorow, 1984).[1] Attributions of objective reality, in other words, are concretizations of subjective truth. As we have observed this process in ourselves and others, we have become aware that it operates automatically and beyond conscious awareness. It belongs to a relatively uncharted area of the unconscious termed the "prereflective" unconscious (Atwood and Stolorow, 1984) and involves the shaping of experience by invariant organizing principles that operate outside a person's awareness.

Adherence to the doctrine of objective reality and its corollary concept of distortion has led both psychoanalytic schools to view pathology in terms of processes and mechanisms located solely within the patient. This emphasis blinds the clinician to the impact of the observer on the observed as an intrinsic, ever-present factor in the psychoanalytic situation, and it obscures the profound ways in which the analyst himself and his theories are implicated in the phenomena he observes and seeks

[1]Although concrete symbolization may serve multiple purposes, its supraordinate function is to cast subjective reality in a reified and material form in order to articulate and consolidate it and buttress one's belief in its validity. The concretization of experience is a ubiquitous process in human psychological life, underlying such phenomena as neurotic symptoms, sexual and other enactments, dreams, fantasies, and psychotic delusions (see Atwood and Stolorow, 1984; Stolorow et al., 1987).

to treat. When the concept of distortion is imposed, a *cordon sanitaire* is established, which forecloses the investigation of the analyst's contribution in depth. The invitation that the patient identify with the analyst's concepts as a condition for a therapeutic alliance is an invitation to cure by compliance. Alternatively, it can trigger the appearance of what seems to be a resistance. Investigation of the patient's experience may reveal, however, an important attempt at self-differentiation, an attempt to protect an independent center of perception and affectivity from usurpation. When the patient reacts adversely to the analyst's explanations, the idea that these disruptive reactions arise from purely intrapsychic causes and are to be explained by the same concepts that are producing the reactions sets the stage for those chronic disjunctions that have been described as negative transference resistances or negative therapeutic reactions (Brandchaft, 1983; Atwood and Stolorow, 1984). When analysts invoke the concept of objective reality along with its corollary concept of distortion, this forecloses and diverts the investigation of the subjective reality encoded in the patient's communications, a reality that is precisely what the psychoanalytic method is uniquely equipped to illuminate.

Considerations of this kind have led us to formulate an intersubjective approach to psychoanalytic treatment:

> In its most general form, our thesis . . . is that psychoanalysis seeks to illuminate phenomena that emerge within a specific psychological field constituted by the intersection of two subjectivities—that of the patient and that of the analyst . . . psychoanalysis is pictured here as a science of the intersubjective, focused on the interplay between the differently organized subjective worlds of the observer and the observed. The observational stance is always one within, rather than outside, the intersubjective field . . . being observed, a fact that guarantees the centrality of introspection and empathy as the methods of observation . . . Psychoanalysis is unique among the sciences in that the observer is also the observed . . . [Stolorow et al., 1987, p. 1].

The intersubjectivity principle was applied to the developmental system as well:

> Both psychological development and pathogenesis are best conceptualized in terms of the specific intersubjective contexts that shape the developmental process and that facilitate or obstruct the child's negotiation of critical developmental tasks and successful passage through developmental phases. The observational focus is the evolving psychological field constituted by the interplay between the differently organized subjectivities of child and caretakers . . . [Stolorow et al., 1987, p. 2]

The intersubjectivity concept is in direct contradistinction to the constricting tendency to view pathology in terms of mechanisms and processes located solely within the patient.

What, from our intersubjective perspective, constitutes the essence of a therapeutic alliance? It is surely not the bond formed by the patient's commitment to follow the insights of the analyst. In our view the foundations of a therapeutic alliance are established by the analyst's commitment to seek consistently to comprehend the meaning of the patient's expressions, his affect states, and, most centrally, the impact of the analyst from a perspective *within* rather than outside the patient's subjective frame of reference (Kohut, 1959). We have referred to this positioning as the stance of "sustained empathic inquiry." Let no one believe that this commitment is an easy one to fulfill—it is frequently like feeling the sand giving way under one's psychological footing. Seeing himself and the world consistently through the eyes of another can pose serious threats to the analyst's personal reality and sense of self, much as the patient must feel threatened when his experience is treated as a distortion of reality.

What are the advantages of this stance? It opens for further psychoanalytic illumination those disruptions of the analytic bond that produce stubborn resistances that threaten to become entrenched. Disjunctions arising from frustration, disappointment, and experiences of misattunement are the inevitable consequence of the profoundly intersubjective nature of the analytic dialogue, the colliding of differently organized subjective galaxies. They are *not* to be regarded as errors in an "objective" sense. They are, however, evidence that the impact of the analyst and his understanding, or lack thereof, is central to the patient's subjective reality, and thus they provide access to crucial areas of the patient's inner world. The commitment to extend empathic inquiry to these experiences of disruption and to view them from within the patient's subjective framework, with the observer as an immanent part of the experience, repeatedly reestablishes and mends the therapeutic bond. Access is then provided to the specific and idiosyncratic ways in which the patient is organizing his experience of the analyst and to the meanings that this experience has come to encode. A window is thrown open for a fresh look into the area of discrepant and conflictful experience, into a room in which are locked the most intimate of secrets and longings and the most personal of happenings. It is from this space that a "new beginning" may take root.

What are the goals that join the participants in the therapeutic alliance? They are the progressive unfolding, illumination, and transformation of the patient's subjective universe. When the analyst and the patient are freed of the need to justify their respective realities, the process of self-reflection is encouraged and vitalized for both. Inevitably, it emerges that the central motivational configurations mobilized in analysis are derailed developmental strivings, and the course of the developmental processes activated by the analysis becomes the focus of inquiry. The experiences of vitality and devitalization, of buoyant aliveness and apathy, which are clues to the unfolding developmental processes and their derailment, can be followed, while the effect of the analyst as he is experienced in this ebb and flow is always kept in view.

It cannot be emphasized too strongly that the analyst's acceptance of the validity of the patient's perceptual reality in the ongoing delineation of intrapsychic experience is of inestimable importance in establishing the therapeutic alliance. Any threat to the validity of perceptual reality constitutes a deadly threat to the self and to the organization of experience itself. When the analyst insists that the patient's perception is a secondary phenomenon distorted by primary forces, this, more than any other single factor, ushers in the conflictful transference-countertransference spirals that are so commonly described as resistances to analysis or negative transferences. These can be recognized as crises or impasses in which each partner in the erstwhile therapeutic alliance becomes engaged in desperately attempting to maintain his own organization of experience against the threat to it posed by the other. Schwaber (1984) has also pointed out that many of our patients suffer from a primary sense of uncertainty about the reality of inner experience. For them the recognition and articulation of vaguely felt affect states or perceptions is especially meaningful (Schwaber, 1984, p. 161). For others the development of the ability to sustain a belief in their own subjective reality was derailed because their perceptions contained information that was threatening to caregivers. The perceptions thereby became the source of continuing conflict and had to be repudiated. This familiar core experience has been dramatized in the "gaslight" genre. We have presented three cases (Stolorow, Brandchaft, and Atwood, 1987) in which the inability to maintain one's own perceptual reality appeared to be a factor predisposing to psychotic states. In these cases delusion formation represented a desperate attempt to substantialize and preserve a perceptual reality that had come under assault and begun to crumble. We stressed particularly the noxious role unwittingly played in therapeutic situations by failures of the analyst to recognize the core of subjective truth encoded in the patient's communications.

The specific attunement to "the role of the analyst and of the surround, as perceived and experienced by the patient . . . as intrinsic to [his] reality . . . draws upon modalities which are significant components of the essentials of parental empathy—attunement to and recognition of the perceptions and experiential states of another" (Schwaber, 1984, p. 160). In the transference such attunement is a constituent of a quintessential selfobject experience serving to reinstate aborted developmental processes of articulating and consolidating self-experience. No more active mirroring is ordinarily required than the analyst's continuing, active interest in, and acceptance of, the perceptual validity of his patient's experience, together with his alertness to cues of disavowed affect states that signal perceptions the patient cannot as yet admit into his subjective world. However, as Schwaber (1984) also points out, "It would be misleading to employ these terms (i.e., the analyst's and the parent's empathy) synonymously, or to suggest that the one 'corrects for' the failure of the other, for they speak to two very different contexts" (p. 160). It is the failure to understand this point that forms the basis of the criticisms of self psychology as being reparenting and psychotherapeutic but not psychoanalytic.

The stance of sustained empathic inquiry consolidates the therapeutic alliance as it enhances and extends the domain of safety and harmony within the intersubjective field. The continuing articulation and consolidation of subjective reality is, however, only a part of the therapeutic experience. The additional goal of the therapeutic alliance is the transformation of subjective experience. We will not focus here on the transformational prospects for the analyst in discovering his impact and that of his inferences on the patient or in reflecting on the invariant principles that organize his experience of himself and his patient. Instead we wish to emphasize that a milieu in which the patient's perceptual reality is not threatened encourages the patient to develop and expand his own capacity for self-reflection. Access is thereby gained into unfolding patterns of experience reflecting structural weakness, psychological constriction, early developmental derailment, and archaic defensive activity—that is, the specific patterns that await transformation.

Often analysts fear that the commitment to understanding from within the patient's own subjective framework, and especially to recognizing and investigating the analyst's contribution to the patient's experience, will result in an obfuscation of the patient's contribution to his own circumstances. We find this fear to be unwarranted. Central to the process of transformation is the understanding of the ways in which the patient's experience of the analytic dialogue is *codetermined* throughout by the organizing activities of *both* participants. The patient's unconscious structuring activity is discernible in the distinctively personal *meanings* that the analyst's activities—and especially his interpretive activity—repeatedly and invariantly come to acquire for the patient.

Self psychology has been mistakenly characterized as a "psychology of the conscious," because of the erroneous impression that the domain of empathic inquiry extends only to the conscious elements of subjective experience. On the contrary, an indispensable part of the work of analysis involves the investigation of how conscious experience is organized according to hierarchies of unconscious principles. These determine the ways in which the patient's experiences are recurrently patterned according to developmentally preformed themes and meanings. It is in the illumination of these meanings, and of the subjective truths they encode, that the therapeutic alliance and psychoanalysis itself finds its most generative purpose.

Consider, for example, the difficulties regularly encountered when attempting to treat patients whose severe developmental deprivations have predisposed them to intense distrust, violent affective reactions, or stubborn defensiveness. In such patients we have become aware of underlying unconscious and invariant organizing principles into which all experience tends to be assimilated. From their early history has crystallized a certain conviction that nothing good could happen to them in relation to another person, that no one could possibly care for them, that they are doomed ultimately to live and die alone, and that any hope for a meaningful life based on an inner design of their own is an illusion and a certain invitation to disaster. Every experience of disappointment or limitation tends to confirm one or another of these principles. The impact of such experiences is not felt to be delimited and temporary, but global and eternal. Consequently, such inevitable experiences lead inexorably to resignation and walling off or to violent affective reactions. The subsequent trajectory of self-experience is codetermined both by the impact of external events and by the invariant ordering principles into which these events are assimilated and from which they derive their meaning. *Developmental traumata derive their lasting significance from the establishment of invariant and relentless principles of organization that remain beyond the accommodative influence of reflective self-awareness or of subsequent experience.*

Our emphasis on investigating the unconscious principles organizing the interacting subjectivities of patient and analyst is an answer to the criticism of self psychology that it involves reparenting or an abdication of the analytic stance. At the same time, we are not unmindful of certain dangers posed by the therapeutic alliance as we have conceptualized it. When the stance of empathic inquiry, for example, facilitates the appearance of archaic longings expressed in concrete demands to occupy a special place or to be given special consideration, there is a tendency for the analyst to be catapulted into a concreteness of his own and to react in either of two ways. On one hand, reacting defensively, he may insist that his patient recognize the unrealistic nature of these demands. On the other hand, he may react from a feeling of responsibility for the patient's disappointment and give covert encouragement to the patient's underlying hope for a relationship purified of any repetition of childhood traumata. Either course diminishes the likelihood of thoroughgoing change through the transformation of existing structures. Only the consistent working through in the analysis of the developmentally determined, invariant organizing principles can achieve the structural change so hopefully envisioned by the pioneers of our calling.

In order to illustrate our view of the therapeutic alliance, we offer some critical commentary on a case report by a well-known and respected psychoanalytic clinician and theoretician that appeared in a recent publication. Kernberg (1987) writes of a woman who "started her psychoanalysis suffering from a hysterical personality, consistent inhibition of orgasm in intercourse with her husband, and romantic attachments in fantasy to unavailable men"(p. 802). After the patient, with the help of the analyst, had overcome her reluctance to speak about her fears of him, she expressed the fantasy that he "was particularly sensual, in fact, 'lecherous,' and might be attempting to arouse her sexual feelings . . . so as to obtain sexual gratification from her" (p. 802). She said that the basis for her fears was that she had heard he came from a Latin American country and had written about erotic love relations. Furthermore, the analyst writes,

> She thought I had a particularly seductive attitude toward the women working in the office area where I saw her. All this, she considered, *justified* her fears. She expressed the fantasy that I was looking at her in peculiar ways as she came to sessions, and that I probably was trying to guess the shape of her body underneath her clothes as she lay on the couch [p. 802, emphasis added].

Her attitude was not seductive. On the contrary, she was "inhibited, rigid, almost asexual in her behavior" (p. 802), and there was very little eroticism in her nonverbal communications. The analyst took notice of all this and noticed also, on reflection, that his own emotional reactions and fantasies about her had a subdued quality and contained no conscious erotic element. On the basis of these observations he concluded "that she was attributing to me her own repressed sexual fantasies and wishes" (p. 802) and that "this typical example of a neurotic transference illustrates the operation of projection,[2] with little activation of

[2]The assumption that transference experiences are to be explained by the operation of defensive measures is undoubtedly shared by a majority of analysts. It is precisely for this reason that we are urging a reexamination of the clinical evidence. We wish to emphasize

countertransference material either in a broad . . . or in the restricted sense" (p. 802).

The report goes on to describe changes that took place during the ensuing year. The patient's fear of the analyst's sexual interest in her was succeeded by expressions of her disgust for the sexual interest older men have for younger women, and she discovered features of her father in these lecherous old men. Her own romantic fantasies, meanwhile, remained fixed on unavailable men, while she was terrified of sexual engagements with men, including her husband, who were available to her. As she became aware, the analyst writes, that her sexual excitement was associated with forbidden sexual relations, there was a decrease in her "repression and projection of sexual feelings in the transference" (p. 803). She stopped feeling that the analyst was interested in her sexually and, as he had anticipated and interpreted from the beginning, she began to have "direct oedipal" sexual fantasies about him.

At one point, in response to her fantasies, the analyst found himself responding erotically and with a fantasy of his own that he in turn would enjoy a sexual relation with her, "breaking all conventional barriers" and providing her "with a gift of the fullest acknowledgment of her specialness and attractiveness" (p. 803). The analyst describes this as a transitory emotional response to her seduction in the transference, which had activated in him "the complementary attitude of a fantasied, seductive oedipal father" (p. 803). Subsequently the patient once more accused the analyst of teasing and humiliating her and, finding no indication of what the patient perceived, the analyst concluded that the patient was projecting onto him experiences with her father from the past.

In this latter series of associations and interpretations, as in the others cited, there is no indication of an attempt to explore fully the *basis* of the patient's experience from within the perspective of her own subjective frame of reference. Perhaps she perceived something in his tone or his manner that he had not intended or even been aware of. Did his initial scrutiny of her for signs of "eroticism" mean something else for her? Did his fantasy of a sexual affair with her, which he believed was reactive, communicate itself to her in some way and stimulate concerns in her?

---

that it is not the particular theory-rooted content of Kernberg's interpretations that we are questioning here. What we are calling into question is the *epistemological stance* according to which the analyst, through his acts of self-reflection, is presumed to have gained privileged access to the objective truth about himself that the patient's discrepant perceptions are then said to distort. This stance does not have to be inferred from Kernberg's clinical material; it is readily demonstrated in his descriptions of how he arrived at transference interpretations. Our growing awareness of the unintended and unexamined impact of this epistemological stance on the course of the therapeutic process was one of the central concerns that motivated us to write this article.

The point here is not that the analyst "objectively" did anything wrong; he clearly kept well within the boundaries of professional behavior. The point is that whatever singular meanings these or other cues from the analyst might have had for the patient are left unexplored. Only what conformed to the theory being employed was attended to. The analyst in this case used as primary data his own self-reflections, and these persuaded him that the patient's experience was the consequence of distorting mechanisms. Here the analyst's subjective frame of reference is elevated to the status of objective fact, and the patient must accept the analyst's view as objective as part of the working alliance. Otherwise, as the report describes, the resistance has to be worked through so that she can come to recognize her defenses against accepting the analyst's perceptions, presumably because she is afraid to face her own impulses. One reality, the analyst's, is apparently real; the other, the patient's, is false! The therapeutic task is to account for the "distortion."

However, a crucial source of data is left unexplored. Access to that source, that is, an investigation in depth of the elements of the patient's experience from within *her* subjective framework, is bypassed when the stance of empathic inquiry is abandoned in favor of doctrinal inference. A process is derailed that might have disclosed how seduction was being signaled for *this* patient. Acceptance of the perceptual (not objective) validity of the patient's experience might have made possible a therapeutic alliance committed to an investigation of the exquisitely personal meanings of seduction and humiliation into which the various cues from the side of the analyst were being assimilated.

It is also possible that such investigation might have provided a safer milieu wherein elements of the patient's experience of her husband that would have illuminated her aversion to his sexual advances could have been articulated. Her extramarital sexual fantasies might then have disclosed, not an oedipal fixation, but sequestered hopes for acceptance, responsiveness, and enrichment not otherwise available to her.

The patient, it is reported, gradually came to realize her defenses against her sexual feelings and produced oedipal wishes toward the analyst. Such expressions are commonly taken as proof of the correctness of the theory of drive and defense. However, nothing illustrates more clearly the need for the analyst to investigate from within the patient's subjective framework the impact of his own theories on the direction and course of the analysis. In the establishment of a therapeutic alliance, *two heads are surely better than one.* Only this can enable patient and analyst to distinguish between a "pseudoalliance" based on compliance with the analyst's viewpoint and a therapeutically mutative alliance based on empathic inquiry into the patient's subjective world.

There is more than an echo here of the quandary Freud encountered that changed the whole course of the evolution of psychoanalysis. Freud found evidence that some of the childhood sexual seductions his patients complained of could not have happened and, it is reported, he felt betrayed. He concluded that these must have been fantasies that expressed the childhood wishes of his female patients, and he built his subsequent theories of psychosexual development and of transference on that foundation. For Freud these fantasies were mental representations of instincts. However, sustained empathic inquiry reveals that such fantasies often encode experiences of traumatic developmental derailment and that Freud's dilemma was a false one. It is common for experiences of abuse and seduction of a nonsexual or covertly sexual nature to be concretized and preserved in sexual symbolism. This insight into the kernel of truth encoded in a patient's fantasies opens up a whole new pathway for exploration, one that remains foreclosed when a patient's perceptions are dismissed as distortion.

Summary

We have offered a critique of the concept of the therapeutic alliance implicit in both traditional ego psychology and Kleinian psychoanalysis. Specifically, we have objected to the notion that the therapeutic alliance requires that the patient identify not only with the analyst's analytic stance of empathic inquiry, but also with his theoretical presuppositions as well. We hold that such an alliance is actually a form of transference compliance, which the patient may believe is necessary in order to maintain the therapeutic bond on which all hopes for his future have come to depend. We have contrasted this "pseudoalliance" with a therapeutic alliance established through sustained empathic inquiry into the patient's subjective world. This latter alliance, in which the perceptual validity of the patient's transference experience is accepted, promotes the illumination and transformation of the invariant principles that unconsciously organize the patient's inner life. Material from a recently published case report is examined in order to illustrate the differing clinical consequences of fostering one or another of these two varieties of therapeutic alliance.

We are aware that analysts of all persuasions approach their patients with preconceived ideas and that any theoretical framework, including our own, can be perceived by patients as something with which they must compliantly identify. What we are emphasizing is that the commitment to investigating the impact of the analyst, of his interpretive activity, and of his theoretical preconceptions, whatever they may be, from within the perspective of the patient's own subjective reality is central to the establishment of a therapeutic context in which the patient's unconscious organizing principles can be most sharply illuminated and thereby become accessible to therapeutic transformation.

References

Abraham, K. (1919), A particular form of neurotic resistance against the psycho-analytic method. In: *Selected Papers On Psycho-Analysis.* London: Hogarth Press, 1948, pp. 303–311.

Atwood, G. & Stolorow, R. (1984), *Structures of Subjectivity.* Hillsdale, NJ: The Analytic Press.

Bibring, E. (1937), On the theory of the results of psychoanalysis. *Internat. J. Psycho-Anal.,* 18:170–189.

Brandchaft, B. (1983), The negativism of the negative therapeutic reaction and the psychology of the self. In: *The Future of Psychoanalysis,* ed. A. Goldberg. New York: International Universities Press, pp. 327–359.

Fenichel, O. (1941), *Problems of Psychoanalytic Technique.* Albany, NY: Psychoanalytic Quarterly.

Freud, S. (1937), Analysis terminable and interminable. *Standard Edition,* 23. London: Hogarth Press, 1964.

Greenson, R. (1954), The struggle against identification. *J. Amer. Psychoanal. Assn.,* 2:200–217.

_____ (1967), *The Technique and Practice of Psychoanalysis.* New York: International Universities Press.

Joseph, B. (1982), Addiction to near-death. *Internat. J. Psycho-Anal.,* 63:449–456.

Kernberg, O. F. (1987), Projection and projective identification: Developmental and clinical aspects. *J. Amer. Psychoanal. Assn.,* 35:795–819.

Klein, M. (1950), *Contributions to Psycho-Analysis 1921–1945.* London: Hogarth Press.

_____ (1957), Envy and gratitude. In: *Envy and Gratitude and Other Works 1946–1963.* New York: Delta, 1977, pp. 176–235.

_____ (1961), *Narrative of a Child Analysis.* New York: Basic Books.

Kohut, H. (1959), Introspection, empathy, and psychoanalysis. *J. Amer. Psychoanal. Assn.,* 7:459–483.

Rosenfeld, H. (1987), Destructive narcissism. In: *Impasse and Interpretation.* New York: Routledge, pp. 105–133.

Schwaber, E. (1983), Psychoanalytic listening and psychic reality. *Internat. Rev. Psycho-Anal.,* 10:379–392.

_____ (1984), Empathy: A mode of analytic listening. In: *Empathy II,* ed. J. Lichtenberg, M. Bornstein, & D. Silver. Hillsdale, NJ: The Analytic Press, pp. 143–172.

Sterba, R. (1934), The fate of the ego in analytic therapy. *Internat. J. Psycho-Anal.,* 15:117–126.

Stolorow, R., Brandchaft, B. & Atwood, G. (1987), *Psychoanalytic Treatment.* Hillsdale, NJ: The Analytic Press.

Stone, L. (1961), *The Psychoanalytic Situation.* New York: International Universities Press.

Strachey, J. (1934), The nature of the therapeutic action of psycho-analysis. *Internat. J. Psycho-Anal.*, 15:127–159.

Waelder, R. (1960), *Basic Theory of Psychoanalysis*. New York: International Universities Press.

Zetzel, E. (1956), Current concepts of transference. *Internat. J. Psycho-Anal.*, 37:369–376.

III

OBJECT VERSUS SELFOBJECT

Object Loss and Selfobject Loss: A Consideration of Self Psychology's Contribution to Understanding Mourning and the Failure to Mourn

ESTELLE SHANE
MORTON SHANE

The child's experience in mourning the death of a significant other has been the subject of considerable interest and debate in the psychological literature for many decades (e.g., Bowlby, 1960, 1973, 1980; A. Freud, 1960; Wolfenstein, 1966, 1969; E. Furman, 1974, 1986; Gardner, 1979; Herzog, 1980; Altschul, 1988). In this paper we are concerned with a particular facet of this topic, the role of adequate parental support in facilitating the mourning process, and with the contributions of self psychology to an understanding of this function. Therefore, the clinical material that follows, as well as our discussion of it, is restricted to that which most closely pertains to the topics of concern here, that is, the lingering effects of the child's profound response to the death of a parental figure as they are manifested in the analysis of an adult patient and the means by which those effects, if unmitigated by parental support, are defended against and disguised over the course of the person's life.

Brief vignettes from the analysis of child patients are included principally to support and illustrate this central thesis. While our review of the literature on the topic of mourning will thus be limited, we want to begin with an examination of the central question raised in that literature: At what age and to what degree can the child mourn? The questions are important because it has been felt that without the capacity to adequately mourn an overwhelming loss, the child's development is significantly impeded. It is postulated that because the child cannot mourn—that is, give up (decathect) the attachment to and investment in the representation of the lost person—or cannot preserve the relationship in the form of identification, the search goes on forever for the parent whose death is unconsciously denied and the person remains, in an important sense, the child at that phase or age when the loss was sustained. Thus, the fantasy that the parent still lives and can be found again precludes the possibility for true replacement, not just in childhood, but throughout life.

Some contributors have taken an extreme view in regard to the child's capacity to mourn. For example, Wolfenstein (1966) concludes that the child is developmentally incapable of decathecting lost objects until the completion of adolescence. It is only then, through object removal, that the parental object can be relinquished. Death of a parent prior to that time, Wolfenstein writes, leaves the person developmentally stunted. Even therapy for the bereaved child, or for the adult who was so traumatized, is futile in terms of completely undoing the developmental impediment.

This is indeed an extreme view. By contrast, the pioneering work of Robert Furman (1964a,b) suggests that children who have attained object constancy before the death of a parent can, if deliberately aided, confront and master the loss. Others, following Furman's work, which involved the analysis of a six-year-old boy, have replicated and advanced his findings (e.g., the Cleveland group, led by Erna Furman, 1974; Lopez and Kliman, 1979; and Cohen, 1980). Further, these contributors claim that when the grown-ups in the surround are able to follow and facilitate the process, a child can mourn even without therapy. The problem lies with the bereaved parents' defenses against their own affects, their impatience with the child's attempts to grieve, or their ignorance of the significance of the loss for the child, all of which impair the child's ability to recover.

This range of responses from pessimism to guarded optimism extends to the prognosis for adults in analytic treatment who have suffered parent loss in childhood. Fleming and Altschul (1963) contend that such treatment too often presents insurmountable problems. Fleming (1972), concludes in her comprehensive paper on the topic that analysis of adults who experienced object loss in childhood reveals that these persons remain immature into adult life and that the immaturity interferes so significantly with the relationship between patient and analyst that ordinary classical analysis cannot proceed. Special technical interventions are required to understand and work with these patients. More recently,

Burgner (1985) came to a similar conclusion. In a research study conducted at the Anna Freud Center on adult analysands who had suffered object loss in childhood, Burgner found that such loss before the oedipal phase results in permanent character defect; analysis can help these patients to some extent, but they still remain tied to the lost parent and unable to resolve oedipal conflicts.

It is important to note that this designation of "difficult patient" is understood as attributable to the inevitable narcissistic damage these patients, as children, suffered as a consequence of their bereavement (e.g., Rochlin, 1953; Pollock, 1978; Perman, 1979). Damaged self-esteem, devaluation of both deceased parent and self, and the threatened or real decrease in availability of and caretaking by the surviving parent and the concomitant decrease in need fulfillment describe the plight of such a child. An inability to trust or depend on the surviving parent complicates the picture.

To summarize the classical literature, then, children who suffer loss and who are denied the benefits of a sustaining environment and the opportunity to mourn are viewed as incapable of giving up the tie to the lost object. They remain forever fixated in this attachment, seeking a continuation of the old relationship in fantasy and in enactment. Psychological development is seriously impeded, with the child remaining at the level attained, regressing to earlier levels, or, at best, progressing in limited ways. These children grow up suffering from significant narcissistic injuries as well as from an unresolved bereavement over the lost parent. If they find their way into therapy, they become the difficult patients described in this literature, requiring special handling and facing a guarded or limited prognosis.

We would like to make the point that one of the difficulties these patients and their analysts have faced is that often the focus of interpretation has been on the blatant manifestations of the loss itself in terms of the person who is missed, rather than on the more silent, more subtle, but more insidious manifestations of the loss of narcissistic support from that person. For example, Fleming (1972) speaks of the patient's clamoring for a relationship in the transference with the preloss object as a significant interference with the therapeutic working alliance. She describes special techniques for dealing with this difficulty, such as confronting the patient with the reality of the parent's death, presumably to avoid isolation of affect, and directly addressing the patient's wish to experience the analyst as a new parent. It seems to us that the patient's defenses against the unbearable, inevitable permanency of the loss are thus directly assaulted. Fleming also resorts to another direct technique, advanced by Greenson (1965) and others for use with patients who require "something extra" to form an alliance: the deliberate use of "we" with the patient in referring to the therapeutic relationship. It is as if she feels the need to force an object relationship rather than address the patient's perceived lack of support in the past, in the present, and in the transference.

This pessimism regarding the ameliorative effects of analysis and the consequent need for analytic measures leads us to the conviction that the classical frame of reference may be insufficient to fully meet the challenge of treating patients who have sustained parent loss in childhood. Self psychology, with its particular focus on narcissistic injury and repair, adds an essential dimension both to understanding and to working with such patients. That is, *object loss,* as it is conceptualized in the object concept of mainstream analysis, may not have the explanatory reach required to encompass the narcissistic damage long recognized as consequent to parent loss. *Selfobject loss,* as it is conceptualized in self psychology in terms of selfobject function, may provide just that needed explanatory reach. While much has been published in terms of the loss of the parent as object, that is, as the target of libidinal and aggressive drives and as provider of global narcissistic supplies, less has been written about loss of the parent in his or her selfobject function, a theoretical framework in which the required narcissistic supplies are particularized. As a theoretical addition, then, self psychology can pinpoint the specific narcissistic injury sustained by the self through such a loss and can indicate as well the remedial steps required to repair the damage.

Using this framework, we can understand that when a parent dies, a child might be threatened in any or all of the three currently acknowledged repairing, sustaining, and regulating relationships of its self. That is, the child's sense of power and importance might be compromised with the loss of a sustaining, mirroring selfobject function. His or her sense of comfort and security might be weakened, the trust and admiration in the idealized parents might be profoundly shaken, and the background of reassuring human connectedness might be disrupted. In short, such functions heretofore provided by the deceased parent would no longer be available. Were the surviving parent able to make up for this loss in a significant way, the child would, of course, be less traumatized. He or she would be able to face the impact of the loss without feeling the risk of being overwhelmed, annihilated, or fragmented. Within such a supportive milieu, compensatory self-structure would be formed not only to repair the weakened aspects of the self, but to facilitate continued or renewed development.

In too many cases, however, the surviving parent is so adversely affected by the death that he or she is less available for support and encouragement than before. So, in effect, the child in his bereavement suffers the loss of self-regulating selfobject functions heretofore supplied by both parents. (And this double loss must be understood to be *in addition to* the loss of mutual affect-sharing experiences with that same deceased other, that is, the post-object constancy, oedipal and postoedipal object-centered dimension of the lost other so central to the classical literature on mourning.)

In attempting to defend against the massive loss of needed functions for the survival of the self, the bereaved child searches for substitute selfobject relationships to shore up and maintain his self-integration. In cases with pathological outcome, such relationships are either inadequate or unavailable, and the self, protected by defensive structures that merely cover over the defect, remains vulnerable.

But how is mourning itself, postulated in the classical literature to be so essential to continued healthy development, to be conceptualized in a framework expanded by self-psychological formulations?

We would like to suggest that given an adequate supportive environment to strengthen the child's total self and aid in dealing with his defensive avoidances, the child will *spontaneously* mourn the death of an important loved one. The pain of loss can be borne and the necessary capacity to think, talk, and reflect about it can be sustained if the child is helped to mourn rather than stifled by unempathic criticism and unrealistic standards for mourning behavior. Therefore—and this is the important point—we consider mourning in children, as it has always been seen in adults, a normal process, neither impossible nor exceptional, although the required optimal selfobject environment, more available to the adult, may be hard to provide for the child.

In addition, we would like to assert that in our experience it is not the failure to mourn per se that is primarily pathogenic, as has been suggested in the classical child analytic literature; rather, it is the absence of an empathic selfobject milieu at a time of crucial need that constitutes the chief pathogenic factor for a child who loses a parent. This is certainly not to say that the loss of a parent in itself does not constitute a major trauma having pathogenic effects. Nor are we saying that the mourning process is not important. It is well documented that if a new other is turned to without such mourning, genuine development in the capacity for relationships beyond the preloss level does not take place. The point is that in order to mourn, the child requires selfobject functions from the surround; moreover, without such selfobject functions the line of self development, as well as the interrelated line of object relations, is impaired.

By introducing the selfobject dimension into the experience of loss and mourning a more thorough appreciation of the process and its facilitation can be achieved, as we hope the preceding remarks and the clinical material to follow demonstrate. There is another point that may be considered in this context. Because selfobject functions are experienced as a part of the self, it may be that the bereaved child can more easily replace these functions from substitute others than he can the object-centered experiences of sharing, loving and hating with a specific, unique, and distinct other. Such avenues for replacement of missing selfobject functions have been emphasized by Kohut (1977), who contends that if there is a deficiency in one or another sector of the self related to selfobject failure emanating from one parent, the child may make up for it by turning to the other parent for compensatory experiences in the same or another sector. This would seem to indicate that the self-centered (selfobject) aspects of the relationship with the lost parent are more easily replaceable and require less mourning than the object-centered aspects of the relationship. In theory, then, it follows that loss of a love object leads to identification (i.e., internalization with object tag), mourning, and turning to a new object. Loss of a selfobject leads to transmuting internalization (i.e., internalization without object tag), less mourning, and a more prompt and peremptory search for new selfobject functions.

Of more clinical importance, however, is the contention we have already made that it is the unavailability of the self-centered aspects of that lost relationship that can most crucially interfere with the mourning process itself. To repeat, children who experience traumatic failure in selfobject function sustain self pathology. They grow up narcissistically damaged. While this has been recognized in the literature, the classical frame of reference has not been adequate to address this clinical issue. Self psychology, with its focus on selfobject function, offers a means both to understand and to rectify this pathology consequent to parent loss.

Now to the clinical material. We are presenting brief vignettes of four latency-age children analyzed by us. All four were asymptomatic following the death of a parent, apparently able to accept that loss without obvious difficulty, according to the surviving parent. Three of these children were placed in treatment several years after the loss was sustained, subsequent to the development of significant symptoms. The three, all girls, lost their mothers and had fathers who responded in a less than optimal way.

Two of the fathers of these three girls actively discouraged the mourning process, conveying in more or less direct fashion their own discomfort with the topic of the mother's death and their belief that it would be better for the child "to get on with her own life." One of the two fathers said that he did not think his daughter really missed her mother and that she was just using her death as an excuse to get his attention, an effort that he felt should go unrewarded. The second reported that he had instructed his daughter to keep all reminders of her mother to herself; she was allowed to have a single envelope to contain any concrete mementos, and all pictures of her mother, including a large portrait of mother and daughter that had previously hung prominently in the house, were removed. When the father remarried, as he did within the year, the child was asked to call her stepmother "Mother" and to not talk, let alone cry, about the mother who was dead. Once a year father and daughter visited the grave site, where she could openly mourn, and that was it.

When these two girls developed symptoms, neither father could accept at first that there might be any causal connection to the mother's death. In analysis what was striking was the fact that both of these girls had understood two things: that their fathers truly loved them and that if they were to keep their fathers' love, support, and admiration, they had to stifle whatever sense of loneliness or longing they might feel for the absent mothers. Both girls guiltily reported in analysis that they had found it shamefully easy to put thoughts of their dead mothers aside and remembered enjoying whatever exclusive attention they were able to get from their fathers, but these issues of conflicts over aggression and oedipal victory were not as crucial to the resultant pathology as the literature appears to suggest.

In contrast to the fathers of these two, the father of the third girl did his best to encourage expression of her grief. He himself was devastated by the loss and openly mourned his wife's death. He was able to understand his daughter's feelings and did not disapprove of her for them. However, the child revealed to her analyst that she remembered being hindered by her father's open distress and feeling, despite his efforts to encourage her to mourn, that it was her responsibility to be supportive of him and to stifle her own neediness. Nevertheless, there is no question that the third father was the most able to provide selfobject functions for his daughter, with the result that she was more able than the other two girls to overcome the effects of the mother's death. While the first two girls suffered pathology that could not be ignored by even the most insensitive of fathers, the third's difficulties were more subtle, and it was a mark of the father's empathy that she entered therapy at all.

We want to make the point that in all three cases there was no question that the fathers, as well as the stepmothers, were intelligent people who loved their daughters, felt kindly toward them, and wanted the best for them. What we are talking about is a capacity in the parent to serve for the child as a needed selfobject, that is, a capacity to appreciate the inner world of the child and to respond appropriately in a way that supports the child's self. These selfobject functions are difficult for even the most empathic of surviving parents to supply when there is death in the family. Our contention is that the pathology in the child is more than the object loss and is consequent to, and proportionate to, the loss of selfobject function.

The fourth child in this series is included to serve as a contrast to the previous three. Scott, who was eight when he lost his father, was also asymptomatic and apparently accepting immediately following his bereavement. Nevertheless, Scott's mother, herself in analysis when her husband died, felt that her son should be helped to deal with his father's death through an analytic experience. In analysis, as in his life in general, Scott defended himself against feelings or preoccupations concerning his father, though their subtle expression could be discerned. For example, in a maze game played repeatedly and with increasingly difficult mazes that he himself had constructed, Scott traced out the path from start, which he invariably labeled "S", to finish, which he labeled "F". It was clear to the analyst that the intense affective striving Scott exerted to connect all the "S's" to all the "F's" was a repeated effort to reconnect Scott to his father, but the analyst said nothing. Finally, in one analytic hour the maze itself was unconsciously designed by Scott in the unmistakable shape of the two initials of his father's name, in addition to including the usual "S" and "F" for start and finish or, as the analyst surmised, Scott and Father. The connection was finally made for him, and it was a moving experience for both patient and analyst to see how strongly Scott missed his father.

Months later, Scott drew a picture of himself and his analyst camping together under the stars. When the stars of one of the constellations were connected, a big "F" appeared. Scott was then able to describe the affect-laden fantasy that his father was not really dead but there, in heaven, from which place he continued his relationship with Scott. Becoming conscious of this fantasy increased Scott's awareness of his loss. While these indications of missing his father were uncovered in the office, in the world outside Scott continued to function without difficulty, as if there were no loss at all. A follow-up of this patient 15 years later, when he was in his 20s, revealed a healthy, enthusiastic, vigorously masculine person who cared about others. Arrests in development at the preloss level, which one might have expected, were nowhere in evidence, the result, we believe, of his mother's sensitive support and her provision of auxiliary support through the relationship with an analyst at a time of great selfobject need. We speculate that this child's development was not impeded because he had been allowed to mourn and because missing selfobject functions were supplied in the process.

In the following exposition of an adult case analyzed by E.S., we will attempt to demonstrate that the early loss of a parental object in the context of an inadequate selfobject milieu leads to the classical picture of an individual arrested at the preloss level. The patient, Mr. W, lost a parental surrogate at age three, after the establishment of object constancy. On the face of it, he should not have suffered to the degree he did, inasmuch as his mother and father remained physically available to him. But neither parent was able to understand or respond to the narcissistic lack the parental surrogate's absence entailed for him. Selfobject functions were compromised and, unfortunately, were not supplied by his parents. Had they been, this patient would not have had to wait until he was in analysis to be allowed to mourn. He would not have had to turn to medication to soothe himself nor to repeat endlessly the search for a lost idyllic relationship.

Mr. W, a 42-year-old trial lawyer, entered analysis because of lifelong feelings of anxiety, depression, and low self-esteem, which he attempted to control through the use of tranquilizers and recreational drugs. These dysphoric affects centered mainly around an inability to commit himself either in love relationships or professionally. He described himself in his relationships with women as being intensely infatuated almost upon meeting the woman and consumed with a desire to win and possess her; then, having reached his goal, he found himself, for inexplicable reasons, having to get away. In analysis, details emerged of this configuration, which he had heretofore kept himself unaware of despite several episodes of therapy in the past. We came to recognize that the process always followed the same pattern. The feelings and fantasies of love would give way to a sense of disappointment, disillusionment, feelings of being trapped and suffocated, and then intense anger and determination to escape. At first an impassioned and effective lover, he would lose interest and, in fact, become impotent, that state serving as a barometer of the fact that it was time to pull out of the relationship. He would then extricate himself with more or less difficulty, and feel an immediate sense of relief and pleasure; then the inevitable feeling of remorse would set in. He would find himself reliving romantic moments with the woman, dream of having found her again, and then awaken weeping when he rediscovered his loss. He would call out to her in his imagination to please come back. The period of truncated mourning would run its course and he would begin to feel both loneliness and aloneness (Adler, 1985). There followed a sense of despair, sometimes with suicidal ideation, extending to fleeting experiences of depersonalization and derealization. These states would prove so unbearable that he was driven to seek out a new relationship, not a difficult undertaking, given his good looks, engaging personality, and intense romantic inclinations. Each new relationship would begin with profound optimism and a sense of great well-being, only to retrace the same course from seeking, to winning, to wanting out, to relief, to regret, and to loneliness and despair. These experiences with women had begun in adolescence when he started dating. He had had many such relationships, some lasting a week, others lasting longer, the longest being for a two-year period. With each affair the anger with the particular woman and the regrets over losing her did not go away; instead of establishing a partnership, or at least the mixed pleasure of bittersweet memories, all he had to show for his efforts was an evergrowing mountain of regret and an ever-renewed reservoir of anger. Finally, 18 months into the analysis, after the pattern itself had become clear to both analyst and patient, it became possible to point out to him during the infatuation phase of one such affair that he didn't even know the woman, that she was, in effect, no more than a fantasy, and yet, as usual, he was planning a life with her that included marriage. He was truly surprised and so impressed that this elaborate pattern was not repeated. Despite this helpful insight, however, and the fact that he was able to cease the actual behavior with women, the underlying sense of loss remained strong with him, along with the anger and regret.

The analysis began with links to the past that demonstrated the oedipal connection to these difficulties with love (and with work as well). Mr. W, an only child, was an infant when World War II ended. His father left for the service just after his birth, returning when he was three. He remembers his father descending upon his intense relationship with his mother and disrupting it. His father, who seemed harsh and cold and displeased with him, threw himself into the task of returning to civilian life. He worked hard to make money and was rarely with the family. The experience of sudden disruption of the close relationship with his mother was repeated at age six, when his sister was born, and at age eight, with the birth of his younger brother.

In the transference the oedipal issues were handled by displacement, with Mr. W finding girlfriends who had physical characteristics similar to mine,[1] even though, as he stated with some embarrassment, I was definitely not his type. In one particular dream, which he had after some romantic experience with a dark-haired woman, a hot dog in the refrigerator appeared split in two, and he awoke in terror. The castration anxiety was easily interpreted and accepted by him. On another occasion, when he found himself having a sexual fantasy about me, he had a sudden image of razor blades inside a vagina. He connected me with his

[1]All first person pronouns throughout this case discussion refer to E.S.

mother, who appeared in dreams as a woman who frowned at him, expressing, he felt, her depressive and undependable nature. He feared that I was similarly unreliable, susceptible to moods, and likely to disapprove of him, reject him, and, most terrifying of all, simply pull away from him and disappear, leaving him bereft and unsteady in his bearings. At such moments the old depersonalization and derealization returned, indicating an anxiety far in excess of what could be characterized as castration anxiety and closer to what Kohut (1977) and others (e.g., A. Freud, 1960) have termed annihilation anxiety.

It was through this transference elaboration of the character of his mother that an understanding of the deeper nature of his problems evolved. I came to see that beneath the Oedipus complex lay something even more profound. The slow discovery of these deeper problems was made in the context of an emerging, predominantly idealizing selfobject transference, which eventually supplanted the positive oedipal transference that had preceded it. Months of experiencing me as one who could be relied on to be there, as steady, predictable, and dependable, indicated the flowering of this new transference constellation. He was reassured and calmed by my presence and by the perception that I was listening and attempting to understand what he was feeling. He came to see me as perfectly attuned to him, and he began to feel very strong and self-contained. In time he was able to give up relying on the various drugs and medications he customarily took to modulate and control his affect states. Only then, in the security established by the smoothly evolving selfobject transference, embedded as it was in the real relationship, could the full story of his early years emerge into consciousness.

The veil of repression was lifted through a dream. The setting in the dream is a courtroom. There is a cage in which a small, deformed creature lies, more dead than alive. The prosecutor points to the figure with a long stick and pokes at it, attempting to get it to move. He turns accusingly to Mr. W. The patient knows he is guilty of doing harm to this creature and feels that all those present know he is guilty as well, but he cannot for the life of him understand what he has done. In associating to the dream, Mr. W first talked about his mother, about whom he has always felt guilty. When she was in a bad mood, he assumed it was due to something he had done. His mother had had the habit of going to her own room and not speaking to anyone for days. He remembered how surprised he was to discover, just a couple of years earlier, that it was not he whom she was mad at, but his father. Mr. W then went on to wonder about the creature in the dream, all shriveled up, more dead than alive. He suddenly recalled, for the first time as an adult, that he and his mother had not lived alone together during the first three years of his life when his father had been away. They had gone to live with his maternal grandmother during that period, and his grandmother had died around the time that his father had come home. He slowly came to the conviction that the small figure in his dream was his grandmother.

The dream, as well as Mr. W's surprising associations to it, was the beginning of an emotion-laden uncovering of the powerful but forgotten relationship between his grandmother and himself and of its tragic end. With lengthy discussions with his mother along the way, the patient dedicated himself to a voyage of discovery about his origins that included trips back home, visits to the graveyard, explorations of the family Bible, and, most importantly, a study of his old baby book. In the sessions that followed, his affect changed from a limited range, which was guarded, flat, and depressed on one end and hostile and angry on the other, to a more authentic and much-expanded range of emotion, best described as buoyant, excited, and lively on the one end and tearful and sad on the other. The patient experienced a change in his sense of himself, which he naively but aptly described as a change from a false self to a real self. The facts that emerged over this time, one year into the analysis, were the following: Mr. W was born one year after the marriage of his teenage mother, at which time several events converged to shape his mother's, and concomitantly his own, experience. First, her husband left for the army; she was shaky and uncertain in her new role as mother and returned to her own mother's home and the support her mother could offer for the duration of her husband's absence. Second, her brother, her mother's favorite, was reported missing in action, presumably dead. At first devastated and inconsolable, the grandmother ultimately responded to these events by regarding the new baby as her dead son restored to her by God, and, sweeping aside her daughter, assumed the full role of mother to the infant. This state of affairs continued for two years until the grandmother became ill and slowly died. His mother told Mr. W that because she herself had been so upset, she had given him no explanation during the time his grandmother was dying or at any time thereafter, though the patient was three years old by the time his grandmother died. From the mother's point of view at the time, the little boy did not notice the loss. She had written in his baby book, "Poor child; his real mother has died. Luckily he shows no signs of missing her," revealing that she had not understood what he was going through or how a child defends himself against painful affect. She now recalls that after his grandmother's death, the patient alternated between refusing to have anything to do with her, and clinging to her, refusing to let her out of his sight. We can assume that Mr. W knew some of this story before his analysis, but all of it was either suppressed or repressed when he started and for the first year thereafter.

We can speculate that it was only in the context of a solidly established and developmentally facilitating selfobject transference that Mr. W could allow himself to face the full impact of the loss of his grandmother and work through in that transference the double loss of her selfobject sustenance and her love-object presence. Working through is often likened to the process of mourning; in this part of the analysis of the case, it was identical to it. Furthermore, it became possible with Mr. W via the quality of the transference that evolved to arrive at the idealizing selfobject nature of the relationship he had had with his grandmother, whom he had apparently experienced as available to him in a kind of asexual, egocentric paradise. But the full sense of what it must have been like for him to lose that idyllic relationship only emerged through an incident in the analysis in which he experienced a profound disruption of the empathy and trust that had been built up between us. That is, the smoothly functioning selfobject matrix, so helpful to the recovery of this patient's early and profound parental object loss, was disrupted by an unempathic response on my part that, I realize in retrospect, expressed my effort to join the patient's derogation of me. When he was exploring his roots in order to understand his connection with his grandmother, Mr. W was simultaneously researching the popular psychological literature in order to understand his connection to me. One day he announced that analysis, according to his reading in Alice Miller, is heavily concerned with empathic understanding as a part of the therapeutic process. He added most sincerely and gratefully that he had always been impressed with my ability to be understanding of him. Then, suddenly, in what appeared to be a humorous mood, he said with a laugh, "Do you really understand me, or are you just bullshitting me?" Joining in what I took to be his joke, I spontaneously laughed. To my chagrin, he was deeply incensed, with the result that I had burst in an instant the sense of well-being and trust in me that had been developing over the previous six months.

There are many ways in which this rupture might be understood. It might be seen as a defensive effort on his part to break the idealizing tie, a tie that threatened a traumatic repetition of the disappointment and disillusionment experienced with his grandmother. But the analyst cannot be left out of the picture. Mr. W's nervous laughter, which was mistaken for humor, was, I realize in retrospect, a defensive distancing that perhaps should have been discerned. Instead, I sided with it for unconscious reasons, no small part of which was relief from the strain and responsibility of being so heavily idealized. In any case, many months after this momentary and seemingly slight breach in empathy, Mr. W sadly recalled the ambience in the analysis prior to it as his long-lost Eden wherein trust, hope, and confidence had been restored, only to be lost again forever. He continued to struggle in the analysis over restoration and loss of that idyllic state, the transference meaning of which became increasingly clear to him. That is, Mr. W came to understand that he had sought all his life for a restoration of the ideal relationship he had experienced with his grandmother but had never been able to allow one to stabilize because he feared that if he dropped his guard, he would suddenly and traumatically be deserted, which is how he experienced both the grandmother's death and his analyst's empathic failure. This fear of traumatic loss had led him from one aborted relationship to another. It was only in the selfobject transference that this repetition could be understood, interpreted, and worked through. To illustrate Mr. W's struggle to defend himself against a recurrence of this trauma, let us present a vignette of a session that occurred during this period of the analysis.

The session takes place on a Friday before a two-week vacation. All week Mr. W described himself as feeling somewhat depressed although, as he told me, work was going very well and he actually should be feeling good. He knows after much experience with me that I will suggest that the depression might have to do with the upcoming separation, but he doesn't accept that. Yesterday, he noted that he could never admit to anyone that he longed for them while he was currently in a relationship. He could only admit to himself his deep need for someone after he had lost that person. He imagined that while I was on vacation, he would think of me as helpful and would miss seeing me, but he was not currently having any of these feelings. He was angry with Sarah (the woman he had lived with for two years) and wished death and destruction on her for marrying someone else; he believed she could not be happily married. He wondered then if I was thinking he was really talking about me and my husband.

Today, a Friday hour, Mr. W comes in struggling again with his low-key mood, which he relates on an intellectual level to my upcoming vacation, of which he again assures me he can feel nothing. He says he only feels numb, a hated feeling that he associates with the way he used to feel all of the time. He would like to say to me, "Don't leave me. What will I do without you?" But he honestly does not *feel* that; he only *thinks* that. When I comment that he seems to still find these feelings difficult to bear, he becomes hurt and very irritated with me. It makes him feel condescended to, as if I am treating him like a small child; he knows he acts like one sometimes, but he doesn't want to be treated like one.

He then pauses nervously and says that a conversation he had last night keeps coming to his mind but that it seems totally off the subject and of no interest or value for discussion. Yet it keeps coming back; he wonders, why is that? He wants to go on, but I bring him back to the recurrent thought. He reluctantly begins to tell me about a conversation he had over dinner with a new friend. His friend described the situation with his own therapist, who makes suggestions to him about what he should do. His friend doesn't follow these suggestions and then feels guilty. Mr. W told his friend that his analyst never tells him what to do. She only listens patiently to what he has to say, makes a few connections, and asks a few questions, and somehow things evolve. Even more hesitantly, Mr. W tells me that he told his friend that he is deeply impressed with all he has learned about himself in analysis and that he admires my dedication and patience very much. He imagines, he tells me, that his dead grandmother must have been like that. He pauses and then says that he guesses he has a hard time telling me that he is grateful to me for what I have done, and continue to do, for him and that he thinks I am really a good analyst, despite all the criticism he directs toward me. He pauses again and says suddenly, in earnest, "Do you plan to give up your practice soon? Are you tired of what you are doing?" He himself, in his law practice, likes to see a client, figure out the legal problem quickly, come to a decision, and then show the client out. He says he couldn't stand to do the work I do; it is too demanding. He wonders, anticipating me, why this comes to his mind now. I tell him that we can understand why he finds it so difficult to admire me or pay me a compliment and that I agree it is hard for him to talk directly about any of his feelings. I tell him that I think it is particularly hard for him to talk about any good feelings he has about me, because he fears not only that that makes him weak and me powerful, but also, more importantly, that I might respond as he tends to when someone expresses a need for him: that is, he wants to run away, to get out of the relationship forever. He is afraid that if he shows me that he depends on me, I will respond by wanting to get away from him, by giving up my practice; he fears I have as much trouble committing myself to him and to my work as he does to others and to his work. He responds, as the hour ends, by saying, "Let's get off this topic; it's getting too heavy."

Recapitulation and Summary

In summary, Mr. W, who had repressed the loss of his parent-surrogate at age three, was able to revive in analysis both the memory and the affective experience of the death. While the analysis began in a positive oedipal transference, it was only in the context of the full flowering of an idealizing selfobject transference that this patient was able to face the task of mourning. Ramifications of his view of the death of the parent-surrogate, including his own feeling of responsibility for it, were explored. A lifelong unconscious character pattern was understood as a defense against intense emotional involvement with women, an involvement that would have recapitulated the early trauma of his parent-surrogate's death. By turning passive into active behavior, the patient abandoned any and all women who threatened to become close to him before they had too much power or could abandon him. In a repeatedly failed effort to master this trauma, he demonstrated the pre-loss fixation on the lost object. The establishment of a selfobject transference that most likely repeated the supportive experiences with the parent-surrogate, but unfortunately was not available with his parents, occurred in the context of the analysis.

In analysis the mourning process was engaged, and signs of the resumption of development became evident. The patient's self-structure was much strengthened through this experience, as evidenced by his increased sense of authenticity, inner harmony, the absence of derealization and depersonalization, and, most impressive to him, his ability to regulate his affect states without medication or recreational drugs.

Here, then, we have attempted to add a self-psychological vantage point to the topic of parent loss. The contentions that mourning in childhood requires adequate selfobject support and that with this support mourning is a more or less spontaneous, effective process are illustrated with both child and adult case material. While we have alluded briefly to the general nature of the selfobject functions required to sustain mourning in childhood, additional work in self psychology is required to particularize these important functions.

References

Adler, G. (1985), *Borderline Psychopathology and Its Treatment.* New York, London: Aronson.

Altschul, S. (1988), *Childhood Bereavement and Its Aftermath.* Madison, CT: International Universities Press.

Bowlby, J. (1960), Grief and mourning in infancy and early childhood. *The Psychoanalytic Study of the Child,* 15:9–52. New York: International Universities Press.

_____ (1973), *Attachment and Loss—Separation.* New York: Basic Books.

_____ (1980), *Attachment and Loss—Loss.* New York: Basic Books.

Burgner, M. (1985), The oedipal experience: Effects on development of an absent father. *Internat. J. Psycho-Anal.,* 66:311–320.

Cohen, D.J. (1980), Constructive and reconstructive activities in the analysis of a depressed child. *The Psychoanalytic Study of the Child,* 35:237–266. New Haven, CT: Yale University Press.

Fleming, J. (1972), Early object deprivation and transference phenomena: The working alliance. *Psychoanal. Quart.,* 41:23–49.

_____ & Altschul, S. (1963), Activation of mourning and growth. *Internat. J. Psycho-Anal.*, 44:419–431.

Freud, A. (1960), Discussion of Dr. John Bowlby's paper. *The Psychoanalytic Study of the Child*, 15:53–62. New York: International Universities Press.

Furman, E. (1974), *A Child's Parent Dies*. New Haven, CT: Yale University Press.

_____ (1986), On trauma: When is the death of a parent traumatic? *The Psychoanalytic Study of the Child*, 41:191–208. New Haven, CT: Yale University Press.

Furman, R.A. (1964a), Death and the young child. *The Psychoanalytic Study of the Child*, 19:321–333. New Haven, CT: Yale University Press.

_____ (1964b), Death of a six-year-old's mother during his analysis. *The Psychoanalytic Study of the Child*, 19:377–397. New York: International Universities Press.

Gardner, R.A. (1979), Death of a parent. In: *Basic Handbook of Child Psychiatry*, Vol. 2, ed. J. Call & R.L. Cohen. New York: Basic Books, pp. 270–282.

Greenson, R.R. (1965), The working alliance and the transference neurosis. *Psychoanal. Quart.*, 34:155–181.

Herzog, J.M. (1980), Sleep disturbance and father hunger in 18- to 20-month-old boys. *The Psychoanalytic Study of the Child*, 35:219–233. New Haven, CT: Yale University Press.

Kohut, H. (1977), *The Restoration of the Self*. New York: International Universities Press.

Lopez, T. & Kliman, G.W. (1979), Mourning in the analysis of a 4-year-old. *The Psychoanalytic Study of the Child*, 34:235–271.

Perman, J.M. (1979), The search for the mother: narcissistic regression as a pathway of mourning in childhood. *Psychoanal. Quart.*, 34:155–181.

Pollock, G.H. (1978), Process and affect: Mourning and grief. *Internat. J. Psycho-Anal.*, 59:255–276.

Rochlin, G. (1953), Loss and restitution. *The Psychoanalytic Study of the Child*, 8:288–309. New York: International Universities Press.

Wolfenstein, M. (1966), How is mourning possible? *The Psychoanalytic Study of the Child*, 21:93–123. New York: International Universities Press.

_____ (1969), Loss, rage, and repetition. *The Psychoanalytic Study of the Child*, 24:432–460. New York: International Universities Press.

Toward a Clarification of the Transitional Object and Selfobject Concepts in the Treatment of the Borderline Patient

STEVEN H. COOPER
GERALD ADLER

The transitional object, poised between the realms of inner and outer reality, has become a focus of attention for psychoanalysts of various theoretical persuasions. The British object relations theorists (e.g., Winnicott, 1953) and their contemporary American counterparts, such as Modell (1963, 1968) and Volkan (1973), view the child's separation as a painfully enforced fact of nature, first hated and eventually appreciated and integrated. From this perspective the transitional object is an object ideally suited, and thus valued, to help mitigate painful separation anxiety and the loss of symbiosis. From the perspective of some self psychologists (e.g., Tolpin, 1986), the transitional object has much less to do with the fact of separation. Instead, the transitional object, like other objects (i.e., selfobjects) is seen as aiding in the transformation of naive infantile omnipotence into core self-esteem and self-confidence. Separation, they believe, has been overemphasized as both a fact and crime of nature. The self psychologists observe a "different transitional object and a different baby" (Tolpin, 1986, p. 1). Other theorists influenced by self psychology, such as Goldberg (1984), view the transitional object and

The authors appreciate the generous assistance of Drs. Dan Buie, Simon Grolnick, Anton O. Kris, and Arnold Modell in the preparation of this chapter. We are particularly indebted to Dr. Marion Tolpin who served as a discussant for the presentation of the paper.

selfobject as embedded in fundamentally different theories and providing contrasting functions.

The purpose of this paper is to discuss our view of the overlapping and distinct domains of the transitional object and the selfobject concepts as applied to the treatment of borderline patients. The transitional object, a concept emanating from Winnicott's version of object relations theory, has been applied to the analysis of borderline (Modell, 1963) and narcissistic patients (Volkan, 1973). The selfobject concept, historically embedded in Kohut's theory of self psychology, is in this chapter viewed as a distinct but complementary concept to that of the transitional object for understanding transference phenomena, conflict, and developmental arrest.

The Developmental Context: Differing Babies, Blankets, and Theories

From the point of view of object relations theorists (particularly Winnicott and, more recently, Modell) the transitional object is viewed as serving multiple functions for the infant's development. First, the transitional object mitigates catastrophic anxiety resulting from loss and separation. Second, it serves to modulate both constitutional aggression and rage reactive to painful separation experiences. Third, the transitional object helps consolidate intrapsychic structure through perpetuation of an idealized maternal object; this function both bridges the gap during the process of evocative memory development and possibly aids in the consolidation of defense mechanisms to help modulate libidinal and aggressive impulses. The transitional object helps perpetuate the idealized maternal object by serving as both an aide-mémoire and an object for displacement of aggression secondary to the loss of the needed relationship. Finally, the transitional object constitutes an early step in the growth of true object relating by helping the infant to recognize an object that exists in the real world (e.g., blanket) even though it is still viewed as exclusively available to the infant's needs for an object. Implicit in these functions is the more global function of the transitional object for infantile development, namely, to ease the strain of reality acceptance.

From this perspective the developmental context for the initiation of the infant's use of the transitional object usually includes a "good enough" holding environment, i.e., a positively experienced, reliable, dyadic or symbiotic relationship, usually with the mother (Winnicott, 1953). The transitional object is, in this view, conceptualized as an offering, either intentionally introduced by the parents or naturally sought out or selected by the infant from a variety of possible objects. If separation difficulties are centrally related to the psychopathology of one or both parents, the transitional object is often prematurely introduced; alternatively, parents' defenses against separation may take the form of discouragement or lack of appreciation of the value of the object, including the infant's interest in such properties of the object as its smell, appearance, or proximity (Winnicott, 1953; Fintzy, 1971; Giovacchini, 1984). In any event, such offerings and handling of the transitional object by primary objects are often reflective of a pathological holding environment that fails the child in a broader framework in addition to the ways in which the transitional object is handled. This general failure of holding renders the transitional object less effective in achieving its multiple developmental functions.

Some self psychologists (e.g., Tolpin, 1986) view the blanket as having some overlapping functions with the selfobject, while others (e.g., Goldberg, 1984) argue for the distinctiveness between the two concepts and the theories from which they emerge. Tolpin (1986) views the baby as transferring the experiences of his parent's care and his own capacity for self-calming to the blanket; this capacity for self-calming is believed to be present from the onset of development. Thus, the blanket becomes the repository of self-selfobject experiences that enable the baby to recapture a sense of equilibrium in the face of everyday psychological frustrations that inevitably assault omnipotence. Through the transitional object the baby has his own means to overcome various types of injury and exhaustion and to restore vigor and a sense of his own or his parent's greatness (Tolpin, 1986).

Thus, Tolpin (1986) views the baby as having a phase-characteristic self-organization, in contrast to the symbiotically merged baby postulated by such object relations theorists as Winnicott. Tolpin argues that the transitional object is not usefully understood as involving even a temporary regression to an earlier state; that is, neither the relationship between the baby and the transitional object (selfobject) nor the function of the transitional object (i.e., self-soothing) are conceptualized as involving regression. Separation anxiety is viewed as disintegration anxiety that is, in Wolf's (1980) terms, "felt by the infant when the absence of the selfobject-caretaker threatens to disintegrate the beginning organization of the precursors of the self." Separation, then, is a threat to infantile omnipotence, not to primary needs for contact and comfort.

Goldberg (1984) discusses the distinctiveness of both the transitional object and selfobject concepts and the larger theoretical frameworks from which they are derived. He persuasively challenges the frequent assumption among psychoanalytic theorists that theory in psychoanalysis is exchangeable. Goldberg develops his argument, in part, by using as an example the differences between transitional object and selfobject concepts in their psychic context, function, and role in development.

Goldberg (1984) views Winnicott's theory, in large measure, as an attempt to explicate the nature of the facilitating environment and, more generally, early environmental influence; the transitional object is seen as a central part of this environmental influence because it involves an object in the real world that thrusts the child toward an even greater adaptation to and appraisal of the surrounding environment. In contrast to Winnicott's explication of the transitional object, Kohut (1971) defines the term *selfobject* as another person experienced as a part of the self. In Goldberg's (1984) terms "a selfobject is recognizable not in terms of any environmental or material factor but rather entirely in terms of an empathic assessment" (p. 127). Furthermore, Goldberg states that while the function of the transitional object is to foster independence during an early point in development prior to the capacity for reciprocity in relationships, the selfobject may be infantile or mature, serving to provide an ongoing source of support and sustenance through the life cycle.

Thus, in Goldberg's (1984, p. 127) terms, only "heroic" attempts to "translate" between the two concepts of transitional object and selfobject can emphasize their equivalence. In summary, Goldberg views the two concepts as embedded in fundamentally different theoretical frameworks, one focusing on experiential referents, the other environmental; one providing ongoing sustenance, the other fostering independence; one a ubiquitous phenomenon or component of all relationships, the other a stage in the development of object relations.

We are in agreement with Goldberg (1984) that the two concepts, transitional object and selfobject are embedded in divergent theoretical contexts, but from our viewpoint each describes essential and differing relational functions as applied to the treatment of the borderline patient. While we view separation as, partially, a threat to infantile omnipotence, we place separation anxiety and experiences of aloneness as primary concerns for the borderline patient (Adler and Buie, 1979; Buie and Adler, 1982; Adler, 1985). For the borderline patient whose early life experiences are often replete with painful separation, the transitional object is an essential but often unavailable aid in mitigating separation anxiety. Over the course of analytic treatment we believe that the functions of the transitional object are rendered successful and meaningful in the context of a self-selfobject relationship. First, we will detail the nature of the divergences between the two concepts as they have been applied to the treatment of the borderline patient.

The Clinical Application of the Transitional Object Concept to the Transference of the Borderline Patient

Numerous psychoanalytic reports have been influenced and enriched by the application of developmental concepts to the understanding of transference in the psychoanalytic psychotherapy and psychoanalysis of the borderline patient. Winnicott's seminal paper on the transitional object and transitional phenomena has been particularly generative in its application to transference issues (e.g., Modell, 1963, 1968; Kahne, 1967; Adler and Buie, 1979; Buie and Adler, 1982). Modell (1963, 1968) has contributed to our understanding of expectable transferences among borderline patients, likening them to the child's relationship with the transitional object.

Modell's (1963) clinical hypothesis that borderline individuals demonstrate a developmental arrest at the stage of the transitional object remains an elucidating account of the particular nature of impaired object relations among borderline patients. Modell proposes that borderline patients have been unable to rely safely on the transitional object as an auxiliary soother, thus precluding the decathexis and subsequent internalization of the transitional object functions. Modell (1963) suggests that borderline patients have unconscious fantasies about the therapist or analyst in which he or she, as in the child's play with the transitional object during development, is recognized as an object existing outside the self but owing both its existence and much of its contents to needs that arise for the object within the individual. Borderline patients often express conscious wishes that the therapist or analyst should exist only for them and exclusively for the gratification of their needs. In their fantasies, both conscious and unconscious, the analyst is regarded as being able to magically provide a feeling of safety in the world through sustained contact. An illusion develops that as long as the relationship is maintained with an analyst of unlimited power, the patient will be protected from potential danger in the environment. Such magical thinking, says Modell, like the transitional object during development, serves to lessen the danger of being alone and unprotected by creating an illusion of a lack of separateness between self and object. Just as the infant attains omnipotent control over his "first possession" or transitional object, the borderline patient clings to the magical belief that he or she can achieve the same degree of control over the therapist or analyst.

Modell's (1970) elaboration of the transitional object as a "watershed" concept emphasizes the dual identity of the transitional object as both a defensive phenomenon and a creative act (an important step in the recognition of externality and the beginning of object relationships). The defensive aspects of the infant's use of the transitional object clearly relate to regressive aspects of borderline psychopathology and transferences of borderline patients. The borderline patient often wishes that his analyst would help him magically alleviate separation anxiety and fears of aloneness.

However, the "creative" (Winnicott, 1953) or generative aspects of the transitional object function, while applicable to the evolving transferences of the borderline patient, require clarification. For example, as Robbins (1976) points out, both the striking instability and fluidity of the borderline individual's relations to others and his inability to make use of their soothing capacities stand in marked contrast to the relative fidelity and reliability of the child's use of the transitional object. The role of the transitional object as the recipient of infantile aggression and its consequent relation to the development of reality acceptance and successful separation differs from the repetitive, stagnant, reactive fury that frequently characterizes the treatment situation with the borderline patient.

There are also other ways in which the very specific function and identity of the transitional object for the infant's play are quite different from the borderline individual's relation to his therapist or analyst. The application of the transitional object concept to the transference phenomena of borderline patients does not sufficiently distinguish the patient's general needs to receive various kinds of psychic mirroring or validation from the particular context in which the analyst, as transitional object, is used in the transference, namely, to ease the strain of separation and to help with reality acceptance (Henderson, 1984). The analogy to the transitional object does not distinguish the use of a transference recipient who is animate and performing specific, active functions from one that is either animate or inanimate and used solely as part of the child's creative need for the transitional object. Thus, interpretation and confrontation, as real or actual functions performed by the therapist or analyst, differ from the inherent functions of the transitional object as something created by the child. To conceptualize and explain these therapeutic activities, Adler and Buie (1979) and Buie and Adler (1982) have suggested that the selfobject concept is necessary and quite useful. This concept is exemplified in those instances in which the borderline patient experiences the therapist or analyst as part of the self. It is important to note here, however, as will be detailed more specifically, that Adler and Buie (1979) and Buie and Adler (1982) use the term *selfobject* in a manner that is not limited to an experience of the analyst as a part of the self, as was defined by Kohut. We use the term *selfobject,* in the context of treating severely disturbed borderline patients, to include those instances in which the analyst or therapist performs some actual function that the patient feels unable to perform for himself. Since the therapist or analyst is experienced as performing selfobject functions, or in actuality does perform certain functions for the borderline patient during the evolution of transference, we believe that the concepts of the transitional object and of the selfobject are both necessary and complementary.

A Comparison of the Transitional Object and Selfobject Concepts in the Treatment of the Borderline Patient

As stated earlier, we view the fundamental problems of the borderline patient as revolving around the experience of aloneness and the inability to use consistently, selfobjects for holding, soothing, and the internalization of holding introjects. Interpretive focus in the analytic treatment of borderline patients is aimed toward understanding the experiences of these patients that preclude or obstruct the use of selfobjects (e.g., the analyst or therapist) to develop capacities for self-soothing or soothing derived from these internalized interactions.

The borderline patient's lack of a solid capacity for self-holding and self-soothing usually emerges in an analytic relationship that revives longings for something the patient desperately needs and is accompanied by wishes to devour and merge with the analyst. These longings threaten the patient's ego boundaries, often leading to defensive withdrawal in the face of increasingly intense wishes and needs. Simultaneously, this experiencing of the analyst or of anyone who fails to fulfill these intense wishes and needs, however defensively attenuated, engenders frightening rage. Primitive guilt related to such rage is also frequently present. The borderline patient often tends to lose his holding and soothing introjects when his rage emerges in treatment (Adler and Buie, 1979; Buie and Adler, 1982). The loss of these holding introjects compromises his capacity to tolerate separation and leads to panic as a manifestation of painful experiences of aloneness. Thus, despite an initial idealization of the analyst and use of his responses to feel understood and momentarily more cohesive, inevitably the borderline patient's fear, panic and dread emerge.

In a series of papers, Adler and Buie (1979, 1982) attempt to apply, in modified form, some of Kohut's (1971, 1977) formulations of selfobject transferences to transference phenomena in the treatment of borderline patients. They describe the way in which transitional objects may be of use in the treatment of adult borderline patients after the patient has had an experience of the therapist or analyst providing holding, soothing, and containing functions. The borderline patient experiencing primitive rage in the transference often regresses to the panic of losing evocative, and sometimes recognition, memory for the therapist in a way that may preclude utilization of transitional objects offered by the therapist. Once the acuteness of the regression is addressed in the treatment and evocative memory is at least temporarily restored, through clarification by the analyst, transitional objects again can become useful for the borderline patient (Adler, 1985). In Adler and Buie's formulation the concept of the selfobject is used in an expanded and thus different way from Kohut's definition of the selfobject concept. Adler and Buie (1979) have addressed the ways in which the therapist must at times actively provide functions such as mirroring, validation of tenuous reality testing, and clarification of precarious self and other differentiation in the treatment of the borderline patient. They refer to these functions as selfobject functions. This differs from Kohut's definition of the selfobject as an experience of the analyst as a part of the self. Adler and Buie (1979) state that these selfobject functions account for the active, normal development of the infant's and the patient's attempts to reach out for the transitional object in the context of an *inevitably* failing, though good enough maternal and therapeutic selfobject relationship. Thus, the selfobject concept as defined by Adler and Buie includes a broad range of psychological and developmental functions for the infant or patient. The transitional object primarily has meaning (i.e., positive affective associations) in the context of a good enough holding and soothing relationship that inevitably fails (Winnicott, 1953; Tolpin, 1971). Modell's clinical description of the borderline patient emphasizes these patients' needs to reach out for objects in the face of an extreme, rather than an inevitable, relative failure.

The transitional object during normal development, in contrast to the therapist or analyst in the treatment of adult borderline patients, is ideally suited to aid in the initial steps toward the recognition of the external world. The context of the treatment situation inherently violates some of the nonreciprocal and predictable conditions necessary for the use of the transitional object. For example, the analyst and the analytic situation introduce separations of all kinds. Additionally, the analyst is not exclusively available to the patient in the way that the transitional object actually does exist only for the infant. While the borderline patient may develop transferences involving the analyst as exclusively available to the patient, many actual events interrupt this development. For example, therapeutic responses to the borderline individual, such as interpretation, clarification, and confrontation, all indicate an independent initiative from a separate object despite the patient's efforts to transform, embellish, or ignore these interventions. Thus, the analytic situation often violates the borderline patient's demands that the analyst not have independent needs. We conceptualize these demands as part of the patient's selfobject needs, despite his defensive efforts involving denial, idealization, and projection to mitigate these repugnant aspects of the treatment situation.

We would further clarify that the psychological context for the transitional object, in Winnicott's formulation, is always one primarily related to separation, in contrast to the broad range of selfobject functions that includes *both* separation and self-esteem regulating functions. The analogy between the therapeutic relationship for the borderline patient and the child's play with the transitional object tends to emphasize the defensive and regressive aspects of the borderline patient's early transference formations (e.g., denial and idealization to lessen painful feelings of aloneness and reactive rage) but less fully addresses the real, positively experienced aspects of the holding environment, which include the patient's positive use of selfobjects as idealizing and mirroring resources over the course of treatment.

A related child development case example cited by Robertson (1971) highlights the child's loss of the ability to utilize transitional objects in the context of failure by parents and others to appreciate the child's tenuously established abilities for evocative memory (Adler and Buie, 1979). In this example, John, a 17-month-old was left in a residential nursery for nine days while his mother gave birth to another child. The staff members, while responsible and caring, changed frequently as a result of shifts and days off; the children who were permanently institutionalized had expertly adapted to this pattern by aggressively securing the attention they needed from a constantly changing staff. As a result, John was unable to obtain the individualized mothering to which he had become accustomed. His tenuous ability for evocative memory of mother's soothing qualities in her absence was temporarily lost, and he gradually regressed to a stance of protest and then to feelings of despair and detachment. The Robertsons demonstrate that John lost the capacity to utilize a potential transitional object to soothe himself when his holding environment failed. John, like many borderline patients, regressed because of the loss of a holding environment that had previously been good enough, rendering transitional objects of very limited value.

From the child or patient's perspective, there is no distinction between a transitional object or selfobject. The child has a need, which is experienced in relation to an inanimate object or a person. The need might be for a transitional object to be utilized, for example, to evoke the qualities of a transiently available, but good enough mother. It is only when that mother fails the child beyond his or her capacity to tolerate failure that the distinction between transitional object and selfobject becomes important.

For the borderline patient in a failing holding environment within the analytic situation, the transitional object function of the therapist or analyst can be lost. At that point the therapist must, interpretively, provide an environment that sufficiently holds or soothes in order to establish or allow for the recovery of the patient's capacity to utilize the therapist as transitional object.

This formulation has important implications in everyday psychotherapy and psychoanalysis. It helps define the therapist's need to monitor regularly the stability of the holding environment for each patient and the patient's capacity to use the clinician as a transitional object as well as a selfobject. In operational terms, it defines the patient's needs for activity, support, clarification, or interpretation from the therapist in response to the therapist's assessment of a faltering holding environment or breakdown of the selfobject transference for the borderline patient.

Clinical Vignette

The case of Ms. A, a divorced woman in her early 30s, helps to illustrate some of the concomitant selfobject and transitional object functions of the psychotherapist in the context of twice-weekly psychoanalytic psychotherapy. Ms. A, a high-level borderline woman with depressive–masochistic features sought treatment owing to chronic debilitating anxiety about feelings of aloneness and massive compromises in her ability to have an intimate relationship with a man and to utilize her considerable intellectual ability in her academically oriented work. The first two years of treatment were characterized by chronic depression and hopelessness about whether her psychotherapist would be able to understand her. Often she would squelch her attempts to speak about her disappointments in relation to her parents and her therapist for fear that it would overwhelm her with a sense of neediness, disappointment, and anger. She had felt ignored by father, who was, in her view, a depressed, perfectionistically driven man, and pressured by her mother to comply, as she did, with father's needs for isolation and few demands from family members. Massive compromise formations in the area of work involved a renunciation of her own abilities as both an expression of rage toward her parents and a way to communicate her yearnings and wishes to be held and understood as she was, not as she felt others demanded her to be. She resented her therapist for asking her to work (in essence, to say what came to mind) in the treatment, and her silences represented, in part, an angry announcement that she would not, once again, comply. At the same time, she sought through her silence to protect her psychotherapist from her rage and powerful yearnings to be held and nurtured.

In approximately the third year of treatment, a fairly positive therapeutic alliance was established. This alliance partly grew out of the therapist's tolerance for her complicated wishes not to be forced to comply and speak, which created an experience of safety in the therapeutic situation. The alliance also developed from the gradual interpretation of Ms. A's self-destructive tendencies to take on projects that were unchallenging and sometimes humiliating. In avoiding the pitfall of feeling pushed to work too hard (by her parents or her therapist), she recreated a historically painful scene in which she felt humiliated and deprived of positive, esteem-building hopes from her parents, particularly as compared to the investment of such hopes toward her younger brother. The compromises that she was making were allowing her to punish herself for having unsatisfied parental longings and hostility toward those who had engendered disappointment; the nature of this disappointment lay in feeling deprived of both the physical holding that she craved as a child and the sense of her parent's aspirations and hopes about her abilities.

With the development of a more positive alliance, Ms. A began increasingly to express dependency feelings and fears of abandonment by the therapist, similar to earlier experiences of aloneness in her family. At one point she described fears that her therapist had plans to move to another city without telling her. She revealed with much embarassment that several weeks earlier she had purchased a piece of material similar to that of a suit of her therapist's that she especially liked and that she touched it at times when she felt alone. In the session that she revealed this practice to the therapist, she also discussed for the first time two memories from her early years. The first was an experience of panic at age four when her teddy bear accidentally fell in the lake at her family's summer home (her father was eventually able to retrieve it for her later that morning). Another memory was of being in a piano recital with other children and feeling extremely panicky when she noticed her mother leave the room for a moment. She revealed over subsequent sessions a practice that she had previously kept secret—that of calling her therapist's answering machine to hear his voice. She had a fantasy of bringing in her current teddy bear to a psychotherapy session so that, by holding her teddy, she might be better able to manage her frustrated yearnings to be held by her therapist. She also spoke during these sessions of often wanting not to talk because she wanted to "fuel up on the therapist until the next session."

The complicated course of Ms. A's psychotherapy and the vicissitudes of her relation to the teddy bear and the piece of material similar to that of the therapist's suit are beyond the scope of this paper. For example, the complex defensive elements of Ms. A's behavior, which included, at times, defensive regression from oedipal conflicts, will not be addressed here. What is important for purposes of the present discussion are the ways in which the establishment of a satisfactory holding environment, which then included a therapeutic alliance, however precarious, allowed Ms. A to creatively use a transitional object, such as the cloth, to remind her of a positive holding experience. We would postulate, as does Tolpin (1971) regarding childhood development, that this creative use of the transitional object helped to internalize the soothing experiences and memories of the therapist. Concomitantly, in genetic associations Ms. A felt freer to explore frightening experiences of aloneness and failures in the parental holding environment. She was able to see how these failures in the holding environment had fostered her withdrawal, inhibitions, and compromise formations, which, from an adaptive point of view, had bound her rage and disappointment but had symptomatically kept her from achieving pleasure in many areas of her life. In many ways, during the period of psychotherapy described here, Ms. A fluctuated between the creative use of a transitional object to remind her of the therapeutic holding environment and, during more painful therapeutic regression, a more basic attempt to mitigate catastrophic anxiety about the failure, or feared failure, of the holding environment itself; the latter was exemplified by fantasies of bringing the teddy bear to a session to help cope with the painful experience of not being held by the therapist as she wished.

We suggest that the patient's needs for the therapist to provide such a holding environment are usefully described as having a selfobject function because borderline patients, as well as neurotic patients at the height of transference regression, experience the analyst or psychotherapist as performing functions that the patient feels unable to provide for him or herself. Only then are the preconditions established for the successful or creative use of the transitional object in aiding internalization of self-soothing functions.

The distinctions between transitional object and selfobject functions in the psychotherapy of borderline patients are also exemplified by those instances in which a psychotherapist is technically required to make provisions other than interpretation. Importantly, these actual functions of the therapist differ from self psychology's definition of the selfobject as referring only to an experience of the analyst as a part of the self. In contrast, the functions described here in the treatment of the borderline patient may also involve explicitly designed parameters to help severely disturbed patients perform functions that they are unable to provide for themselves. Specifically, stalemates in the analytic treatment of the borderline patient often occur secondary to the patient's difficulties in maintaining object constancy, particularly during separations. For example, particularly in the treatment of more severely disturbed borderline patients, it is sometimes necessary for the therapist to arrange for a colleague to meet with a patient during a long break in a psychotherapy. In these instances the covering therapist is often experienced as evoking the memories of either the therapist's person or aspects of the psychotherapy. Sometimes this takes the form of actual interventions geared toward reminding the patient of previously consolidated understandings of conflicts or painful affect. At other times the covering therapist may remind the patient of his availability during times of crisis. The covering therapist's activity may often include questioning the patient about the therapy and therapist in a way that evokes the image of the psychotherapist and the fact that he or she will return, particularly for patients whose ability for evocative memory is relatively undeveloped or subject to regression in the context of the therapist's absence. Often these interventions provide a sense of the holding environment sufficiently so that the patient's ability to use transitional objects is restored or solidified. In contrast Kohut's use of the term selfobject refers not to actual functions of the analyst, but instead to the patient's experience of the analyst in response to the latter's listening and interpretive activity.

We believe that the need for transitional objects is ubiquitous. For better integrated individuals, as compared to severely disturbed borderline individuals, the expression of wishes and conflicts surrounding selfobject and transitional object functions of the analyst is more often accomplished through verbalized fantasy, rather than actual behavior; often these wishes are expressed within a more highly organized and adaptive defensive structure. Such patients demonstrate greater distance from the accompanying painful affect, as illustrated by their ability to work with these affects through expression of wishes rather than through the experience of needs that are felt to be desperately essential, such as is the case for the borderline patient. For example, we believe that analysands sometimes attempt to solidify or restore the analytic situation as a safe, holding environment, even as they proceed to examine and work through conflicts at a variety of developmental and psychosexual levels.

Clinical Vignette

The case of Ms. B, a divorced woman in her mid-20s, exemplifies some of the ways in which neurotic patients may express wishes for transitional phenomena to aid or restore the experience of the analyst's holding, selfobject function. During the second year of analysis, Ms. B began to experience many old feelings of aloneness and loneliness in the form of memories of painful separation experiences from her family during latency and adolescence. These memories were salient at this point in the analysis at the same time as some of her modes of enactment in her outside life, such as a longstanding affair with an unavailable man, became much less satisfying. Many of these memories of being separate from the family were related to ways in which she had felt it necessary to hide parts of herself from her family, particularly rebellious and hostile feelings; through lack of disclosure and, in some instances, deception she hid activities that her parents had forbidden. As she began to explore more fully these experiences in her analysis, she began to feel a sense of isolation centering around family members "not knowing who I really am". Dream content often began to include wishes to internalize and utilize soothing experiences of the analytic situation. For example, she dreamed of placing her feet inside the couch, which, in her dream, was specially equipped with pouches for such purposes. She also had dreams in which she would rise from the couch and tape record our sessions, take notes during the analytic session, and be held by the analyst for as long as she liked. In her associations to such dreams she spoke of the comforting aspects of these activities.

Although such wishes were partly understood as a form of defensive regression in which she could safely take in the analyst at a variety of levels as an asexual little girl rather than as a woman, there were also indications that at the same time, faced with exploring earlier experiences of hiding and exile from the family, she sought to buttress the analytic situation as a safe and holding experience. Thus, as part of the transference, she expressed wishes for transitional objects, such as the pouch in the couch for her feet and the tape recorder to preserve analytic sessions, to help cope with these experiences, rather than engage in the actual use of transitional objects to restore soothing and safety, as in the case of Ms. A.

A Note on the Application of the Transitional Object Concept to the Treatment of Narcissistic Patients

A brief vignette from the lengthy three-times-a-week psychotherapy of Mr. E, a divorced and remarried man in his early 30s, illustrates some of the complex functions of the "teddy bear" for patients with narcissistic character disturbances.

Mr. E sought treatment due to chronic, debilitating shame and humiliation as a result of sexual fantasies about pubescent boys and to ongoing rage toward his wife for what he experienced as ridicule and rejection. In his sexual fantasies Mr. E dominated the boys as they performed fellatio or allowed him to have anal intercourse with them. In addition to the experience of shame, these fantasies were accompanied by conscious feelings of pleasure and ejaculation during masturbation, largely deriving from the sense of omnipotent control that he had over the boys.

After several months of treatment, Mr. E began to tell his therapist about his teddy bear. Teddy, as he referred to "him", (Teddy was referred to as masculine, but the patient was often quick to qualify that teddy bears have neither penises nor vaginas) was used during childhood, and Mr. E had continued to use him in a variety of contexts intermittently since his early 20s. Teddy was often called upon to soothe and calm the patient when he felt misunderstood or mistreated by others; most often this involved feeling slighted by authority figures. Mr. E would feel especially angry if he sensed that someone underestimated his professional abilities or talents.

In the transference during the first several years of treatment, Mr. E would often feel envious and enraged with his therapist, feeling that the therapist was bigger, smarter, and more accomplished than he. Mr. E felt that his therapist was secretly contemptuous of him and viewed him as a small boy who was always aspiring and never measuring up. He also felt that the therapist would be critical of his relationship to Teddy. Occasionally he had pleasurable fantasies that his therapist might have a teddy bear which, as he put it, gratified his wish that his therapist, father, and four older brothers be men who also experienced self-doubt, weaknesses, and needs for holding. During this period he would often go home from sessions beset with rage and competitive strivings and find transient tension relief through masturbatory fantasies involving sexual domination of young boys or by looking at himself in the mirror while masturbating. He would also find some solace from Teddy's unchallenging acceptance of and compliance with his wishes.

During a large portion of the treatment, Mr. E's use of the teddy bear centered on the restoration of self-esteem in the face of memories of humiliating and rejecting experiences in childhood and adult life, including his feelings of inadequacy as a male during his oedipal phase. Clearly, he used the teddy bear as a way to restore empathic failures in the psychotherapy and as a way to supplement postive feelings about being male that he felt unable to obtain or maintain from his therapist. Genetic material discussed over the course of treatment revealed that between the ages of three and six Mr. E. had carried a teddy bear and blanket around the house as a source of soothing and comfort. He recalled feeling that his brothers and occasionally his father would laugh at him about his reliance on the blanket and bear. At age seven he felt confused and humiliated by an operation for an undescended testicle, which exacerbated his sense of being inferior to his brothers and father. He was prone to serious tantrums throughout childhood and would often cuddle and play roughly with his teddy bear when sent to his room.

As an adult Mr. E relied on his fantasies and his teddy bear in a variety of ways, but none of these emphasized separation conflict as a *primary* conflict. Teddy was a safe spokesperson for the patient's needs to be mirrored, loved, and seen as a person who was strong and in control of his interactions with others. Teddy provided a haven for the beleaguered little boy who, as an adult, often felt rejected and mocked by his wife and therapist, as he had felt by his brothers as a child. Mr. E's fantasies were partly retaliatory in nature, not to avenge or repair painful separation, but instead to dominate the pubescent self projected onto the young boys as objects in his fantasies. Rather than feel victimized by and ashamed of his emerging sexuality and his yearnings for holding and support, as he had felt within his family, he sought outlets for his disappointment and rage through identification with his father and brothers as the persons in control. In the transference the therapist became the object of his wishes to dominate and control; to do otherwise would have meant that he felt helpless in the face of his experience of the therapist's ridicule toward him. The teddy bear helped Mr. E titrate his yearnings and his rage toward the therapist, allowing him to try to express and integrate these feelings.

Mr. E's use of the teddy bear, as well as his fantasies, functioned as a soothing resource to help him cope with the severe vicissitudes that he experienced in his self-esteem regulation in both the preoedipal and oedipal sectors of his psychopathology. Using Winnicott's definition of the transitional object as an aid in the denial of separation, we would not characterize the teddy bear's function as primarily transitional in nature because it appeared that whatever separation anxiety Mr. E experienced (in fact quite minimal), it was secondary to his relative inability to use people to help him regulate self-esteem. However, Tolpin's (1971) expansion of the functions of the transitional object to include resources for the restoration of vigor and equilibrium seem quite applicable to Mr. E.

Volkan (1973), in describing the analysis of a narcissistic man, characterized his patient's fantasies and associative content during the first four years of analysis as transitional in nature. These fantasies—mostly involving the patient seducing numerous women and at other times visualizing himself as a bull entirely dominating his environment—were conceptualized as transitional because they provided the patient a means of having omnipotent control over the analyst and, thus, not needing the analyst. This conceptualization partially confuses the phenomena of defensive self-sufficiency and needs for omnipotent control, so common among narcissistically disturbed individuals, with the complex functions of the transitional object, which include attempts to mitigate separation anxiety but also to help create a capacity for new forms of object appraisal and object relating.

This terminological confusion also involves a failure to differentiate between the creative or development-building functions of the transitional object and the transferences of borderline and narcissistic adult patients, which often involve massive and basic defenses against disappointment and reactive rage. For the borderline patient the formation of the transitional object transference, as described by Modell, reflects the early and somewhat rigid establishment of the denial of the analyst as a separate person. Such a transference may be viewed as partly providing protection from excessive aggression resulting from disappointment with others. Winnicott (1971) distinguishes between what he terms the "positive" aspects of aggression and aggression as a response to conflict with the reality principle. He formulates the positive use of aggression, "destructiveness," in the analytic situation as a process through which the patient is gradually able to place the analyst outside the area of omnipotent control. Eventually, in successful treatment, the patient views the analyst as able to survive the full strength of the vicissitudes of his instinctual experience. Thus, "maximal destructiveness" (p. 91) is associated with maximal separateness between patient and analyst.

For Winnicott, the positive use of aggression in the analytic situation involves a progressive step for the patient in shedding the denial of separateness. However, the immediate formation of the wish for omnipotent control by the narcissistic patient differs in important ways from the progressive or "positive" functions of aggression inherent in the use of the transitional object during development. The transitional object helps "make reality" for the infant, despite being a reality that is imbued with projected internal processes. In contrast, for the borderline and narcissistic patient such immediate transference phenomena involve more centrally the denial of limitation, separateness, and dependency. Once again, the analogy of the borderline and narcissistic adult's transference to the child's play with the transitional object may partially blur our understanding of the infant's use of the transitional object as an adaptive step in the normal development of object relations and the infant's use of the transitional object as a defense against painful separation anxiety.

General Implications and Conclusions

In recent years there has been an increasing appreciation and elaboration of the holding environment in psychoanalysis and psychoanalytic psychotherapy as an agent of therapeutic action that is complementary to notions of conflict resolution and insight. It is probable that the holding environment comprises both transitional and selfobject functions and that it is here, to some extent, that the work of Winnicott, Modell, and Kohut converge (Tolpin, 1986).

Numerous analysts in recent years emphasize the ways in which the holding environment may usefully create a "background of safety" (Sandler, 1960) that permits and enhances the unfolding of the analytic process for all patients. We believe, additionally, that many phenomena observed during the analytic process have referents to transitional and selfobject concepts. Often such phenomena as carrying the analyst's bill on the analysand's person may, without being spoken of in analysis, help to remind the patient of either the analyst's presence, the holding aspects of the analytic situation, or newly emerging and precariously internalized analytic insights. Such interpretations of these phenomena clearly do not contradict or supplant other important meanings of these behaviors; carrying around the analyst's bill may have many meanings, such as enactment or displacement of sexual or hostile impulses, depending on the patient and the particular phase of the analysis. But, additionally, such examples may represent attempts of the analysand to buttress the analytic holding environment by linking the analysand to the selfobject functions of the analyst or the analytic process. Thus, patients may express transference enactment of anxiety surrounding expression of affects while concomitantly expressing or enacting anxiety about the precariously experienced analytic holding environment.

The therapist or analyst of the borderline patient benefits from multiple pespectives for understanding the complex transferences of such patients. These transference phenomena are illuminated by both the transitional object and selfobject concepts.

The transitional object as a concept for understanding these transferences (Modell, 1963, 1968) allowed for an expanding appraisal of aspects of borderline psychopathology as a form of developmental arrest. Modell emphasized the reparative and compensatory efforts of the borderline patient to use the therapist or analyst to defend against and mitigate the painful aspects of separation anxiety; Modell's work also addressed the "creative" (Winnicott, 1951; Modell, 1970) aspects of the borderline patient's use of the therapist or analyst, as reflected in attempts to create an object where, presumably, one was missing. Additionally, the transitional object concept takes almost exclusively as its focus the affects and conflicts projected onto both the environment and the analyst; within this formulation the object-analyst is seen largely as a projective entity owing its very existence to needs arising within the individual for such an object.

The selfobject concept allows for the understanding of transferences among borderline patients that may partially include, but are not embedded in, the context of separation. This concept, as it has been applied to the treatment of the borderline patient, allows for the opportunity to appraise the borderline patient's projections of intense object hunger and oral rage, as well as to suggest the ways in which the borderline patient experiences a variety of forms of empathic failure on the part of the therapist or analyst: thus Kohut's description of the analyst as a selfobject focused exclusively on the interpretive efforts of the analyst as experienced by the patient. The selfobject concept as applied to the treatment of borderline patients (Adler and Buie, 1979; Buie and Adler, 1982), in contrast to Kohut's formulation, has additionally addressed the ways in which the therapist or analyst actively provides such functions as mirroring, validation of tenuous reality testing, and clarification of precarious self and other differentiation. It is our hope that these distinctions help characterize and define the analyst's ongoing need to assess the stability of the analytic situation as a holding environment from which analytic work may proceed for all patients.

REFERENCES

Adler, G. (1980), Transference, real relationship and alliance. *Internat. J. Psycho-Anal.* 61:547–558.

_____ (1985), *Borderline Psychopathology and Its Treatment.* New York: Aronson.

_____ Buie, D. (1979), Aloneness and borderline psychopathology: The possible relevance of child development Issues. *Internat. J. Psycho-Anal.*, 60:83–96.

Buie, D. Adler, G. (1982), Definінitve treatment of the borderline personality. *Internat. J. Psychoanal. Psychother.*, 9:51–87.

Fintzy, R. (1971), Vicissitudes of the transitional object in a borderline child. *Internat. J. Psycho-Anal.*, 52:107–114.

Giovacchini, P. (1984), The psychoanalytic paradox: The self as transitional object. *Psychoanal. Rev.*, 71:81–92.

Goldberg, A. (1984/1985), Translations between psychoanalytic theories. *The Annual of Psychoanalysis,* 12&13:121–135. New York: International Universities Press.

Henderson, J. (1984), Play in the psychotherapy of selfobject relating. *Can. J. Psychiat.*,

29:417–424.
Kahne, M. (1967), On the persistence of transitional phenomena into adult life. *Internat. J. Psycho-Anal.*, 48:247–258.
Kohut, H. (1971), *The Analysis of the Self.* New York: International Universities Press.
_____ (1977), *The Restoration of the Self.* New York: International Universities Press.
Modell, A. (1963), Primitive object relationships and the predisposition to schizophrenia. *Internat. J. Psycho-Anal.*, 44:282–292.
_____ (1968), *Object Love and Reality.* New York: International Universities Press.
_____ (1970), The transitional object and the creative act. *Psychoanal. Quart.*, 39:240–250
Robbins, M. (1976), Borderline personality organization: The need for a new theory. *S. Amer. Psycho-Anal. Assn.*, 24:831–845.
Robertson, J. (1971), Young children in brief separation: A fresh look. *The Psychoanalytic Study of the Child,* 26:264–289. New Haven, CT: Yale University Press.
Sandler, J. (1960), The background of safety. *Internat. J. Psycho-Anal.*, 41:352–356.
Tolpin, M. (1971), On the beginnings of a cohesive self: An application of the concept of transmuting internalization to the study of the transitional object and signal anxiety. *The Psychoanalytic Study of the Child,* 26:316–352. New Haven, CT: Yale University Press.
_____ (1986), Discussion of paper, "Toward a clarification of the transitional object and selfobject concepts in the treatment of the borderline patient." Presented at the fall meeting of the American Psychoanalytic Association, New York City.
Volkan, V. (1973), Transitional fantasies in the analysis of a narcissistic personality. *J. Amer. Psychoanal. Assn.*, 21:351–376.
Winnicott, D. W. (1953), Transitional objects and transitional phenomena. A study of the first not-me possession. *Internat. J. Psycho-Anal.*, 34:89–97.
_____ (1971), *Playing and Reality* New York: Basic Books.
Wolf, E. (1980), On the developmental line of selfobject relations. In: *Advances in Self Psychology,* ed. A. Goldberg. New York: International Universities Press, pp. 117–130.

IV

THEORETICAL AND HISTORICAL CONTRIBUTIONS

On Postanalytic Amnesia

MARK TREWARTHA

The impetus for this paper arose out of a series of discussions with two colleagues on the issue of what our patients found meaningful about their analytic treatment. What we discovered was how little they seemed to remember about the content of their treatments; this, in turn, prompted us to speculate about what actually happens in an analysis and what it is that is curative. My two colleagues and I recorded unsolicited accounts from our patients during treatment hours of material that they identified directly or indirectly as meaningful during that hour or preceding hours. Later we added both solicited and unsolicited replies to questions about what was meaningful, important, or helpful in their treatments. In addition, I wrote several analytic colleagues asking for similar information about their own and their patients' analyses. While admittedly this was not a rigorous study (e.g., the sample is small and no standardization of questions was attempted), some interesting "data" did emerge, which prompted me to wonder about and explore the area of postanalytic amnesia.

A vignette from a woman in analysis with me in the midst of an intense transference neurosis will serve as a not atypical response. Unsolicited, she revealed the following:

> Yesterday I think at the end when the issue of trusting you and my perception of you—are they right and so much depends on that. I don't remember what you said but whatever it was it seemed you really appreciated that and understood. The way you sounded it was like you had an appreciation of the way it was—just the opposite of I can talk straight for forty-five minutes sometimes and you'll sift it through and come out with one major thing; it gets reduced to one major thing. But yesterday wasn't that at all. I was talking about a whole lot of different

> feelings that are hard to feel at the same time—a feeling you were right there with me—it's the sort of moment that, after I carry it with me, it stays.

And in another hour:

> Do you have any idea why it is I have so much trouble remembering what happens from one session to the next? On Monday and yesterday it doesn't seem that either day I came in and talked about what I wanted to. It's just such a blank—I don't know how I could have so much to say and not remember it—I mean sometimes it feels like I go into some other state or something—when I get up it's like I wake up or something.

Though her "loss of memory" turned out to be in part defensively derived, this vignette is similar to what my two colleagues reported: their patients remembered their analyst's support, listening, and "being there" but didn't remember much about the content, the interpretations, or reconstructions in their analyses. The following description of a patient in the termination phase is from a colleague.

> He started the hour by telling his analyst his [patient's] wife told him he is hardly fighting with her anymore. When he started analysis, one of his chief complaints was irrational jealousy about his wife. He feels flickers of this still but much diminished. He wonders why the change. He thinks maybe his mother's attention to his younger sister who was born when he was young? Maybe his greater freedom in his sexual life? But he feels these are textbook explanations. He really doesn't know why. He says after he reflects on it that "It's like I was sick and I was healed—it took time and it took analysis." His analyst asked, "What about analysis?" He said, "Well, it was something I did for myself; I came three times a week and you supported me. That's what I remember, not the textbook explanation but our relationship—the feeling that you supported me." His analyst asked him at one point, "Is the healing like getting over a cold?" He said, "No, more like getting over a chronic infection."

One respondent claimed that "if people don't remember their analysis, not much was memorable"; later in his letter he noted that what several patients thought was helpful in their work was the climate of opening up and understanding. However, this colleague did not specify if these patients remembered much of the content of their analyses. He himself claimed to remember a great deal from his own analyses. Another analyst I wrote to had a similar experience in his training analysis though he remembered "almost nothing" from his first analysis when he was a psychology intern. My two colleagues and I had analytic experiences more closely resembling our patients'. We remembered little of the content of our analyses though, interestingly, one of us found that as our discussions proceeded, some of that content became "more available".

As Calef (1982) notes of the responses he received from former analysands, patients admit to change in themselves but generally regard this as having happened without their knowing how. Most of his correspondents, even those whose outcome was relatively unsuccessful, seemed to identify with a process but had little memory of the unconscious content unveiled. As Calef tersely puts it, "In a manner of speaking, the analysand (as with any analysand) did not know what hit him" (p. 105).

There have been others who have commented on postanalytic amnesia, but, as Stein (1965) points out, "many authors have commented on the forgetting of dreams, not nearly so many on the forgetting of analytic content" (p. 65). There has been no systematic investigation of what is remembered and what is forgotten from an analysis. Freud never specifically addressed the forgetting of the content of one's analysis. If he had, he might have attributed it to "after repression," wherein new or old conflicts are rerepressed, or repeated his aphorism that psychoanalysis helps one to remember so that one may forget.

Kris (1956) mentions the relative infrequency, except perhaps in some analysts, of the connections and patterns between past and present remaining available after analysis. He proposes "systematic analytic catamnesis" (p. 85) as a way of studying whether insight into personal history remains operative after analysis and whether such insight can be correlated with therapeutic results. His own speculation is that there is not a high correlation between results and awareness of the "biographical picture."

Deutsch (1959) coined the term "pseudoamnesia" to describe the forgetting of the events of one's analysis. "The patients claim that the content of their memories of a long, successful analysis can be expressed in 'two sentences.' They simply do not remember more" (p. 446). Deutsch attributes this "pseudoamnesia" to cathexis being shifted away from the outer world during analysis onto the intrapsychic experience so that the reliving in the transference creates a "climate" that is stronger than the external one. When, after analysis, there is a recathexis of external reality, the world of analysis becomes "pale, unreal and without content" (p. 474).

Herbert Schlesinger (1970) describes a chance encounter with a patient some years after termination during which the patient spontaneously described an event that had been most helpful to him: Schlesinger had made a special effort to accommodate him by seeing him at an unusual hour. However, when asked if he could recall some of the things that he had felt were important during the analysis or truths he had discovered about himself, he was distressed at not being able to remember more than some generalizations about these personal discoveries, generalizations that lacked much of the specificity and intensity that Schlesinger remembered they had had at the time. Schlesinger believes that such incidents are not at all unusual and would be attributed to rerepression by most analysts but that an alternative explanation could be that the repressed memories and fantasies, once worked through, are no longer invested with "drive energy." That is, once the purpose for learning them has passed, they tend to fade from memory and become a part of the person who underwent them—essentially, Freud's psychoanalysis helps one to remember so that one may forget.

Follow-up studies, notably by Pfeffer (1959, 1961, 1963) and Schlessinger and Robbins (1983), reveal the now generally accepted experience of revival of the analytic experience in miniature, the "Pfeffer Phenomenon," as Calef calls it, but little attention is devoted to what the patient remembers of the content of the analysis or to what the patient thought was meaningful or helpful in it. Both studies are evaluations of results of analysis based on the analyst's estimation of the importance of what the former analysand describes as having changed and on the recrudescence and subsiding of the revived transference during follow-up; they are not based on what the patient remembers or ascribes as meaningful. Pfeffer (1963) describes the patient as retaining after analysis "an important and complicated intrapsychic representation of the analyst" (p. 238) and Schlessinger and Robbins (1983) elaborate on the preconscious self-analytic function they believe is one of the hallmarks of a successful analysis, but these explanations are again from the analyst's vantage point. This is not to discredit such explanations, but to note that such follow-up work does not add significant understanding to the phenomena being investigated here, namely, the forgetting of a majority of the process and content of one's analysis and the identification from the analysand's viewpoint of what has been meaningful.

There are, of course, the exceptions to the many analysands who seem to remember so little. A rereading of Calef's (1982) retrospective evaluation of his analytic work reveals that while he claims it is unusual for analytic patients to achieve a clear recognition of what happens in their analyses, some of his patients (two analytic candidates and a noncandidate psychiatrist) seemed to retain not only knowledge of the dynamic and genetic issues, but a recollection of the intensity of the emotional experiences. Kris (1956) speaks of some analysts successfully pursuing self-analysis as either a concomitant part of their work or at times of personal crisis. He believes a wide area of awareness of their past remains available to them after analysis, but he cautions that even in these cases detailed information is not available. Kramer (1959), in describing her own "autoanalytic function" postanalytically, does not detail what she actually remembered from her analysis but elaborates on certain insights derived largely spontaneously (without active attention) that she believes involved activation of an ego function derived from the analytic process. Likewise, Myerson (1960), in writing about an experience of self-analytic work postanalytically, describes not what he remembers from his analysis but what he implies is a major outcome of analysis: the ability to do just such self-analytic work—work that is only partially conscious.

As I've mentioned, two colleagues I wrote to seem to remember a significant amount from their analyses, but, apropos of Kris's cautionary note, they did not explicitly detail what they do remember. Norman and associates (1976), writing on the fate of the transference neurosis after analysis, describe in detail the follow-up interview of an analytic institute graduate who had completed his analysis five years before the follow-up study. Not only did this analysand reveal the usual "Pfeffer Phenomenon," but he remembered a wealth of dynamic and genetic issues and was able to describe at some length the subjective experiences in his analysis. Norman and his associates were also impressed that the other four subjects they followed up, two of whom were not graduate analysts, were able to remember and discuss so much of their analyses. Oremland, Blacher, and Norman (1975) followed up two nonanalyst analysands two years after completion of their analyses and were likewise impressed with these analysands' recall and with their knowledge of the sequence of their analyses. Oremland and associates admit the unexpectedness of such findings since they are at variance with the commonly held belief that patients remember little of their analyses. However, they don't pursue the question of why some analysands seem to remember so much while many remember so little. I return to this problem later.

Despite what appears to be a significant number of exceptions, I think it is still safe to conclude that many, if not most, patients remember little of the content of their analyses. And as a number of authors have noted, it is not just a forgetting of painful experiences, but pleasant and seemingly unconflicted experiences as well. Rerepression, change of cathexis, and fading from memory once issues have been worked through and de-invested of drive energy all could play a part. But I believe other explanations deserve exploration. Knowledge derived from memory research and investigation of altered states of consciousness is crucial to understanding this forgetting.

Squire (1986), writing in *Science* on mechanisms of memory, describes two types of knowledge or memory. What he terms "declarative memory" is explicit and accessible to conscious awareness. It includes the facts, episodes, lists, and routes of everyday life and can be "declared," that is, brought to mind verbally as a proposition or nonverbally as an image. "Procedural knowledge" or memory on the other hand is implicit and accessible only through performance, that is, by engaging in the skills or operations in which the knowledge is embedded. Exposure to stimulus material, called "priming," activates the preexisting representations, and the information acquired through priming is fully accessible only through the same sensory modality in which the material was presented initially. Procedural learning is likely phylogenetically old while the capacity for declarative knowledge is phylogenetically recent, reaching its greatest development in mammals with greater elaboration of certain brain structures, that is, the hippocampal formation and associated cortical areas.

These two forms of memory or knowledge are thought to involve different information storage systems and to involve either primarily conscious (declarative memory) or unconscious (procedural knowledge) processes. In most cases an experience is thought to engage both memory systems. For example, perception of a word transiently activates the preexisting assembly of neural elements through the priming effect, an unconscious process that temporarily facilitates processing of the same word and associated words, and is followed by the establishment of longer-lasting declarative (conscious) memory that the word was seen—and seen at a particular time and place.

Obviously, there are similarities here to what has been described as state-dependent retrieval, in which memory is activated or primed by exposure to conditions or a stimulus similar to that in response to which the memory was laid down in the first place. Perhaps the most famous example is the memory crystallized by Proust's Madeleine: when he inhaled the lime-perfumed cup-cake, seven volumes' worth of memories—which would become his *Remembrance of Things Past*—were "primed" in his brain. I return to state-dependent retrieval shortly.

Reiser (1985), in striving to develop an approach to the interface between mind and brain, psychoanalysis and neurobiology, summarizes Mishkin's work on memory in the monkey and speculates that there could be an analogy between Freud's ideas of two parallel and independent, that is, primary and secondary, modes of processing information and Mishkin's research, which suggests two shared-memory systems in the monkey. The system Mishkin terms "habit memory" involves corticostriatal complexes and is noncognitive, likely older, and closer to preverbal visual representations. The other, which Mishkin labels "cognitive memory," involves corticolimbic systems and is preceded in development by the striatal complex. Reiser suggests it could be closer to conscious representations.

In parallel to this anatomic work, Bucci (1985) offers convincing evidence derived from current experimental work in cognitive psychology that there is dual coding, in which nonverbal and verbal information are each encoded, in symbolic form, in separate systems specialized for such representation. The two systems are thought to be connected by a complex system of referential relations, and both nonverbal and verbal representation may become conscious, be temporarily inaccessible, or remain repressed. However, it is thought that repression is, in general, more likely to affect material stored in the nonverbal system, since emotion is linked more closely to perceptual (nonverbal) representations. Bucci believes this dual code model for mental representations can account for the fact that it may be difficult at times to find the right words to express ideas, images, or feelings and that we often seem in some sense to know what we want to say without being able to put it into words. In other words, variation in style of delivery could be accounted for in terms of differences in initial input. Information stored in verbal schemata would be easier to recount than that in nonverbal schemata.

Without recourse to the foregoing research, Schachtel (1959), writing on memory and childhood amnesia, describes two types of memory: the "autobiographical" memory and the "useful" memory. The "useful" memory, like Squire's "declarative memory," includes the facts, dates, episodes—the past shorn of the richly textured, complex experience that it once was. This "useful" past is remembered because, in contrast to the "autobiographical" past, it is constantly reexperienced and used and because it is essential to the orientation and adaptation of the child and adult to the environment. The "autobiographical" memory—memory of the personal past—remains elusive. The period richest in experience, the period of childhood, is difficult, if not impossible, to remember. It increasingly assumes the form of clichés and, like procedural knowledge, gains awareness only by being primed by contexts and stimuli associated with the original. Schachtel acknowledges that in actuality these two types of memory are not clear-cut and the two types of content are continuously and everywhere interrelated. And while his examination of the forgetting of childhood experience leads him to conclude that it is the adult culture, with its "language, biases, emphases, and taboos" (p. 297), that is, its different schemata, that precludes a reliable rendering of childhood, it is, nevertheless, interesting that his conceptualization of different types of memory shares such a close resemblance to that posited by his more biologically oriented contemporaries.

Returning now to state-dependent retrieval and the relationship of different memory systems to postanalytic amnesia, I think it possible that our forgetting the content of our analyses can be explained in part by the fact that the experiences that arise in analysis are similar to "procedural knowledge," "habit memory," "nonverbal representation," or "autobiographical memory" and that while this knowledge can become partly conscious during the analytic hour and even between hours and can be intense and vivid, it quickly "sinks" from awareness. Yet it can be revived or "primed" when the patient is again "in analysis." Obviously, there is a complex relationship here with repression of content; as Schachtel points out in comparing the repression of objectionable material with forgetting that is due to the schemata of the adult being unable to accommodate childhood experience, the "two mechanisms of forgetting shade gradually and imperceptibly into one another" (p. 285). It is Rapaport (1950) who reminds us that the hypothesis that all forgetting is due to repression was advanced not by Freud, but by Jones. Freud was reluctant to claim a general validity of his theory of repression for the forgetting of isolated words, facts, and knowledge but readily claimed it for the tendency to forget childhood memories, dreams, and intentions. Even in the forgetting of dreams, however, he did not claim an absolute role for repression (Whitman, 1963).

Human state-dependent retrieval has been a topic of experimental investigation for nearly two decades. Retrieval operations complete the act of remembering that begins with encoding or registration of information about an event into the memory store. The information is stored or retained and, according to the encoding specificity principle (Eich, 1980; Tulving and Thompson, 1973), what is stored is determined by what is perceived and how it is encoded, and what is stored determines what retrieval cues are effective in providing access to it. That is not to imply that once an event has been encoded, its trace cannot undergo further change. There are many possible modifications of stored information that occur prior to the act of explicit retrieval. Nevertheless, in experimental work what has been focused on is the accessibility (retrieval) of a stored trace, and what seems crucial besides the strength, quality, and durability of the trace itself is the context or environment during encoding and whether or not such a context is available at retrieval. In other words, how well something is remembered depends not only on what it is, but how it is stored in memory and whether those cues are available at retrieval. Tulving and Thompson detail the long history of research into learning that has concluded what Bartlett (1932) in his early work on remembering had emphasized—the conditions of the prior perceptions in determining recall and recognition are important.

In terms of the analytic situation then, it appears that what might be required to remember more of the content and experiences of our analyses is not just an overcoming of resistance to painful rerepressed content but a context or cues not too dissimilar from the analytic experience itself. Some of these cues must have been triggered in one of my colleagues during our discussions, for he began to have more memories of his analysis. It certainly has to be an important factor in the appearance of the "Pfeffer Phenomenon" on follow-up interviews.

But what about the cues? What is the context or environment in which analytic experience takes place that is akin to "procedural knowledge" and that must be duplicated, at least in part, if remembering is to ensue? I believe there is evidence that the analytic experience takes place, in part, in an altered or fluctuating state of consciousness.

Stein (1965) mentions that initially in psychoanalysis there was an all-absorbing interest in the psychology of consciousness, which was surpassed by the development of interest in the study of character and defenses. However, in the 1950s such investigators as Rapaport, Fisher, and Klein explored the field of consciousness once again, and Lewin investigated the similarities between the manifest content of the analytic situation and that of the dream. Stein grants to Lewin the most inclusive discussion of variations of awareness during analysis. Lewin (1973) studied the analytic patient as a quasi sleeper or quasi dreamer, noting Freud's (1900) similar description of the patient who is free associating, having undergone "the establishment of a physical state, which in its distribution of psychical energy (that is, of mobile attention), bears some analogy to the state before falling asleep—and no doubt also to hypnosis" (p. 102). Lewin traces some of the historic reasons we may resist the idea that analytic theory and technique are related to sleep and hypnosis but reminds us that the psychoanalytic session is an outgrowth, historically, of the hypnotic trance: "In most patient's experience the nearest thing to what they are asked to do on the couch is what they have sometimes done in bed, when, with a fluctuating state of consciousness somewhat influenced by the anticipation of sleep, they have let idle thoughts run through their mind, with whatever consequence" (p. 243).

Other writers describe the analytic context in a similar vein. Zinberg (1977) compares meditative states and psychoanalysis, stressing the contemplative and introspective approaches of both in which the press of stimuli from the external environment is minimized and the awareness of one's inner state of being is maximized. Paralleling Lewin's comments on our resistance to our historical roots in the hypnotic trance, "a truth many of us would rather ignore" (Stein, 1965, p. 65), Zinberg writes about the doubt the scientific community has to the respectability of altered states of consciousness, since there is still an association in the minds of many between such states, illicit drug use, and Eastern sects. Bodaracco (1975) describes psychoanalysis as evoking and facilitating altered states of consciousness, regression with different levels of awareness, and a "meditative atmosphere" of alternating relaxation-experiencing and effort-reflecting. Stein (1965) believes it likely that we miss many covert changes in states of consciousness in the analytic situation, and although his attention was drawn to the issue by a special group of patients who had experienced early physical trauma and had powerful tendencies to forget the material of their analyses (they were subject to periods of what he called "pseudo stupidity"), he extends his discussion to modifications of consciousness in general and to the laws, similar to those regulating the forgetting of dreams, governing the extensive forgetting of analytic content in certain patients.

Marsh (1977) notes, as have others, that a characteristic of consciousness is that it is constantly changing and quotes William James as describing consciousness as a continuous stream, ever moving, never the same, from moment to moment. Marsh believes Freud's use of the term "states of consciousness" implies that there might be an almost infinite number of such different states. Klein (1959) describes consciousness as a useful structural convention that permits us to speak of a wide variety of patterns of awareness or states of consciousness and believes that the term "preconscious" is more misleading than helpful, since it refers to little more than "registrations not in awareness" (p. 31). He develops the theme, using evidence from research studies, that subjects are more responsive to subliminal stimuli during reverie-like states and that these subliminal registrations are more amenable to voluntary recall if attention is deployed towards a passive, eidetic-imaging state. He advances the proposal that there are processes other than repression, "in the sense of a 'pushing out' process" (p. 31), that deny awareness to these registrations and offers different states of consciousness in the waking state as an explanation. Kalman (1975) prefers to drop the term "altered" altogether, since he feels it gives an erroneous impression of there being something special or unique about the altering going on in consciousness, a "sequence of patternings" that he believes is going on all the time, as is "our attending to these patternings as our attending focuses now inward and now outward" (p. 193). Basch (1981) also eschews the concept of levels of consciousness and explicates the work of cognitive psychologists to advance the thesis that in the normal course of events "thought" (or what we think of as "conscious thought") is but a very minor part of the thought-processing activity of the brain. He believes that the transformations that take place in analysis take place largely outside of conscious awareness.

In conjunction with the patient as quasi sleeper or quasi dreamer, Lewin (1973) conceived of the analyst as sleep maker or waker, comparing the dream as the guardian of sleep with the analyst as the guardian of free association. This, of course, is not an unfamiliar aspect of analytic technique; in addition to interpretations and other operations, we encourage more free association, more reverie or quasi sleep, if you will. And, in parallel with the promotion of such a state in our patients, we too sink into a semi-reverie in our listening attitude, a state perhaps not too unlike the intermediate area between wakefulness and sleep Lewin describes in the analysand. We often breathe sighs of relief when our patients accept analysis and the couch, feeling ourselves relaxing, feeling time on our side, directing our attention and efforts less stringently and allowing more "free play," and roaming over our thoughts and feelings as they are stirred by our patients' associations. Or, as Freud stated (1922):

> Experience soon showed that the attitude which the analytic physician could most advantageously adopt was to surrender himself to his own unconscious mental activity in a state of evenly suspended attention, to avoid so far as possible reflection and the construction of conscious expectations, not to try to fix anything that he heard, particularly in his memory, and by these means to catch the drift of the patient's unconscious with his own unconscious [p. 239].

Again, in parallel with our patients, we too can have difficulty in remembering, though I think not to the same degree, the content of their analytic hours. Like our patients, we frequently need a context or priming to remember or remember vividly. The "Monday morning crust" is true not just of the analysand.

I am not advocating an interpretationless, drifting "sleep therapy"; I am attempting to highlight the shift in the usual deployment of attention both in our analysands and, to a lesser degree, ourselves that, I hypothesize, is partially responsible for our difficulty in recapturing the content and process of individual hours and the analysis as a whole without contextually derived clues.

Fleiss (1942), analyzing the analyzing analyst, calls the "evenly suspended attention" of Freud "conditioned daydreaming." The analyst reciprocates his patient's motor restrictions, thereby obtaining one of the prerequisites for daydreaming, and oscillates between the states of full and partial differentiation. It was Fleiss who coined the term "trial identification" to explain empathy. Olinick and associates (1973) likewise stress the parallel and partial regression required of the analyst if trial identification or empathy is to take place. As they put it, "The two observing egos regress—the work ego for the purpose of empathy, the patient's observing ego for the purpose of transference gratification" (p. 147). While then stressing that to be effective the work ego must return to an observing, information-processing function, they also point out and give examples to show how, at times, the interpretive formulations are derived outside of awareness, how the functions of the work ego are often silent, and how we become aware of them only after the fact. They attribute this phenomenon in part to the "intangible quality of the material, the primary data with which one works" (p. 149). Their quote from Bion captures, I believe, some of the essence of this "procedural knowledge" with which we work:

> Anyone who has made careful notes of what he considers to be the facts of a session must be familiar with the experience in which such notes will, on occasion, seem to be drained of all reality; they might be notes of dreams made to ensure that he will not forget them on awakening. To me it suggests that the experience of the session relates to material akin to the dream . . . the dream and the psychoanalyst's working material both share dreamlike quality [p. 149].

Calef and Weinshel (1980) speak directly of the analyst being in an altered state of consciousness or "intermittent" altered state in which to achieve "evenly suspended attention" he "puts to bed" but not to sleep certain censorship functions so that he may "hear" his patient's free associations, which are conceptualized as "serving the same functions as the day residue of a dream in providing the stimuli from above which trigger internal processes and associations within the analyst" (p. 287). The comparison is to "a state of being able to dream while still awake" (p. 285), that is, a state of controlled fantasy and daydreaming, stimulated by the patient's associations.

Are there parallels to the forgetting of analytic content and the forgetting of dreams and childhood amnesia? It is a commonplace experience that dreams, not unlike analytic content, can quickly slip from memory, and many people, analysts and more poetic authors alike, have commented on the necessity of remaining still with eyes closed to try to "fix" the dream. As previously mentioned, Whitman (1963) called attention to the fact that Freud (1900) was careful not to claim an absolute role for repression and resistance in the forgetting of dreams: "The forgetting of dreams depends *far more* upon resistance than upon the fact, stressed by the authorities, that the waking and sleeping states are alien to each other" (p. 520, italics added). Whitman attempted to explain the nonmotivated aspect of forgetting on the basis of primal repression—material never available to consciousness or available only before the erection of the repression barrier.

Wolpert (1972) elaborated the two classes of factors, motivated and unmotivated, affecting dream recall. He cites four "laws" representing parameters of a basically physiological nature that affect recall or failure of recall of a dream. Briefly stated, these four laws involve consolidation, a parameter that requires that the dream presentation be registered or consolidated for a finite period; decay, a parameter requiring that the consolidation occur within a certain period after the dream ceases; stimulus characteristics, namely, externally imposed limitations on what can be recalled from a series; and awakening characteristics, which indicate that remembering depends in part on how the dream is interrupted. The second class of factors affecting the recall are those described by Freud as repression, and, as Wolpert points out, any complete account of remembering and forgetting of dreams must take into account both sets of factors: "Memory thus is determined both by the limitations imposed on the nervous system by its biological structure and by psychological conflict interfering with its function. Because the absence of dreaming never occurs, the presence of forgetting may or may not indicate current psychological conflict" (p. 57).

I believe it is likely that another set of factors, different from the physiological variables Wolpert writes about, could be significant in dream recall. Not only is the analytic patient as quasi sleeper or quasi dreamer in a state in which, through free association and resistance analysis, connections are made that can undo the repression of the dream, but the state itself is conducive to priming or cuing the memory system of dreaming. Just as moving our limbs and opening our eyes may prevent consolidation and cause us to lose the memory of our dreams, (Proust dared not stir lest his exhilarating visions and memories disappear), so returning to a similar context and allowing our thoughts to drift may be the retrieval cues that help provide access to our dreams.

In their attempt to understand childhood amnesia, Wetzler and Sweeney (1986) propose a "marriage" of cognitive psychology and psychoanalysis. They question whether this form of amnesia is truly an amnesia or a normal forgetting, defined as a "constant and homogeneous process of forgetting across all periods of life as a function of time" (p. 676). I won't explicate their experimental design, but they conclude that childhood amnesia exists. From the psychoanalytic perspective they present the usual undoing of resistances and reliving that occurs in the transference as important to recall of childhood events. In cognitive psychological terms, this analytic explanation for the amnesia would be a "motivated retrieval failure," in which well-formed memories from childhood are in storage and available to the adult but are inaccessible due to repression.

Wetzler and Sweeney group the more purely cognitive psychological explanatory contributions into encoding deficit theories and encoding specificity theories. The encoding deficit theory proposes that a child does not encode as many experiences or encodes them in a less schematic fashion than an adult. Thus these experiences decay more rapidly, are more easily interfered with, or are not accessible to adult retrieval strategies, which require richer and more elaborate memory traces. I believe the encoding specificity theory, along with repression, best explains our forgetting the content of our analyses. This theory refers to the discrepancies between the contextual circumstances at encoding and those at retrieval. In childhood amnesia the discrepancies have to do with discontinuities in cognitive functioning from early childhood into adulthood; in analysands who have forgotten the content of their analyses, the discrepancies are the discontinuities between the altered state while "in analysis" and later recall. Childhood memories are at times accessed through psychoanalytic treatment, by lifting repression, strengthening the ego, or providing contextual cues. It would appear that the analysis of resistance and contextual cues would go hand in hand; that is, regression in the transference, which would take place with analysis of the multitude of resistances to it, would be required to provide the cues and context for recall of childhood memories.

Having hypothesized that we need similar contextual circumstances to remember our analysis, I return to the investigation of the extent of such amnesia and of the exceptions to those who have only vague or few recollections of the content of their analysis. As Kris (1956) mentioned, there has been no "systematic analytic catamnesis" done, and only with such an investigation would we be able to get a better idea of just how widespread among analysands and how extensive in the individual analysand this amnesia might be. Of course, such an investigation would require, among other things, standardization of the length of time between termination of analysis and investigation of the recollections, as well as a method of questioning that would not "pull" for certain responses. Calef's (1982) letter to his former supervisees and former analysands might serve as a beginning model. Most follow-up studies take place two to five years after termination, and none of the analysands to whom Calef sent his letter had been seen for at least four years. It would be interesting to know whether the amnesia is as great soon after termination as it is later, my own hypothesis being that while there is some normal "decay" of recollection over the years, the amnesia is significant soon after termination, just as it can be for individual hours.

Obviously, remembering is more than quantitative. It involves not only the amount, detail, and accuracy of the content, but the affective quality and intensity as well. Therefore, another aspect of such an investigation would be to study the intensity and quality of affect associated with what is remembered. Still another would be the degree of memory for the unfolding of the process, how well the analysand can remember the sequential order of his treatment.

The other point Kris (1956) makes, that of attempting to investigate whether insight into one's analysis—memory for the content and process—can be correlated with therapeutic results, would be a concomitant line of investigation. As already mentioned, Kris doubts a high correlation between results and such awareness. Deutsch (1959) concludes that lack of awareness of the working-through process and of the amnesia and resistance conquered does "not depend on the skill of the analyst, on the resolution of the infantile conflicts, nor on the quality of the psychological insight, and above all—not on the duration of the treatment" (p. 448).

Most accounts of analysands who have significant recall involve the analysis of analytic candidates, though Oremland and associates (1975) and Norman and associates (1976) mention several noncandidate analysands with remarkable recall. The follow-up studies by Pfeffer (1959, 1961, 1963) and Schlessinger and Robbins (1983) on noncandidate analysands do not detail what the patient remembers of his or her analysis per se. Why certain analysands, and in particular, analytic candidates, might remember more of their analyses is remarked on but, again, is not well explored. Deutsch (1959) believes that "pseudoamnesia occurs less frequently and intensely in persons for whom the analysis was strongly intellectualized" (p. 447) and that episodes of acting out are much better remembered than other aspects of the process. As already mentioned, Kris (1956) has suggested analysts remember more because they pursue self-analysis, either as part of their work or at times of personal crisis. It would be interesting to know if many analysts have experienced what my colleague did who wrote that while little was remembered of his first analysis, a great deal was of his training analysis.

My speculation is that for some, but by no means all, analysts the significant recall of their analyses reflects a stirring up of the process in themselves through identification with similar issues in their analysands—in a sense, identificatory cue-dependent retrieval. In simple memory theory, one could hypothesize that analysts are prone to remember more because they "rehearse" or "relive" their memories through their study and interest in the field, as well as through their work with their patients. Of course, one must then answer why many analysts don't experience such revival of their analyses through their study and work with patients.

Finally, I would like to turn to what significance this phenomenon of forgetting the content-process of one's analysis has for what is meaningful or curative about analysis. What is this "ineffable process," as Calef (1982) calls it and how does it heal? I will not review the numerous contributions to the "therapeutic action" of psychoanalysis, but I propose another possible explanation, derived from exploration of the forgetting I have been describing.

What most people seem to remember from their analyses is some aspect of the "holding environment"—the climate, if you will—that allowed the process to unfold but little of the inner process of change itself. As I have considered in this paper, the failure to remember much about the process itself could be accounted for by, in addition to repression of the painful, the fact that the process itself is a different form of knowledge—more dreamlike—and is accessed most readily by reinstating a similar context. What might happen, it seems to me, is that we, by continuing to focus on the manifold and repetitive defenses and evolving transferences, set in motion an ever-deepening process, which is increasingly intense and increasingly dreamlike—the altered state or states of consciousness (transference neurosis?)—and results in the disorganization and reorganization of existing memory schemata that analysts have referred to as restructuring. Typically, analysts have described this process of restructuring from a metaphoric or macro level in accord with whatever their prevailing theory is (Levey, 1984/1985) but have paid little attention to their patients' explanation or lack thereof. And even though the process can again be set in motion, the "Pfeffer Phenomenon," are our patients able to describe even then what this inner process of change is all about? Or can we rely on what graduate analysts say about what affected them? After all, as Schachtel (1959) argues and research on memory supports, our explanations for what happened and what was meaningful are likely to be couched in prevailing clichés and currently useful language schemata—in this case, the language analysts use with each other. Could it be that this process is "ineffable" because it is a process that, for the most part, is not conscious and remains so? That what we remember, or remember with the appropriate cues—the insights, transferences, reconstructions—are, by and large, epiphenomena of a process that is largely nonverbal?

Perhaps Freud (1913) had something like this in mind when he wrote the following:

> The analyst is certainly able to do a great deal, but he cannot determine beforehand exactly what results he will effect. He sets in motion a process that of the resolving of existing repressions. He can supervise this process, further it, remove obstacles in its way, and he can undoubtedly vitiate most of it. But on the whole, once begun, it goes its own way and does not allow either the direction it takes or the order in which it picks up its points to be prescribed for it. The analyst's power over the symptoms of the disease may thus be compared to male sexual potency. A man can, it is true, beget a whole child, but even the strongest man cannot create in the female organism a head alone or an arm or a leg; he cannot even prescribe the child's sex. He, too, only sets in motion a highly complicated process, determined by events in the remote past, which ends with the severance of the child from its mother (p. 130).

Similarly, Weinshel (1984) suggests a process "beyond" insight when he says, "the process-resistance issue is closely connected to the energetic-biological-quantitative postulates of our science; the transference and its vicissitudes become the principal (although not the only) vehicle by which we can observe, study, and deal with the resistances" (p. 72). Weinshel stresses the "work" in the sense of the "persistent labor" we employ in overcoming our patient's resistances and believes it is this work, rather than the more dramatic product of this work, insight, that is the most important ingredient in the psychoanalytic process. "Most of the central psychoanalytic work," he says, "takes place with the analyst not in a starring role" (personal communication).

Basch (1981), in his exploration of the experimental work done by cognitive psychologists, also advances the notion of a process "beyond," or in his case "before," insight. Through elaboration of the work of Piaget, Vygotsky, and others, Basch stresses how much of learning and maturation in the child, and the "thinking" that enables the changes observed in analysis to take place, is not conscious and not verbal. He believes that the mutative interpretation frees or expands "the capacity for thought as indicated by the greater maturity and freedom of behavior" (p. 152) but that this "thought" is not yet at a conscious level:

> When a successful interpretation is made the patient may not understand consciously what has happened to him. He may realize that something has happened to make him understand a connexion between his present behavior and his past without, however, connecting this change with the interpretation; not infrequently even such insight is lacking, though the material that comes up in associations indicates the accuracy and effectiveness of the interpretation. The patient's mental functioning and adaptation to reality may change dramatically

> without the patient's conscious reflection on the reasons for this, perhaps aware only that 'things are better,' or 'I feel more grown up,' etc. (p. 152).

It is helping the patient make conscious for himself what has happened, by giving words to the experience, describing it, and understanding it, that is the "insight." The "thinking" that enables the changes to take place need not be conscious; insight requires additional verbal-descriptive ability.

All of this accords with what I am hypothesizing, namely, that with continued resistance analysis and analysis of transference a process develops in which new learning takes place, and this learning is some form of reprogramming or formation of new memory schemata. It is the relationship to the analyst (real and transference) that serves as a powerful and catalytic day residue that sets in motion this process of restructuring or new memory organization; that is, the relationship to the analyst and its interpretation make the inner change possible, but this is not the inner change per se. These intensely meaningful interpersonal transactions are facilitators of new learning, and while we can with adequate contextually derived cues reexperience these transactions and understand the insights and reconstructions that derive from them, what takes place as a result of this facilitation is, as our patients keep telling us, not known.

As Kramer (1959) recognized, the self-analytic function, the identification with the analytic process that results in increased self-observation, would not initially be conscious. Only when attention and speech are added would we attain self-conscious awareness of this function. We recognize its presence "from above" not "from below"—the expanded pathways that leave us experiencing ourselves as richer and changed but not knowing how.

Stern (1985), in line with Basch's formulations, is closer to this learning "from below" when describing the cued recall memory for affective experience, perceptual experience, and motor experience in infants (less than one year old) that exists before the development of language. Infant research reveals not only remarkable capacity for such "memory without words" (Piaget's sensorimotor learning), but when such memory is exercised, there is an enhanced "self-affirming" and "world-affirming" experience—the well-known "smile of recognition"—in the sense of Winnicott's "going on being." I believe there could be parallels here to the enhanced sense of self-continuity (well-being that ensues from a correct interpretation and from a successful analysis but which is difficult to capture verbally), because while the new learning was facilitated verbally, it is largely, as Basch explains and Stern describes in the infant, a nonverbal experience.

Despite the tangled thicket of brain versus mind issue, or as Reiser (1985) puts it, we do not know "how nonphysical stimuli (meanings, symbols) are transduced into physical physiological events somewhere in the brain-body or in the opposite direction, how physiological brain events in brain-body are transduced into meanings" (p. 17), I will, nevertheless, offer a further explanation "from below."

Neurobiological research has been elaborating how learning and experience can alter the "molecular grammar of memory" (Reiser, 1985, p. 30). Synaptic transmission is largely a chemical process, and learning involves many alterations in these neurotransmitter systems (Thompson, 1986). Kandel's studies of the marine snail Aplysia (Reiser, 1985) and neuroscientists' studies of the microanatomy of the visual cortex (Barnes, 1986) reveal that learning and experience result in changes in the effectiveness of synaptic terminals and thus of synaptic organization. Of course, I'm not doing justice to the complexity of this whole process, but, following in the speculative vein of my previous hypothesis, I suggest that what we catalyze in our patients is a synaptic reorganization, a restructuring, and that the working-through process is a form of continual reliving in which new synaptic organizations are strengthened, thus promoting more permanent memory traces. The fact that this new organization is never permanent and old conflicts are never once and for all resolved might be explained by prior synaptic organizations never being completely overridden. Why one couldn't be "told" the insights, a form of cognitive therapy, rather than having to go through the long, intense, and frequently painful reliving that occurs in an analysis might have something to do with the profound effect of emotions on the ability of humans to learn and remember (Rapaport, 1950; Thompson, 1986). To put it all too simply, there is evidence that emotions may serve both to index and fix (i.e., make indelible) memories.

I will not resist a last analogy to analysis promoting "unrememberable" change by citing an experiment on young owls described by Rosenfield (1986) in his review of Edelman's work on memory and perception. Edelman's research suggests that memory is not an exact repetition of events, but a recategorization and rearranging based on strengthening of synaptic connections between different neuronal groups. There can be a constant recategorization in the service of adaptation. A series of experiments with young owls that were raised with one ear plugged (thus shifting the perceived location of sound relative to its actual location) revealed that within four to six weeks these owls learned to localize sound accurately. It was believed that the owls adjusted to the altered mapping of sound by rearranging their internal maps, that is, by strengthening synaptic connections between different neuronal groups. While we don't plug an ear, we do arrange a setting in which we use a "third ear" to promote in our patients attention to certain "sounds" (associations, dreams, fantasies) and not others, thereby rearranging their internal maps in the service of better adaptation.

In summary, I have attempted to investigate the phenomenon "I've changed but I don't know how." I have not attempted to undertake the systematic study of such amnesia but have tried to make a case for an explanation based on memory research and altered states of consciousness research that includes these phenomena, along with repression, in accounting for such amnesia. In addition, I have made some comparisons with other forms of amnesia; forgetting of dreams and childhood amnesia. Finally, I have speculated on the significance of such forgetting for what is curative or healing about psychoanalysis. My sweep has been broad, with scant justice done to the voluminous body of research in learning and memory, altered states of consciousness, dreams, neurobiology and neuropharmacology. But perhaps I've set out some cairns on trails that will aid future explorers and researchers to find more definitive answers to the phenomenon of postanalytic amnesia.

REFERENCES

Barnes, D. (1986), Brain architecture: Beyond genes. *Science,* 233:155–156.

Bartlett, F. (1932), *Remembering.* Cambridge: Cambridge University Press.

Basch, M. (1981), Psychoanalytic interpretation and cognitive transformation. *Internat. J. Psycho-Anal.,* 60:151–175.

Bodaracco, M. (1975), Psychoanalysis as altering states of consciousness. *J. Amer. Acad. Psychoanal.,* 3:205–210.

Bucci, W. (1985), Dual coding: A cognitive model for psychoanalytic research. *J. Amer. Psychoanal. Assn.,* 33:571–607.

Calef, V. (1982), An introspective on training and nontraining analysis. *The Annual of Psychoanalysis,* 10:93–114. New York: International Universities Press.

_____ & Weinshel, E. (1980), The analyst as the conscience of the analysis. *Internat. J. Psycho-Anal.,* 7:279–290.

Deutsch, H. (1959), Psychoanalytic therapy in the light of follow up. *J. Amer. Psychoanal. Assn.,* 7:445–458.

Eich, J. (1980), The cue-dependent nature of state dependent retrieval. *Memory and Cognition,* 8:157–173.

Fleiss, R. (1942), The metapsychology of the analyst. *Psychoanal. Quart.,* 11:211–217.

Freud, S. (1900), The interpretation of dreams. *Standard Edition,* 4 & 5. London: Hogarth Press, 1953.

_____ (1913), On beginning treatment. *Standard Edition,* 12:121–144. London: Hogarth Press, 1958.

_____ (1922), Two encyclopedia articles. *Standard Edition,* 18:233–259. London: Hogarth Press, 1964.

Kalman, H. (1975), Altered states of consciousness in therapy. *J. Amer. Acad. Psychoanal.*, 3:187–204.

Klein, G. (1959), Consciousness in psychoanalytic theory: Some implications for current research in perception. *J. Amer. Psychoanal. Assn.*, 7:5–34.

Kramer, M. (1959), On the continuation of the analytic process after psychoanalysis (a self observation). *Internat. J. Psycho-Anal.*, 40:17–25.

Kris, E. (1956), The recovery of childhood memories in psychoanalysis. *The Psychoanalytic Study of the Child*, 11:54–88. New York: International Universities Press.

Levey, M. (1984/85), The concept of structure in psychoanalysis. *The Annual of Psychoanalysis*, 12/13:137–153. New York: International Universities Press.

Lewin, B. (1973), *Selected Writings of Bertram D. Lewin.*, ed. J. Arlow. New York: *Psychoanal. Quart.*

Marsh, C. (1977), A framework for describing subjective states of consciousness. In: *Alternate States of Consciousness*, ed. N. Zinberg. New York: Free Press, pp. 121–144.

Myerson, P. (1960), Awareness and stress: Post psychoanalytic utilization of insight. *Internat. J. Psycho-Anal.*, 41:147–156.

Norman, H., Blacher, K., Oremland, J. & Barrett, W. (1976), The fate of the transference neurosis after termination of a satisfactory analysis. *J. Amer. Psychoanal. Assn.*, 24:471–498.

Olinick, S., Poland, W., Grigg, K. & Granatir, W. (1973), The psychoanalytic work ego: Process and interpretation. *Internat. J. Psycho-Anal.*, 54:143–151.

Oremland, J., Blacher, K. & Norman, H. (1975), Incompleteness in "successful" psychoanalysis: A follow-up study. *J. Amer Psychoanal. Assn.*, 23:819–844.

Pfeffer, A. (1959), A procedure for evaluating the results of psychoanalysis. *J. Amer. Psychoanal. Assn.*, 7:418–444.

_____ (1961), Follow-up study of a satisfactory analysis. *J. Amer. Psychoanal. Assn.*, 9:562–571.

_____ (1963), The meaning of the analyst after analysis—a contribution to the theory of therapeutic results. *J. Amer. Psychoanal. Assn.*, 11:229–244.

Rapaport, D. (1950), *Emotions and Memory*. New York: International Universities Press.

Reiser, M. (1985), Converging sectors of psychoanalysis and neurobiology and mutual challenges and opportunity. *J. Amer. Psychoanal. Assn.*, 33:11–34.

Rosenfield, I. (1986), Neural Darwinism and a new approach to memory and perception. *NY Rev. Books*, 33 (15):21–27.

Schachtel, E. (1959), *Metamorphosis*. New York: Basic Books.

Schlesinger, H. (1970), The place of forgetting in memory functioning. *J. Amer. Psychoanal. Assn.*, 18:358–371.

Schlessinger, N. & Robbins, F. (1983), *A Developmental View of the Psychoanalytic Process*. New York: International Universities Press.

Squire, L. (1986), Mechanisms of memory. *Science*, 232:1612–1619.

Stein, M. (1965), States of consciousness in the analytic situation: Including a note on the traumatic dream. In: *Drives, Affects, Behavior, Vol. 2*, ed. M. Schur. New York: International Universities Press, pp. 60–86.

Stern, D. (1985), *The Interpersonal World of the Infant*. New York: Basic Books.

Thompson, R. (1986), The neurobiology of learning and memory. *Science*, 233:941–947.

Tulving, E. & Thompson, D. (1973), Encoding specificity and retrieval processes in episodic memory. *Psycholog. Rev.*, 80:352–373.

Weinshel, E. (1984), Some observations on the psychoanalytic process. *Psychoanal. Quart.*, 53:63–92.

Wetzler, S. & Sweeney, J. (1986), Childhood amnesia: A conceptualization in cognitive psychological terms. *J. Amer. Psychoanal. Assn.*, 34:663–685.

Whitman, R. (1963), Remembering and forgetting dreams in psychoanalysis. *J. Amer. Psychoanal. Assn.*, 11:752–774.

Wolpert, E. (1972), Two classes of factors affecting dream recall. *J. Amer. Psychoanal. Assn.*, 20:45–58.

Zinberg, N. (1977), The study of consciousness states: Problems and progress. In: *Alternate States of Consciousness*, ed. N. Zinberg. New York: Free Press, pp. 1–36.

*Freud and Hypnosis: The Development of an Interactionist Perspective**

STEVEN M. SILVERSTEIN
BARRY R. SILVERSTEIN

Even though Freud abandoned the use of hypnosis as a therapeutic tool, he never lost interest in achieving a satisfactory theoretical understanding of the phenomenon.[1] In this paper we shall review Freud's continuing theoretical confrontations with hypnosis, from his prepsychoanalytic days to his final major statement on the subject. In addition, we shall explore the complementary influence of Freud's attempts to answer questions concerning hypnosis and his development of psychoanalytic concepts.

The Prepsychoanalytic Era

Freud's first major experience with hypnosis was in 1886 when he studied with Charcot at the Salpêtrière in Paris. This began a period of several years of combined theoretical and clinical interest in hypnotism. For example, soon after he returned to Vienna in 1886, Freud gave two lectures on the subject, one before the Vienna Physiological Club and one before the Psychiatric Society (Jones, 1953, p. 229). Freud's first publication on hypnosis came early in 1888, a brief favorable review of Obersteiner's 1887 monograph, *Der Hypnotismus mit besonderer Berücksichtig ung Seiner Klinischen und Forensischen Bedeutung* (Hypnotism with special consideration of its clinical and forensic significance). A few months

*The authors would like to thank Dr. Joseph Masling for his helpful comments on an earlier draft of this manuscript.

[1]See Polgar (1951) and Gravitz and Gerton (1981) for claims that Freud continued to use hypnosis well into the 20th century.

later, Freud published his first extensive consideration of hypnosis, the preface to his translation of Bernheim's book, *De la Suggestion et de ses Applications à la Thérapeutique.* In this work a clear picture of Freud's earliest views on hypnosis is presented. These were summarized in a letter to Fliess, dated August 29, 1888, in which he wrote, "I do not share Bernheim's views, which seem to me one sided, and have tried to defend Charcot's point of view in the preface . . ." (Masson, 1985, p. 24). Thus, this work also represents Freud's first attempt at a resolution of the controversy over the competing positions of Charcot and Bernheim. This struggle was to continue even until Freud's last psychoanalytic theory. Equally important here, however, is that out of this and other early attempts at a theoretical resolution, several ideas emerged that would serve as precursors of later psychoanalytic theories.

Early in the preface to Bernheim's book, Freud contrasted Bernheim's and Charcot's positions. According to Freud (1888c), Bernheim saw all hypnotic phenomena as "effects of suggestions" and, as such, understandable solely in terms of psychical and cortical functioning (p. 77). Charcot, on the other hand, believed that the forms of hypnotic phenomena were, in large part, predetermined by physiological factors, that is, by "displacements of excitability in the nervous system" (p. 77). After a discussion of the lawfulness of hysterical phenomena, the role played by autosuggestion in their production, and their similarities to Charcot's reports of "grand hypnotisme" (the most profound form of hypnosis), Freud concluded that these phenomena are "of a real, objective nature" and are not due to the effects of externally given suggestions (p. 70). Thus, in regards to "grand hypnotisme" Freud rejected Bernheim's position. Regarding minor hypnotism, however, Freud was more sympathetic to Bernheim's view. In comparing hypnosis and sleep, he noted that sleep is often brought on by suggestion, that is, "by mental preparedness and expectation of it" (p. 81). Even in this case, however, Freud acknowledged that physiological changes take place, changes due to an associated link between cortical representations and their physiological and anatomical counterparts. In Freud's view, this associative link was a built-in property of the nervous system and it allowed psychical changes to produce effects in the physical realm, and vice versa, regardless of which type of change occurred first. As a way out of the impasse over causation (psychical vs. physiological), Freud offered a middle ground resolution: "There are both psychical and physiological phenomena in hypnotism, and hypnosis can be brought about in one manner or the other" (p. 81).

Nevertheless, Freud agreed with Bernheim that "the partitioning of hypnotic phenomena under the two headings of physiological and psychical leaves us with a most unsatisfied feeling: a connecting link between the two classes is urgently needed" (p. 81). In pursuing this connecting link, Freud reached several conclusions that foreshadowed his later work. As part of his defense of Charcot, Freud insisted that autosuggestions, such as those implicated by Charcot as precipitating factors in spontaneous hysterical paralysis, were intervening variables in hypnosis that affected various conditions of innervation or excitation in the nervous system. However, even though autosuggestions are psychical processes, argued Freud, "they are no longer exposed to the full light of consciousness which falls upon direct suggestions" (p. 83). Thus, Freud was saying that one should not equate "psychical" with "consciousness"; there are unconscious ideas, and they can affect conditions in the nervous system. One also should not equate "cortical" with "consciousness," Freud asserted, because consciousness "is not attached to every activity of the cerebral cortex, nor is it always attached in an equal degree to any particular one of its activities; it is not a thing which is bound up with any locality in the nervous system" (p. 84). Finally, Freud believed that one should not view the functioning of the cerebral cortex as if it were separate from the rest of the nervous system; the nervous system functions as a whole in that functional changes in the cerebral cortex associated with hypnosis are not likely to occur "unaccompanied by significant changes in the excitability of the other parts of the brain" (p. 84).

In sum, by focusing on autosuggestion as an intervening variable, Freud managed to defend Charcot's assertions about major hypnotism and to point out the weakness of Bernheim's "one sided view" by concluding that "the question whether hypnosis exhibits psychical or physiological phenomena cannot be accepted in this general form" (p. 85). Even if the psychical and the physiological were qualitatively different phenomena, Freud asserted, in hypnosis both types of processes generally existed as interactive variables in a singular process. Thus, when explaining hypnosis, a two-sided view was called for.

Freud's two-sided view, presented in his consideration of hypnosis, would remain characteristic of his thinking throughout his career. Freud's two-sided view of the mind-body relationship was both dualistic and interactionist (Silverstein, 1988, 1989a). In an article on the brain, written in the same year as his preface to Bernheim's book, Freud (1888a) stated that although the mechanical process was not understood, there was a connecting link between changes in the material conditions in the brain and changes in the state of the conscious mind. "Although the essence of this coupling is incomprehensible to us, it is not haphazard, and on the basis of combinations of the experiences of the outer senses on one hand and inner perception on the other we can determine something about the laws which govern this coupling" (p. 69). Here Freud was granting the psychical independence in the sense that, as he stated three years later in his monograph "On Aphasia" (Freud, 1891a), he did not regard mental processes simply as effects produced by mechanical brain processes (p. 55). He took consciousness as a given, an enigma, whose *existence* could not be explained by reference to the mechanics of brain functioning. Consciousness might be correlated with certain cortical functions, but it was a unique phenomenon that required its own methods of study and its own explanatory concepts. Freud also granted the psychical some independence in the sense that, as he stated two years after the Bernheim preface (Freud, 1890), "the relationship between body and mind . . . is a reciprocal one . . ." (p. 284). In other words, psychical changes produced effects in the body, as well as vice versa.

Although the question of the connecting link between mental phenomena and mechanical brain processes was of some concern to Freud early in his career, his dualistic-interactionist position and his tolerance for a lack of comprehension of the mechanisms involved in the coupling of mind and body left him free to investigate mental phenomena in their own right After 1895 Freud abandoned any hope that he might explain the linking of mind and body through explanations focused on brain functioning. By that time, however, he had found a new way of looking at mind–body interaction by focusing on sexuality as a prime issue around which such interaction takes place (Silverstein, 1985). Sexuality had a mental side, in terms of wishes and fantasies, and a physical side, in terms of glandular secretions and their exciting effect upon the nervous system. Sexuality became the organic foundation upon which Freud would build his models of the mind. When Freud told Fliess, on September 22, 1898, that he must "behave as if only the psychological were under consideration" (Masson, 1985, p. 326), he was declaring that, with sexuality as his organic base, he would start from the data of consciousness and explain the determination of consciousness by reference to inferred unconscious mental processes that were not accessible to consciousness. These unobservable, unconscious mental processes were portrayed by Freud as intentional, as highly influenced by physiological processes, and as exerting a greater influence on somatic processes than that of consciousness.

As we examine Freud's later writings on hypnosis with respect to his two-sided view, we shall see that the viewpoint he put forth in 1888 remained essentially the same, although more complex and implicit in later works. Specifically, Freud (1905b) first viewed hypnosis as a type of transference based on libidinal fixations and later (Freud, 1921) as a type of transference based on the effects of desexualized libidinal forces. In other words, in his later works, Freud saw the mechanism underlying hypnosis as transference, which in turn was rooted in human sexuality. This essential continuity in Freud's work was highly significant, for it enabled him, soon after writing his 1888 preface, to agree much more with Bernheim without changing his fundamental position, Indeed, although Freud would come to be much more sympathetic to Bernheim's position, he would still criticize it on the point that suggestion itself was not satisfactorily explained. Freud (1896) stressed this point when he had the opportunity to write a short preface for the second German edition of Bernheim's book: "And, while he explains all the phenomena of hypnotism by suggestion, suggestion itself remains wholly unexplained, but is veiled by a show of its needing no explanation" (p. 87). As noted above, this major issue of the prepsychoanalytic era was later resolved by Freud himself with his conceptualization of transference.

The beginnings of Freud's departure from Charcot's view of hypnosis can be seen in his 1889 review of August Forel's book, *Der Hypnotismus, seine Bedeutung und seine Handhabung (Hypnotism, its Significance and its Management).* This review consisted of two sections. The first was written in July of 1889, before Freud visited Bernheim and Liebeault at Nancy. The second section, however, was written in November of 1889, after his return. It is in this latter section of the review that the influence of the Nancy school on Freud is most pronounced. Before discussing this, however, several interesting points in the first section should be considered.

In the first section of the Forel review, Freud stated that hypnotic treatment depended upon bringing about a hypnotic state and then conveying a suggestion to the hypnotized subject. Here he characterized the hypnotic state as "nothing other than ordinary sleep" (Freud, 1889, p. 93). While the equation of the hypnotic state with sleep was commonplace at the time, Freud was using it to playful advantage to argue against Meynert's view of the injurious effects of the hypnotic state; such a state was, Freud was asserting, no more hazardous then going to sleep. However, a year later, Freud felt it necessary to point out differences between the mental state of hypnosis and normal sleep.

By the time Freud began writing the second half of the review of *Der Hypnotismus,* his position on the Charcot–Bernheim controversy had shifted. Having just returned from Nancy, he was growing dissatisfied with what he now saw as Charcot's one-sidedness, his "exclusively somatic view of hypnosis" that "disregards the influence of ideas . . ." (Freud, 1889, p. 97). At the same time, Freud (1889) was becoming a proponent of Bernheim's position:

> Here it need only be remarked that a physician who desires to study hypnosis and form an opinion on it will undoubtedly be best advised to adopt the suggestion theory from the first. For he will be able to convince himself of the correctness of the school of Nancy at any time on his own patients whereas he is scarcely likely to find himself in a position to confirm from his own observations the phenomena described by Charcot as 'major hypnotism," which seems only to occur in a few sufferers from grand hystérie [p. 98].

While it is clear from this passage that Freud had by then sided with Bernheim, this association stopped short of being complete. To Freud, who sought a more two-sided view, a crucial issue still remained: the essential nature of suggestion itself. In his next work on hypnosis, Freud began to speculate on what this might be, thus beginning an investigation that was to lead directly to the development of psychoanalytic concepts.

In an 1890 paper entitled "Psychical (or Mental) Treatment," Freud elaborated upon several of the ideas he had discussed earlier. For example, although he had described hypnosis as "nothing other than ordinary sleep" (Freud, 1889, p. 93), in the Forel review, as noted earlier, he began to differentiate the two, writing ". . . hypnosis is in no sense sleep like our nocturnal sleep or like the sleep produced by drugs. Changes occur in it and mental functions are retained during it which are absent in normal sleep" (Freud, 1890, p. 295). This position, virtually unchanged, was to remain a part of Freud's theory of hypnosis even in his last writings on the subject (e.g., Freud, 1916–1917, 1921).

An additional topic covered by Freud in the 1890 paper was hypnotic induction. He considered three types of procedures as being effective. The first involved exposing the subject to repetitive, monotonous stimuli. This included "getting him to stare fixedly at a bright object for some minutes, or by holding a watch to his ear for a similar length of time." (Freud, 1890, p. 294). The second method of induction involved "describing the onset of the state of hypnosis and its characteristics quietly and firmly to the subject—that is, by 'talking him into' hypnosis" (p. 294). The third type of induction procedure involved a combination of these two methods.

After describing these methods of induction, Freud set out to explain their effectiveness. He noted that "all the procedures have in common a fixing of the attention" (Freud, 1890, p. 294). Beyond this, their mechanisms seemed to differ. With the first method, he saw that "the attention is fatigued by slight and monotonous sensory stimuli" (p. 294). For the second method, though, Freud had no explanation. All he could say of this was that "it is not yet satisfactorily explained, however, how it comes about that mere talking produces exactly the same state as the other procedures" (p. 294). Here, once again, we see Freud dealing with the issue of the essential nature of suggestion. This time, however, he would not be satisfied with merely posing the question.

Freud noted that one characteristic of the hypnotic state was that "the influence of the mind over the body is extraordinarily increased" (p. 295). On another level this meant "an increase in the physical influence of an idea" (p. 296). Both of these statements are extensions of the interactionist position Freud put forth in his translation of Bernheim's *De la Suggestion*. Specifically, while in that work he argued that changes in the cerebral cortex produced by suggestions cause certain concomitant changes in other parts of the nervous system, in this paper Freud (1890) argued that the degree to which these changes are effected is increased during hypnosis. By making this leap, Freud had now specified the necessary factors in producing hypnosis, that is, the induction procedures, as well as the results of these procedures. What still remained, however, was the identification of the crucial intervening variable, namely, an answer to the question, Why did these procedures produce these effects?

While in 1890 Freud could not explain how a hypnotist could come to exert such power over a subject, a remark near the end of this paper foreshadowed his later explanation of the phenomenon with the notion of the transference. He wrote:

> It may be remarked by the way, that outside hypnosis and in real life, credulity such as the subject has in relation to his hypnotist is shown only by a child towards his beloved parents, and that an attitude of similar subjection on the part of one person towards another has only one parallel, though a complete one—namely in certain love relationships where there is extreme devotion. A combination of exclusive attachment and credulous obedience is in general among the characteristics of love [p. 296].

Here we see Freud's first association of hypnosis with anything resembling what would later be termed "transference." Interestingly, Freud did not follow up on this theme in his next few writings on hypnosis, preferring instead to concentrate on more well-known topics. Indeed, it seems as if it was only after several critical personal experiences with hypnosis that Freud felt the need to give this issue theoretical consideration again.

A final matter discussed by Freud in his 1890 paper was hypnotizability. He was careful to point out that "different people show a varying degree of suitability for hypnosis" (p. 300). In addition, he noted that the effect of a suggestion is in some sense up to the subject, that is, that motivational factors are important in hypnosis. Both these points were made to emphasize that hypnotized persons do not lose total control of their decision-making capacities, as was commonly believed. In later works (e.g., Freud, 1891b, 1921) Freud continued to emphasize these points. For example, in 1921 he would argue that differences in hypnotizability resulted from differences in the susceptibility to activation of the unconscious submissive response of the members of the primal horde to the primal father. On the issue of conscious motivation to be hypnotized however, Freud's discussions always remained detached from theoretical consideration.

Freud's next work on hypnosis was an article that appeared in 1891 in a medical dictionary, Anton Bum's *Therapeutisches Lexikon*. This article (Freud, 1891b), entitled "Hypnose" ("Hypnosis"), contained practical information for physicians intending to use hypnosis and included little in the way of theoretical considerations. Nevertheless, Freud did use the opportunity to reemphasize some points made earlier. For example, he again summarized various means of hypnotic induction, writing that all had in common the "arousing, by an association of thought, the picture of falling asleep and of fixating attention by means of a persistent sensation" (p. 111). In addition to restating such points as these, Freud noted that when the hypnotic state is achieved, "we shall find some of the somatic phenomena which characterize hypnosis will emerge" (p. 110). This belief in characteristic signs, like the ideas of a hypnotic state and an association with sleep, was commonly held in Freud's time, and although in his later focus on theoretical issues he never returned to this point, it was incorporated into several post-Freudian psychoanalytic theories of hypnosis (Silverstein and Silverstein, this volume).

Freud's continued clinical work with hypnosis led to his publication in 1892 of "A Case of Successful Treatment by Hypnotism," a work consisting of a case history but with no theoretical insights into hypnosis. It was not until the next year that Freud again made his position clear. In an obituary of Charcot (Freud, 1893), Freud stated once again that he no longer held to Charcot's views on hypnosis. Of these he wrote:

> The exclusively nosographical approach adopted at the School of the Salpêtrière was not suitable for a purely psychological subject. The restriction of the study of hypnosis to hysterical patients, the differentiation between major and minor hypnotism, the hypothesis of three stages of "major hypnosis," and their characterization by somatic phenomena—all this sank in the estimation of Charcot's contemporaries when Liebeault's pupil, Bernheim, set about constructing the theory of hypnotism on a more comprehensive psychological foundation and making suggestion the central point of hypnosis [pp. 22–23].

It is clear from this that by 1893 Freud's position on hypnosis was significantly different from what it had been five years earlier. Summing up his position at this time, Freud was to write many years later (February 20, 1930, to A. A. Roback), "Over the question of hypnosis I sided against Charcot, even if not entirely with Bernheim" (E. Freud, 1961, p. 394). Interestingly, soon after the publication of his Charcot obituary, Freud was to have several experiences with hypnosis that would force him to question Bernheim's position more than he had previously. These experiences would ultimately have the effect of leading him away from a continued concern with the Charcot-Bernheim debate and towards the development of his own radically different theory of hypnosis.

The first indications of Freud's dissatisfaction with hypnosis as a clinical tool appeared in "Studies on Hysteria" (Breuer and Freud, 1895). In describing the case of Frau Emmy Von N., Freud wrote:

> It was while I was studying Frau Von N.'s abulias that I began for the first time to have grave doubts about the validity of Bernheim's assertion, "tout est dans la suggestion" ("suggestion is everything") and about his clever friend Delboeuf's inference: "Comme quoi, il n'y a pas d'hypnotisme" ("that being so, there is no such thing as hypnotism") [p. 101].

In addition, in the case of Miss Lucy R, Freud wrote that he now believed that "the percentage of cases amenable to somnambulism was very much lower than what Bernheim reported" (Breuer and Freud, 1895, p. 108). Both of these statements were reactions to Freud's difficulty in hypnotizing various patients. Indeed, this problem was so great that in 1910 he cited it as his main reason for giving up hypnosis. In 1925, however, Freud gave a more complete account of his motivations at this time. He stated first his realization that successful results could be reversed if the hypnotist-patient relationship became disturbed. This "proved that the personal emotional relation between doctor and patient was stronger than the whole cathartic process" (Freud, 1925, p. 27). What appears to be the crucial event in Freud's abandonment of hypnosis was an experience that occurred with a patient. Freud wrote:

> One day I had an experience which showed me in the crudest light what I had long suspected. It related to one of my most acquiescent patients, with whom hypnotism had enabled me to bring about marvellous results . . . As she woke up on one occassion, she threw her arms around my neck. The unexpected entrance of a servant relieved us from a painful discussion, but from that time onwards there was a tacit understanding between us that the hypnotic treatment should be

> discontinued. I was modest enough not to attribute the event to my own irresistible personal attraction, and I felt that I had now grasped the nature of the mysterious element that was at work behind hypnotism. In order to exclude it, or at all events to isolate it, it was necessary to abandon hypnotism [p. 27].

One of the reasons Freud (1910) was able to abandon hypnosis was that he believed he could continue to use the cathartic method without it. In making this decision he remembered a demonstration by Bernheim in which he had shown that with a great deal of effort memories usually retrieved only under hypnosis could be retrieved in the normal state. Immediately after he stopped using hypnosis, Freud began to use the "pressure" technique of placing his hands on the patient's forehead to assist in the recall of memories. This, however, "was a laborious procedure, and in the long run an exhausting one; and it was unsuited to serve as a permanent technique" (p. 23). An additional method used by Freud at this time was the "concentration hypnosis." This too proved inadequate. An example of the difficulties Freud faced with this technique can be found in an 1895 draft on paranoia that Freud sent to Fliess (Freud, 1895). In the end, none of the hypnosis-type treatments proved satisfactory. As a result, Freud turned to a new technique and, in doing so, to an entirely new way of understanding the human mind.[2]

Freud's Early Psychoanalytic Views of Hypnosis

According to Chertok (1977), the earlier erotic episode with his patient that Freud revealed in 1925 represented "the starting point of the discovery of transference" (p. 102). This discovery would finally provide the answers to some long-standing questions. For example, in 1890, Freud had written, "It is not yet satisfactorily explained, however, how it comes about that mere talking produces exactly the same state as the other procedures" (p. 294). Even as late as 1895, he had written, "And to this day I cannot understand how it can be supposed that by merely holding up a finger and saying once 'go to sleep' I had created in the patient the peculiar psychical state . . ." (Breuer and Freud, 1895, p. 101). By 1905, however, Freud felt that he had the answer. In "Three Essays on the Theory of Sexuality," Freud (1905b) wrote:

> I cannot help recalling the credulous submissiveness shown by a hypnotized subject towards his hypnotist. This leads me to suspect that the essence of hypnosis lies in an unconscious fixation of the subject's

[2]See footnote 1.

> libido to the figure of the hypnotist, through the medium of the masochistic components of the sexual instinct [p. 150].

Ferenczi (1909), agreeing with Freud's views on hypnosis, would later clarify this by noting that masochism "is pleasurably obeying, and this one learns in childhood from one's parents" (p. 81).

By 1910 this idea of an unconscious libidinal fixation would come to be known as transference. Freud now believed he understood the mechanism underlying both suggestion and hypnosis. He stated in 1910 that "a study of transference, too, can give you the key to an understanding of hypnotic suggestion" (p. 51). Likewise, in 1912, Freud defined suggestion as "the influencing of a person by means of the transference phenomena which are possible in his case" (p. 106). By going further and analyzing the transference itself, Freud saw its roots in human sexuality. This, however, was not the manifest sexuality of an aroused individual. Instead, Freud (1912) saw that the bases of the transference "are genetically linked with sexuality and have developed from purely sexual desires through a softening of their sexual aim, however pure and unsensual they may appear to our conscious self-perception" (p. 105). This idea, that underlying hypnosis is an attenuated form of the sexual drive, was to continue to be a major part of Freud's theories of hypnosis, especially the one advanced in 1921 in "Group Psychology and the Analysis of the Ego."

By postulating the transference reaction as the mechanism underlying hypnosis, Freud felt he had achieved what Bernheim had stopped short of achieving: explaining the nature of suggestion. On this subject Freud (1916–1917) wrote:

> Bernheim . . . based his theory of hypnotic phenomena on the thesis that everyone is in some way "suggestible." His suggestibility was nothing other than the tendency to transference . . . He did not know that his "suggestibilité" depended on sexuality, on the activity of the libido. And it must dawn on us that in our technique we have abandoned hypnosis only to rediscover suggestion in the shape of transference [p. 446].

By 1917 then, well into the "topographical period," Freud had consolidated his views on suggestion within the psychoanalytic framework. Regarding hypnosis in particular, however, he was still influenced by several prepsychoanalytic ideas that he did not try to explain according to psychoanalytic principles. This is evident in his continued adherence to the idea of a similarity between hypnosis and sleep. On this matter, he stated:

> There is an obvious kinship between the hypnotic state and the state of sleep . . . The psychical situations in the two cases are really analogous. In natural sleep we withdraw our attention to the whole external world; and in hypnotic sleep we withdraw it from the whole world, but with the single exception of the person who has hypnotized us and with whom we remain in rapport [p. 104].

This comparison implies that Freud saw hypnosis as more than a transference reaction. Indeed, this was necessary as it was obvious to him that transference occurs in many contexts other than hypnosis. What was added to the transference in hypnosis was a special state of focused attention, one in which the subject is able to disregard external stimuli not coming from the hypnotist.

Freud's next and final theoretical statement on hypnosis was put forth in 1921 in "Group Psychology and the Analysis of the Ego." The view advanced there included some major theoretical revisions. Before we examine these, though, another psychoanalytic theory from the pre-1921 period will be considered.

Ferenczi's Views of Hypnosis

Ferenczi, writing during the time when psychoanalysis was concerned mainly with infantile sexuality and transference, also contributed to the psychoanalytic theory of hypnosis. He took Freud's 1905 view that the essence of hypnosis was an unconscious libidinal fixation and narrowed the concept to one of a "parental complex." Ferenczi (1909) saw that

> the capacity to be hypnotized and influenced by suggestion depends on the possibility of transference taking place, or, more openly expressed, on the positive, although unconscious, sexual attitude that the person being hypnotized adopts in regard to the hypnotist; the transference, however, like every "object-love," has its deepest roots in the repressed parental complexes [p. 67].

Moreover, Ferenczi made a distinction between paternal and maternal hypnosis. In the former the hypnotist unconsciously represents the "stern, all-powerful father" (p. 69) who must be obeyed. In the latter the hypnotist, as the result of a gentler demeanor, reawakens the subject's attitudes towards the mother. Ferenczi pointed out, however, that the purpose of this distinction was not to stress that two different types of hypnosis exist. Rather, it was to "call attention to the way in which the situation during hypnosis tends to favor a conscious and unconscious imaginary return to childhood, and to awaken reminiscences, hidden away in everyone, that date from the time of their childhood obedience" (p. 70). Consequently, Ferenczi saw as a prerequisite of hypnosis that

> the hypnotist shall figure as a "grown up" to the hypnotised subject; i.e., the former must be able to arouse in the latter the same feelings of love or fear, the same conviction of infallibility, as those with which his parents inspired him as a child [p. 71].

Just as Freud had seen an analogy between sleep and hypnosis in the psychical processes involved, Ferenczi saw "a far-reaching analogy between hypnosis and neurosis" (p. 84). This was based on the idea that "unconscious ideational complexes determine the phenomena, and that among these ideational complexes in both cases the infantile and the sexual, especially those concerned with the parents, play the greatest part" (p. 84). In addition, Ferenczi believed that hypnosis involved not a "giving of ideas," but instead, a setting in motion of "unconscious, pre-existing auto-suggestive mechanisms" (p. 85). The similarity to neurosis lies in the view that neuroses, too, are caused by the activation of unconscious thought processes.

While Ferenczi wished to stress certain similarities between hypnosis and neurosis, he stopped far short of equating them. His emphasis in comparing them was only

> to point out that the high percentage of normal people that may be hypnotised can, according to the experience gained by psycho-analysis, be cited as an argument rather for the universality of the predisposition to suffer from a psychoneurosis than against the essential sameness of hypnosis and neurosis [p. 85].

As previously discussed, Freud first argued that hypnosis required the intervening factor of unconscious autosuggestion in his 1888 preface to Bernheim's *De la Suggestion*. There, however, Freud was arguing against Bernheim's position that hypnosis was reducible to suggestion. In 1909, however, Ferenczi's and Freud's positions were an extension of Bernheim's earlier view. This apparent paradox can be resolved if several points are considered. First, Freud had earlier attempted a resolution of the physiology/psychology dichotomy with regards to hypnosis by taking a two-sided view: he stressed the inseparability of the psychical and physiological effects of suggestions on the nervous system. Furthermore, this intertwining of the psychical and the physiological was an important part of Freud's dualistic–interactionist conception of the mind–body relationship, and later, of his theory of the sexual drive. Viewed in this way, Ferenczi's (1909) and Freud's pre-1921 ideas on the importance of the libido and the unconscious in (auto) suggestion and hypnosis can be seen as a direct extension of Freud's (1888) earlier position, rather than a contradiction of it.

Freud's Final Theory

Freud's 1921 theory of hypnosis represented a major extension of his earlier views. He began by comparing the state of hypnosis to being in love, an idea left untouched by him since 1890. The difference between the two states, according to Freud, was that in hypnosis sexual satisfaction is excluded due to an inhibition of the sexual impulses.

In this first application of the structural model to the theory of hypnosis, Freud stated that "no one can doubt that the hypnotist has stepped into the place of the ego-ideal" (p. 114). By also ascribing the functions of reality testing to the ego-ideal, Freud hypothesized a "structural" explanation of the power of the hypnotist: in essence, the hypnotist, as the subject's ego-ideal, serves as the subject's tester of reality and thus has control over subsequent behavior as well.

Before continuing, it should be noted that later developments in Freud's general psychoanalytic theory rendered this view problematic (Chertok, 1977). Specifically, just two years later, in "The Ego and the Id," Freud (1923) wrote of the ego ideal:

> The considerations that led us to assume the existence of a grade in the ego, a differentiation within the ego, which may be called the "ego-ideal" or "super-ego", have been stated elsewhere. They still hold good . . . Except that I seem to have been mistaken in ascribing the function of "reality testing" to this super-ego—a point which needs correction. It would fit in perfectly with the relations of the ego to the world of perception if reality testing remained a task of the ego itself [p. 28].

As "Group Psychology and the Analysis of the Ego" contained his last major statement on hypnosis, Freud (1921) never resolved the quandary created by this later revision. Despite his failure to bring his 1921 theory of hypnosis in line with later advances in structural theory, Freud's new emphasis on the ego in hypnosis was to be the starting point for several later psychoanalytic theories of hypnosis, especially those approaching hypnosis from the viewpoint of ego psychology.

Even with these two additions to his theory (i.e., love and the ego ideal), Freud (1921) realized much still remained to be explained about hypnosis: "There is still a great deal in it which we must recognize as unexplained and mysterious" (p. 115). After listing some of the areas that needed further exploration, for example, the exact nature of the relationship between hypnosis and sleep, Freud commented once again on the inability of the hypnotist to remove wholly the will of the subject. He attributed this "to the fact that in hypnosis as it is usually practiced some knowledge may be retained that what is happening is only a game, an untrue reproduction of another situation of far more importance to life" (p. 116).

It will be recalled that in 1890 Freud distinguished between two methods of inducing a hypnotic state: by repetition of monotonous stimuli and by talking a subject into hypnosis. At that time it was the latter method whose mechanism Freud could not explain. By 1921, however, he had derived an explanation and in doing so had changed his earlier view regarding the reasons these methods were effective. In 1891 Freud had written that induction procedures worked by "arousing by an association of thought, the picture of falling asleep and of fixating attention by means of a persistent sensation" (p. 111). Now, however, Freud (1921) wrote:

> It is true that hypnosis can also be evoked in other ways, for instance by fixing the eyes upon a bright object or by listening to a monotonous sound. This is misleading and has given occasion to inadequate physiological theories. In point of fact these procedures merely serve to divert conscious attention and to hold it riveted . . . the subject is in reality unconsciously concentrating his whole attention upon the hypnotist, and is getting into an attitude of rapport, of transference on to him [pp. 125–126].

After restating the psychical similarities between sleep and hypnosis, Freud next elaborated upon the idea that the subject–hypnotist relationship is like the child–parent relationship. In this view the hypnotist revives those thoughts and feelings that are associated with a child's submissive attitude towards its parents. Interestingly, while it appears that Freud agreed with Ferenczi's distinction between maternal and paternal hypnotism, he saw only the latter as operating in the fully developed state, relegating the former to having a possible value in describing a type of hypnotic induction. In other words, Freud saw the subject–hypnotist relationship as being modeled on the child–father relationship, seeing Ferenczi's maternal hypnotism as being relevant only to the extent that a soothing, coaxing attitude might help to induce a hypnotic state. This emphasis on the child–father relationship was stated clearly when he wrote: "What is thus awakened is the idea of a paramount and dangerous personality, towards whom only a passive-masochistic attitude is possible, to whom one's will has to be surrendered" (p. 127).

Freud's almost exclusive focus on paternal hypnotism was a necessary step towards his next theoretical development; the subject–hypnotist relationship was modeled not only on that of a child to its father but, more importantly, on the relationship of an individual member of the primal horde to the primal father. This extension of Freud's social theory, originally advanced in "Totem and Taboo" (1913), allowed him to solidify his thesis of a similarity between the relationship of an individual to a group leader and the relationship of a subject to a hypnotist. According to Freud (1921), both relationships had their roots in the history of the human species. Hypnosis, seen this way, was "an inherited deposit from the phylogenesis of the human libido—hypnosis in the form of a predisposition . . ." (p. 143). In this view, when people enter hypnosis, they reenact the relationship of an individual to the primal father, the extreme submissiveness being the result of an inherited predisposition to behave in this way. Freud described this situation in another way: "The primal father is the group ideal, which governs the ego in place of the ego-ideal. Hypnosis has a good claim to being described as a group of two" (p. 127).

To sum up, in "Group Psychology and the Analysis of the Ego" Freud saw the state of hypnosis as being similar to being in love but with the sexual aims inhibited. This inhibition of the sexual drive was assumed to enforce a separation between the ego and the ego-ideal, thus setting up a situation where the cathexes constituting the ego-ideal could be bound up with the image of the hypnotist, and was seen as an inherited predisposition from early in the phylogenetic development of the human species that had originally served to bind the members of the primal horde to the will of the primal father.

As discussed previously, Freud's earliest (post-1888) writings on hypnosis expanded Bernheim's view of the importance of suggestion. Later he discussed libidinal elements, in their relationship to transference, as the factor underlying suggestion. In "Group Psychology and the Analysis of the Ego" Freud (1921) further specified the nature of this transference by postulating its origins in a predetermined behavior pattern. Ironically, this last revision appeared to return him to his original position regarding Bernheim's theory, in that he was again asserting the existence of intervening variables in hypnosis in the form of preexisting unconscious autosuggestive mechanisms. Freud now defined suggestion as "a conviction which is not based upon perception and reasoning but upon an erotic tie" (p. 128), and regarding hypnosis he concluded as follows:

> It seems to me worth emphasizing the fact that the discussions in this section have induced us to give up Bernheim's conception of hypnosis and go back to the naif earlier one. According to Bernheim all hypnotic

> phenomena are to be traced to the factor of suggestion, which is not itself capable of further explanation. We have come to the conclusion that suggestion is a partial manifestation of the state of hypnosis, and that hypnosis is solidly founded upon a predisposition which has survived in the unconscious from the early history of the family [p. 128].

The "naif earlier" view was, of course, that of Charcot, who saw hypnosis as being based upon a physiological predisposition for disordered neurological functioning.[3] Freud's last theoretical statement on hypnosis represents only a partial return to his earliest position, however, because he was not advocating a reacceptance of Charcot's views. For Freud the predisposition to unconscious autosuggestion, which he saw as present in all humans and which was pivotal in hypnosis, was a *psychical phenomenon* similar to the idea that the memory of the primal father remains alive in the human unconscious.[4] The predisposition to relate to the hypnotist with the submissiveness required by a primal father was presumed by Freud to have an organic base in the sexual physiology underlying the libido. Freud, however, did not attempt to account for psychophysiological changes associated with hypnosis. As previously noted, although the issue of the coupling of psychical and physiological phenomena had originally been of some concern to Freud in his earliest writings on hypnosis, understanding the physiological side of the coupling no longer remained a major concern for him after 1895, when he adopted sexuality as the organic base for his psychology and (from 1898) proceeded "as if only the psychological were under consideration" (Masson, 1985, p. 326).

---

[3]Charcot believed that a hereditary constitutional defect lay behind the disorders of his patients, thus accounting for both their hysterical symptoms and their susceptibility to "grand hypnotisme."

[4]Freud based his conception of a transpersonal, inherited predisposition to reexperience, in psychic form, events that actually occurred in human prehistory on the questionable biological principles of the inheritance of acquired characteristics (Lamarckism) and on recapitulation theory (ontogeny recapitulates phylogeny). These principles gave Freud a platform from which he could assert that certain psychical characteristics of the child or adult mind were predetermined factors. Thus, in his *Introductory Lectures on Psycho-Analysis,* Freud (1915–1917) stated:

> It seems to me quite possible that all the things that are told to us today in analysis as phantasy—the seduction of children, the inflaming of sexual excitement by observing parental intercourse, the threat of castration (or rather castration itself)—were once real occurrences in the primaeval times of the human family, and that children in their phantasies are simply filling in the gaps in individual truth with prehistoric truth [p. 37].

For accounts of Freud relating features of the contemporary psyche to events in human prehistory, which he decided not to publish, see Grubrich-Simitis (1987) and Silverstein (1989b).

Freud's psychological approach to hypnosis remained a two-sided one because he assumed an underlying sexual foundation whose physiology was not identified or understood when he limited his attention to the psychical mechanisms and predispositions involved in the phenomenon. In his final, two-sided view of hypnosis, then, the "psychoanalytic" Freud was content with his assertion that the physiological substrate of hypnosis lay in human sexuality (even though the precise nature of this organic foundation remained unknown to him); realized that transference could not account for hypnotic phenomena *in general;* and saw the unique aspects of hypnosis in the interaction of transference elements with both an extreme state of focused attention and (in 1921) an inherited psychical predisposition involving a submissive attitude, which was a transpersonal factor, rooted in the prehistory of the human species.

In 1908 Freud told Jung (McGuire, 1974): "In the sexual process we have the indispensable 'organic foundation' without which a medical man can only feel ill at ease in the life of the psyche" (pp. 140–141). Freud's approach to hypnosis, like his approach to mental phenomena in general, was not exclusively psychological. In differentiating his psychoanalytic technique, which was purely psychological, from his psychological theory, which was two-sided, Freud (1905a) made the following remarks about the psychoneuroses, which could also apply to his theoretical confrontations with hypnosis:

> The theory does not by any means fail to point out that neuroses have an organic base—though it is true that it does not look for that basis in any pathological anatomical changes, and provisionally substitutes the conception of organic functions for the chemical changes which we should expect to find but which we are at present unable to apprehend. No one, probably, will be inclined to deny the sexual function the character of an organic factor, and it is the sexual function that I look upon as the foundation of hysteria and of the psychoneuroses in general. No theory of sexual life will, I suspect, be able to avoid assuming the existence of some definite sexual substances having an excitant action [p. 113].

Freud's psychological theorizing always saw mind and body as linked, but since he could not explain the mechanism of the coupling, he created speculative organic foundations to serve as a logically consistent base for his psychological theory. Thus, his sexual theory was anchored to a speculative sexual physiology and, eventually, a hypothesized phylogenetic inheritance and the predisposition for ontogenetic recapitulation. His theoretical confrontations with hypnosis helped move Freud toward the creation of a speculative organic base for his psychology, and the development of that organic base led Freud to revise his views on hypnosis several times, although he continued to maintain a consistently two-sided view.

REFERENCES

Breuer, J. & Freud, S. (1895), Studies on hysteria. *Standard Edition,* 2. London: Hogarth Press, 1966.

Chertok, L. (1977), Freud and hypnosis: An epistemological appraisal. *J. Nerv. Ment. Dis.,* 165:99–109.

Ferenczi, S. (1909), Introjection and transference. In: *Sex and Psychoanalysis.* New York: Basic, 1950, pp. 35–93.

Freud, E., ed. (1961), *The Letters of Sigmund Freud: 1873–1939.* London: Hogarth Press.

Freud, S. (1888a), Gehirn [Brain], ed. A. Villaret. *Handwörterbuch der gesamten medizin, Band 1.* Stuttgart: Ferdinand Enke, pp. 684–697.

_____ (1888b), Review of Obersteiner's "*Der Hypnotismus.*" *Internat J. Psycho-Anal.,* 70:401–403, 1989. (English trans. Dr. Mark Solms).

_____ (1888c), Preface to the translation of Bernheim's *Suggestion. Standard Edition,* 1:75–85. London: Hogarth Press, 1966.

_____ (1889), Review of August Forel's *Hypnotism. Standard Edition,* 1:91–102. London: Hogarth Press, 1966.

_____ (1890), Psychical (or mental) treatment. *Standard Edition,* 7:282–302. London: Hogarth Press, 1953. (See also *Standard Edition,* 1:63).

_____ (1891a), *On Aphasia.* London: Imago, 1953.

_____ (1891b), Hypnosis. *Standard Edition,* 1:105–114. London: Hogarth Press, 1966.

_____ (1892), A case of successful treatment by hypnotism. *Standard Edition,* 1:117–128. London: Hogarth Press, 1962.

_____ (1893), Charcot. *Standard Edition,* 3:9–23. London: Hogarth Press, 1962.

_____ (1895), Draft H: Paranoia. *Standard Edition,* 1:206–212. London: Hogarth Press, 1966.

_____ (1896), Preface to the second edition of Bernheim's *Suggestion. Standard Edition,* 1:86–87. London: Hogarth Press, 1966.

_____ (1905a), Fragment of an analysis of a case of hysteria. *Standard Edition,* 7:3–122. London: Hogarth Press, 1953.

_____ (1905b). Three essays on the theory of sexuality. *Standard Edition,* 7:130–243. London: Hogarth Press, 1953.

_____ (1910), Five lectures on psychoanalysis. *Standard Edition,* 11:9–55. London: Hogarth Press, 1957.

_____ (1912), The dynamics of transference. *Standard Edition,* 12:99–108. London: Hogarth Press, 1958.

_____ (1913), Totem and taboo. *Standard Edition,* 13:1–161. London: Hogarth Press, 1953.

_____ (1916–1917), Introductory lectures on psycho-analysis. *Standard Edition,* 15&16. London: Hogarth Press, 1963.

_____ (1921), Group psychology and the analysis of the ego. *Standard Edition,* 18:69–143. London: Hogarth Press, 1955.

_____ (1923), The ego and the id. *Standard Edition,* 19:12–66. London: Hogarth Press, 1961.

_____ (1925), An autobiographical study. *Standard Edition*, 20:7–74. London: Hogarth Press, 1959.

Gravitz, M. A. & Gerton, M. I. (1981), Freud and hypnosis: Report of post-rejection use. *J. Hist. Behav. Sciences*, 17:68–74.

Grubich-Simitis, I. (Ed.). (1987), *Sigmund Freud: A Phylogenetic Fantasy*. Cambridge: Harvard University Press.

Jones, E. (1953), *The Life and Work of Sigmund Freud, Vol. 1*. New York: Basic Books.

Masson, J. M., ed. (1985), *The Complete Letters of Sigmund Freud to Wilhelm Fliess: 1887–1904*. Cambridge, MA: Harvard University Press.

McGuire, W., ed. (1974), *The Freud-Jung Letters*. Princeton, NJ: Princeton University Press.

Polgar, F. J. (1951), *The Story of a Hypnotist*. New York: Thomas Nelson.

Silverstein, B. (1985), Freud's psychology and its organic foundation: Sexuality and mind-body interactionism. *Psychoanal. Rev.*, 72:203–228.

_____ (1988), Will the real Freud stand up, please? *Amer. Psychol.*, 43:662–663.

_____ (1989a), Freud's dualistic mind-body interactionism: implications for the development of his theory. *Psychol. Rep.*, 64, 1091–1097.

_____ (1989b), Oedipal politics and scientific creativity: Freud's 1915 phylogenetic fantasy. *Psychoanal. Rev.*, 76. 403–424.

*Post-Freudian Developments in Psychoanalytic Views of Hypnosis: From Libido Theory to Ego Psychology**

STEVEN M. SILVERSTEIN
BARRY R. SILVERSTEIN

Starting with his 1888 preface to the German translation of Bernheim's *Suggestion,* Freud repeatedly attempted to conceptualize theoretical explanations for the phenomenon of hypnosis (Silverstein and Silverstein, this volume). His final major theoretical statement on the issue came in 1921, in "Group Psychology and the Analysis of the Ego." Here, Freud presented a view of hypnosis that, while distinctly psychoanalytic, nevertheless remained in harmony with his first major statement on the issue in that he consistently opted for a two-sided view of hypnosis. For Freud hypnosis had to be understood both in terms of psychical functions and an organic substrate. By 1905 Freud believed that (a) the organic substrate of hypnosis lay in human sexuality (even though the physiology of this organic foundation remained unknown to him) and (b) the psychical factor was transference, "an unconscious fixation of the subject's libido to the figure of the hypnotist" (p. 150). By 1921 he asserted that the unique aspects of hypnosis lay in the interaction of transference elements with both an extreme state of focused attention and an inherited psychical predisposition to assume a submissive attitude to the primal father, that is, a transpersonal factor rooted in the primeval times of the human family.

In this chapter we review the major psychoanalytic theories of hypnosis that followed Freud's final statement of 1921. In examining post-Freudian theoretical developments concerning hypnosis, we can observe

*The authors would like to thank Dr. Joseph Masling for his helpful comments on an earlier draft of this manuscript.

a correlation between the presentation of new psychoanalytic theories for this phenomenon and changing directions and emphases within the psychoanalytic field.

Rado

The first major post-Freudian psychoanalytic theory of hypnosis was offered by Rado. Following Freud (1905, 1921) and Ferenczi (1909), Rado (1925) elaborated on the idea that "the hypnotist activates in the patient the latter's infantile erotic relationships to the parents" (p. 36). In addition, he saw the "hypnotic fascination" shown by the subject as a neurotic symptom; libido is transferred from symptoms to the hypnotic experience, being "discharged, in all probability through the silent affective and somatic processes in hypnosis" (p. 36). Like a neurotic symptom, hypnotic fascination was seen as a compromise in that while there is some libidinal discharge in the direction of an actual object, this gratification is "inhibited in its aim" (p. 37).

Concerning the structural dynamics of hypnosis, Rado (1925) believed that "the hypnotist takes the place of the patient's ego ideal, usurping the functions of the super ego" (p. 39). (The ego ideal here is not quite the same as Freud's (1921); rather, it is the post-1923 concept used in psychoanalysis today.) In this way the subject "borrows from the hypnotist the forces necessary for repression, thus regressing as far as aims and means of instinctual mastery are concerned, to the stage of childhood at which the father's omnipotence is supreme" (p. 39). The subject's own desire for omnipotence is then gratified since this regression occurs alongside alterations in the ego that result in an identification with an omnipotent figure (i.e., the hypnotist). On these points Rado agreed with Jones (1923) and with Schilder and Kauders, 1927, (see following section), who further speculated on the importance of a sense of omnipotence in hypnosis. This was also the first discussion of the role played by identification in hypnosis.

According to Rado (1925), the process by which the hypnotist partially takes over the functions of the subject's superego is that of introjection. Initially the hypnotist becomes an object for the ego through oedipal libidinal investment. This investment activates a "feminine masochistic" attitude in the ego (p. 42). In an effort to counter this attitude, the ego tries to replace the object by identifying with it. This identification is never totally successful, however, and the object cathexes that remain are transformed into aim-inhibited feeling. At this point the unity of the ego is threatened, since any remaining cathexes connected with the masochistic attitude are incompatible with the ongoing attempt at identification. A resolution occurs as the identification separates itself from the masochistic content of the ego. This identification then begins to attract to itself "the natural cathexis of the topographically differentiated superego" (p. 40). The result is that the superego is "subjected to a new authority and the hypnotist is promoted from being an object of the ego to the position of a parasitic super-ego" (p. 40). In the end, "masochism ultimately gains a free hand in the ego and unites with the sadism of the introjected parasitic super-ego to bring about the results of hypnosis" (p. 42).

The hypnotic state, as seen by Rado, results from a feminine masochism interacting with a process of identification with an omnipotent figure. Rado appears, however, to have stressed the former factor: "The feminine masochism of the ego has to be regarded as the decisive factor in hypnotic fascination . . ." (p. 43). In stressing this, he acknowledged that it was "wholly in keeping with Freud's first fundamental observation on this matter," p. 43, (i.e., Freud's 1905 position). Beyond this, though, Rado felt that "much yet remains to be explained" (p. 45) about hypnosis.

In an interesting theoretical turn, Rado (1925) objected to the idea of hypnosis as an artificial sleep, noting its similarity instead to an "artifical dream." He also expressed the view that the hypnotic state was an "aim inhibited derivative of coitus." These two ideas were tied together with the assumption "that there is a close relation between the course of the sex act and that of dream processes (i.e., not merely of sleep!)" (p. 43). The importance of this theoretical development lay in its redirection of focus for psychoanalytic investigation. Specifically, while previous theories had concentrated on the drive elements and the unconscious processes involved in hypnosis, this view, through its analogy with dream processes, suggested that some understanding of the hypnotic state might be gained by investigating its conscious manifestations.[1] As will be demonstrated shortly, this was the direction in which psychoanalytic theory later turned, most notably in the form of ego psychological theories that focused on ego regressions and alterations. This development was gradual, however, and did not come before further contributions were made to the original theoretical position.

[1]While Rado was the first to suggest that hypnosis could be studied in a similar manner to dreams, Freud (1921) had earlier stated that the subject experiences the commands of the hypnotist in a "dream-like way" (p. 114).

Schilder and Kauders

Schilder and Kauders (1927) extended the views of earlier psychoanalysts and, in addition, attempted to provide a physiological explanation of hypnosis. They started with the recognition that "hypnosis is as a rule an erotic state with inhibited goals" (p. 39). In particular, they saw the hypnotic state as an opportunity for a subject to experience a revival of "the still strong libidinous fixation to his father" (p. 38).

In addition to viewing hypnosis as fundamentally an erotic state, Schilder and Kauders saw a second "root" of hypnosis, the subordination to the authority of another: "hypnosis is an attitude of subordination, an attitude of self-subjection" (p. 39). Both of these attitudes are characteristics of masochism and thus, in the end, go back to the sexual instinct, in the manner originally discussed by Freud (1905). One difference, however, between the view of Schilder and Kauders and that of Freud is that the former's focus on subordination emphasizes the dynamics of the individual and has nothing to do with the history of the species.

Schilder and Kauders saw two muscular phenomena as characteristic of hypnosis: absolute relaxation and catalepsy. Furthermore, both these somatic phenomena were seen as manifestations of the masochistic attitude. The assumption that there are specific identifiable signs of the hypnotic state originated with the earliest theories of hypnosis. Freud (1891) also took this position; when the hypnotic state is achieved, he stated, "We shall find that some of the somatic phenomena which characterize hypnosis will emerge" (p. 110). Freud, however, never returned to this point in his subsequent writing on hypnosis. The belief in somatic characteristics of hypnosis clearly implies a further belief in an hypnotic state that can be distinguished from other states of consciousness, a question still debated today (e.g., see Kihlstrom, 1985; Hilgard, 1986).

According to Schilder and Kauders (1927), the hypnotized person adopts a submissive attitude in order "to have a share in the greatness of the hypnotizer" (p. 42). In the view of the subject, the hypnotist is "the great magician," capable of altering reality. This view, however, does not come from the hypnotist; rather, it is a projection of the subject's own desire for omnipotence. Thus, by "unconscious manipulation" the longing for omnipotence is fulfilled through a process of projection and, later, by identification.

Schilder and Kauders saw this process as paralleling the phase of infantile experience in which the child, after realizing that it is not omnipotent, ascribes this quality to its parents. Through the process of identification, the child is later able to share in this power. Because they saw this parallel, Schilder and Kauders categorized hypnosis as a type of regressive phenomenon; they described it as only a partial regression, however, recognizing that a portion of the person remains in contact with reality.

Schilder and Kauders (1927) did not see the regression involved in hypnosis as limited to the psychic sphere. They viewed this "primitive archaic regressive phenomenon" (i.e., hypnosis) as having physiological correlates as well. According to them, hypnosis alters the relationship between the higher cortical functions and the vasovegetative functions (i.e., those of the phylogenetically more primitive brain structures). In the normal waking state, "fully developed cortical function is connected with clearly defined images which are productive of expedient action" (p. 79), in contrast to the hypnotic state where cortical functioning regresses to a "primitive stage" as a result of increased vasovegetative activity. This increased activity of the lower brain centers arises from increased affective activity. The latter, of course, results from an activation of the transference and its derivatives. Thus, according to Schilder and Kauders,

> the attitude of the suggested person, in its goal-inhibited masochistic trend recognizing authority in a magic degree, is very evidently archaic and represents a primitive experience. It should not surprise us to learn that this attitude has particularly close relations with the phylogenetically deep-lying vasovegetative realm [p. 79].

Interestingly, the physiological explanation of hypnosis advanced by Schilder and Kauders corresponds with Rado's (1925) view that hypnosis is a dreamlike state. Specifically, Schilder and Kauders (1927) stated that as higher cortical functions become less predominant, "dislocations, condensations, defective differentiation of details ensue, and modes of thought familiar to us from the primitive state and from childhood put in their appearance" (pp. 78–79). Thus, while Schilder and Kauders never explicitly pointed to the similarity between hypnosis and dreaming, the association is obvious in their work.

In a sense, the theory of Schilder and Kauders seems to have anticipated the next major psychoanalytic theory of hypnosis, that of Kubie and Margolin (1944). The similarity between these theories lies in their emphasizing both the psychodynamic and the physiological mechanisms involved in hypnosis, both being seen as necessary and interrelated factors.

Kubie and Margolin

Prior to adding anything new to psychoanalytic theorizing about hypnosis, Kubie and Margolin (1944) stressed the importance of separating hypnosis into two distinct phenomena: the process of hypnotic induction and the fully developed hypnotic state. They saw hypnotic induction as analogous to (not as an approximation of) the creation of a condition of partial sleep, partial in the sense that one or two channels of communication to the outside world (i.e., the hypnotist) are left open. This reduction in communication channels was seen as leading to a dedifferentiation of the boundaries between a subject's sense of self and the external world. The consequence of this focused attention combined with a loss of ego boundaries is a state of psychological fusion between the hypnotist and the subject. Through this process of fusion, hypnotists exert their influence over subjects.

> It is this dissolution of ego boundaries that gives the hypnotist his apparent "power"; because his commands do not operate as something reaching the subject from the outside, demanding submissiveness. To the subject they are his own thoughts and goals, a part of himself [Kubie and Margolin, 1944, p. 612].

In a sense, Kubie and Margolin's idea that the hypnotist operates by controlling a portion of the subject's ego can be seen as an extension of Freud's (1921) theory, with its thesis that the hypnotist usurps some of the reality-testing functions of the subject's ego-ideal. As will become apparent shortly, however, this similarity to Freud's 1921 position was the closest Kubie and Margolin ever came to the earlier psychoanalytic theories. While these all relied on some dynamic process (e.g., transference, identification, masochism, etc.) to explain the influence of the hypnotist, Kubie and Margolin saw none of these as necessary components of the hypnotic state.

Working with a Pavlovian perspective, Kubie and Margolin (1944) saw a physiological prerequisite of the hypnotic state to be the "creation of a focus of central excitation" in the brain "with surrounding areas of inhibition" (p. 613). The achievement of this state depends on two factors: relative immobilization and monotonous, low-intensity stimulaton. Both these requirements were met by the hypnotist by having the subject focus on one aspect of sensation and remove attention from everything else. It is here that other theorists believe transference elements help to induce hypnosis, since subjects must allow themselves to be put through the hypnotic process. Kubie and Margolin, however, did not discuss the mechanics of this transference: they did not see it as a necessary factor in hypnosis. Indeed, they did not even see the presence of another human being as a necessary factor in hypnosis (to be explained shortly).

While they did not see transference as a necessary component of either hypnotic induction or the hypnotic state, Kubie and Margolin (1944) did not deny that elements of transference might be observed during either of these situations. To clarify this point they used the following analogy regarding dreaming: transference elements that arise during the induction process may be carried over into the hypnotic state in the same way that day residues are made use of in dreams; however, "the carry-over from the pre-hypnotic transference relationships are not the essence of the hypnotic state itself any more than the 'Tagesrest' is the essence of the dream" (p. 618). The similarity lay in the observation that thought content concerning the hypnotist might undergo transformations characteristic of the dream work (e.g., condensation), making material from the unconscious accessible. Kubie and Margolin noted that since the hypnotic state is usually produced with a hypnotist, transference elements often appear, thus leading to the false assumption that transference is at the core of the hypnotic state. In fact, "if the hypnotic state could be produced without the use of any personal prehypnotic maneuvers, the hypnotic subject's thought content would then arise solely out of the depths of his own personality" (p. 618).

According to Kubie and Margolin (1944), a major difference between the process of induction and the hypnotic state is that in the fully developed state there is a reopening of communicative channels to the world. The subject can get up, walk around, and behave as a normal person would. The difference between this state and the normal state, then, is one of psychological organization. Specifically, the hypnotist retains a degree of control over the subject by acting as an "unconscious component of the new personality that has emerged" (p. 619). This psychic subsystem

> delimits memories and contacts, dictates purposes, distributes inner rewards and inner punishments, and engenders strong affects. In some measure therefore, it temporarily dispossesses the earlier authorities (i.e., the superego), or merges with them . . . the buried (incorporated) image of the hypnotist becomes an experimentally induced superego figure [p. 619].

Thus, although subjects in the hypnotic state may interact with the world more fully than they can during the process of induction, Kubie and Margolin argued that there are limits on this behavior as well, limits imposed by the altered state of psychological organization.

The initial theory of Kubie and Margolin (1944) can be summed up as follows: During the induction process [there is] "a state of maximal attention to one group of stimuli, combined with an alteration of all others, which results in a loss of ego boundaries and an incorporation of the hypnotist in the subject" (p. 619). This can be distinguished from the fully developed hypnotic state in which "a diffusion of sensor-motor relations occurs with a retention of a dominant but repressed link to the hypnotist by the incorporation of a fragmentary image of him in the reexpanded borders of the ego" (p. 620).

Later Kubie (1961, 1972) extended the original theory. An important addition was the idea that neither psychodynamic nor psychophysiological factors alone are sufficient for the production of a hypnotic state; both are necessary, a concept clearly in contrast to several earlier views (e.g., Ferenczi's) that discussed the process solely in psychological terms. Interestingly, Freud (1915–1917) in his "Introductory Lectures on Psycho-Analysis" noted that although transference was an essential element in hypnosis, an extreme focusing of attention was also necessary. This focusing of attention, while not given physiological correlates by Freud, would nevertheless correspond, in Pavlovian terminology, to extreme excitation of cortical points leading to inhibition of surrounding areas through the process of negative induction. Indeed, Pavlovian discussions of physiology are basically descriptive, rather than anatomical or functional. In sum, when Kubie discussed physiological aspects of hypnosis, he was discussing hypothetical cortical processes, not actual physiological processes with anatomical referents. Thus, his theory need not be seen as a radical departure from all nonphysiological earlier theories, but can be seen as a departure from those using only dynamic concepts as causal factors. In addition, by taking a two-sided view. Kubie's approach is in the tradition pioneered by Freud.

A second major point of Kubie's later theory (1961) was that "there is nothing remarkable about the psychological ingredients in the phenomenology of hypnotism, nothing to differentiate them from their manifestations in other psychological states, whether normal or pathological" (p. 41). Later Kubie (1972) extended this beyond the realm of the psychological, writing, "It is impossible to establish clear correlations between this state and physiological, psychophysiological, psychiatric, psychoanalytic, or clinical data in general" (p. 211). Research strongly supports this statement in that there is as yet no sign by which the hypnotic state can be distinguished from other states (e.g., relaxation, meditation, role playing, etc.; see, e.g., Edmonston, 1968; Morse et al., 1977). While such evidence supports Kubie's position, it also points out the difficulties in testing it, since to compare hypnosis to what is not hypnosis, one must know when hypnosis exists. Kubie himself recognized this problem and concluded that much research still had to be done before hypnosis would be properly understood.

A third point in Kubie's later work concerned the concept of hypnosis as a form of regression. This concept was used by earlier theorists such as Schilder and Kauders, and by several later ones as well (see following discussion). Kubie (1961) noted, however, that there was no evidence to support this idea, especially that "it must always constitute a return to so called 'archaic levels'" (p. 41). Again, research suggests that Kubie was correct in this warning; there is a great deal of variability in the amount of regression observed during hypnosis (e.g., see Gruenwald, Fromm, and Oberlander, 1979). There is also the question of what is regressed, this concept often being employed in an overly vague manner.

A fourth major point in Kubie's theory involved the issue of transference. From the beginning Kubie saw transference elements as products of hypnosis, not as its cause or as its essence. Moreover, Kubie believed that the hypnotic state could be produced without the presence of another human being (i.e., through relative immobilization and monotonous stimuation). While transference, as it is commonly understood, was not seen as essential to hypnosis, Kubie did see a form of transference, which he called "transference in the purest culture," as a necessary ingredient. This type of transference reflects an "unseen and unacknowledged presence, sometimes consciously perceived but more often preconsciously and/or unconsciously. This presence may represent the earliest protective figures of infancy, or much later figures of authority and protection." In this way, "the past makes its inevitable contribution to the process of induction" (Kubie, 1961, p. 43).

What all of this means is that the "experimentally induced superego figure" may be the psychical representation of the hypnotist or, in cases where no hypnotist is present, the representation(s) of past authority figures. The important point here, according to Kubie, is that this "transference in the purest culture" is an integral component of the hypnotic state. In this view, there need not be a developing transference between two participants for the hypnotic state to occur.

To support the idea that transference is not necessary for hypnosis, Kubie (1961) described an experiment by Kubie and Margolin (he also cited an independent replication) in which a hypnotic state was induced by playing back to a subject through headphones his own respiratory sounds recorded by a microphone placed against the subject's neck at the trachea.

> When into this hypnoidal state with its diffused ego boundaries and orientation in time and space the observer's words were introduced quietly, they became one with the patient's own free-flowing associative stream. This comes close to demonstrating that the phenomenon of suggestibility is an expression of the degree to which the hypnotist's words become the subject's own purposes and thoughts. It is this which converts the hypnotists words into effective "suggestions"; and this can happen only when the boundary between the hypnotist and the subject is in some measure erased. In fact, this is an experimental induction of what in analysis is called "introjection," a step towards incorporation [p. 48].

How different this approach was from the way in which Freud (1905) discussed the mechanisms underlying suggestion: "an unconscious fixation of the subject's libido to the figure of the hypnotist, through the medium of the masochistic components of the sexual instinct" (p. 150).

All four of these points led Kubie to a crucial final argument: that such crucial concepts as suggestion and regression should not be used to explain hypnosis. In his opinion, using such concepts was equivalent to explaining a phenomenon by its consequences and was thus invalid. According to Kubie, a true understanding of hypnosis can only be gained when its essential nature is examined apart from its epiphenomena.

The theory of hypnosis put forth by Kubie and Margolin clarified several aspects of hypnosis. Its influence can be seen in the fact that the next major psychoanalytic theory of hypnosis, that of Gill and Brenman (1959), took as its starting point several of its concepts. Rather than continue to disentangle what Kubie and Margolin saw as the essence of the hypnotic state from its artifacts, however, Gill and Brenman believed that Kubie and Margolin were mistaken in assigning epiphenomenal roles to several aspects of the hypnotic situation. Their theory represented a return to a more traditional psychoanalytic perspective.

Gill and Brenman

Gill and Brenman (1959) defined the hypnotic state as "an induced psychological regression, issuing, in the setting of a particular regressed relationship between two people, in a relatively stable state which includes a subsystem of the ego with various degrees of control of the ego apparatuses" (p. xxiii). Later, Gill (1972) would add that "hypnosis is a state of regression in the service of the ego and that that aspect of this regressive state which comprises the subject's relationship to the hypnotist is what we call transference" (p. 229). Unlike Kubie and Margolin, Gill and Brenman saw the interpersonal factor as crucial to hypnosis. In his 1972 paper, Gill summed up this theoretical difference as follows:

> To me transference *is* crucial in hypnosis. The hypnoidal states Kubie describes are doubtless regressive states and, since there furthermore is always an introjected object to which a helpless human being will turn, there are surely some major resemblances between these hypnoidal states and hypnosis. But for me hypnosis does reguire an outside hypnotist and the transference is of the essence [p. 230].

Gill (1972) hypothesized two types of transference to occur in the hypnotic relationship. The first type

> is the one underlying the hypnosis itself. It is the existence of the capacity for this transference which makes the real characteristics of the hypnotist so apparently unimportant at first, because this transference is present from the beginning and is a predisposition evoked but not created by the hypnotist [p. 230].

The second type of transference is the type that develops in therapy; this reaction involves "that complex amalgam of feelings and attitudes, in part justified and in part unjustified by the real relationship with the hypnotist" (p. 231).

In postulating two types of transference underlying hypnosis, Gill and Brenman's theory paralleled that of Kubie and Margolin. Moreover, Gill and Brenman's first type of transference greatly resembled Kubie and Margolin's "transference in the purest culture." The fundamental difference between the two theories lay in the importance of Gill and Brenman's second type of transference, which they saw as a necessary factor in hypnosis whereas Kubie and Margolin did not. In the end, this theoretical difference was only a definitional one, representing a contrast between a broad (Kubie and Margolin's) and a narrow (Gill and Brenman's) definition of hypnosis. The evidence necessary to transform the latter into the former would involve demonstrating, as Kubie did, that many hypnoidal phenomena can occur without the presence of a hypnotist. Gill and Brenman would not have considered this evidence acceptable, however, since the lack of a transference would mean to them that the phenomenon was not hypnosis.

Throughout their work Gill and Brenman emphasized two aspects of hypnosis, both of which are found in their definition previously cited (Brenman, Gill, and Hacker, 1947; Brenman, Gill and Knight, 1952; Gill and Brenman, 1959; Gill, 1972). The first theme involves transference; the second concerns the idea of hypnosis as an altered state of consciousness. In Gill and Brenman's view, the subject's ego is altered because part of it comes under the control of a newly established "subsystem of the ego" representing the will of the hypnotist. They saw this subsystem as developing in the following manner: First, deautomatization of various ego apparatuses occurs as the result of the interference with the normal sensorimotor relationships with the environment. This idea was similar to Kubie and Margolin's idea about dedifferentiation of ego boundaries and its consequences. Second, the hypnotist gains control of these functions and in this way is able to exercise an influence over the subject. Gill and Brenman's subsystem of the ego is thus like Kubie and Margolin's unconscious component of the personality (see their description of this psychic subsystem in the previous section). Both concepts describe similar steps leading to the incorporation of the hypnotist by the subject.

It is interesting to note that while the concept of incorporation in psychoanalytic theories of hypnosis goes back to 1925 (Rado), the emphasis in 1959 was much more on ego functions and less on drive elements. This development paralleled the increased interest and emphasis on ego functioning in psychoanalytic theory as a whole. For example, while the earliest theories concentrated on the sexual drive and its vicissitudes in the transference (e.g., Freud, 1905, 1921; Ferenczi, 1909; Rado, 1925), later theorists, such as Kubie and Margolin and Gill and Brenman, while recognizing the importance of transference, focused their attention on alterations of the ego. This trend was continued by later theorists, such as Bellak and Fromm. Before examining their theories, however, a final issue on Gill and Brenman's theory remains to be considered. While Gill and Brenman saw a portion of the subject's ego functions as being usurped by the hypnotist, they believed that the rest of the ego remained in contact with reality. In addition, they believed that the ego could retain control over the subsystem at any time, thus preventing the subject from becoming a helpless automation. This idea of a portion of ego independence goes back to Freud's writings: "The person under hypnosis is still able to form a judgement on his own state . . ." (Freud, 1891, p. 109); and in 1921, Freud wrote, "It is noticeable that even when there is complete suggestive compliance in other respects, the moral conscience of the person hypnotized may show resistance" [p. 116]. . . . Some knowledge that in spite of everything hypnosis is only a game, . . . may, however, remain behind and take care that there is a resistance against any too serious consequences of the suspension of the will in hypnosis" (p. 127). However, Gill and Brenman's position had additional connotations beyond the belief that the hypnotic subject is not being completely dominated by the will of the hypnotist.

By believing that the ego could retain control over the hypnotically produced subsystem, Gill and Brenman were able to classify hypnosis as an example of "regression in the service of the ego," a concept borrowed from Kris (1952) and greatly extended by Schafer (1958). The classification of hypnosis in this way implies that it shares some characteristics with other regressed states, such as creativity, as opposed to the type of regression in which the ego is overwhelmed.

Later Psychoanalytic Developments

Bellak (1955), following up on the early work of Gill and Brenman, concentrated also on the role of the ego in hypnosis. He saw hypnosis as "a special case of self-exclusion of the ego" (p. 375). That is, a regression in the service of the ego takes place wherein the ego relinquishes a portion of its reality testing functions to the hypnotist. As a result of this regression, according to Bellak, preconscious functioning becomes the dominant cognitive mode and the hypnotist determines the direction of attention.

Bellak (1955) agreed with Gill and Brenman's contention that hypnosis and sleep are both cases of ego regression: "It must be concluded that psychodynamically there are no systematic differences between sleep and hypnosis except the quantitative one of degree of ego exclusion" (p. 377). This comparison was made inevitable by classifying hypnosis as a case of ego regression, since this concept was used to describe various other conditions, including sleep.

While Bellak saw hypnosis as a case of ego regression, he did not specify what it was that differentiated it from other such states. This task was left to later theorists, who moved even further away from dealing with physiological or libidinal elements as a means of formulating a theory of hypnosis purely in ego psychological terms.

Van der Walde (1965, 1967) defined "the basis of hypnosis as the presence of a specific attitude in which the subject feels that he can uncritically accept complete participation in a specifically defined relationship wherein one partner is expected to do what the other tells him to" (van der Walde, 1965, p. 44). He noted, however, that this attitude is also present in role playing, waking hypnosis, and task-motivated behavior. What differentiated hypnosis from these other behaviors was the context in which this attitude appeared. Specifically, hypnosis could be understood by exploring its motivational, interpersonal, and state-of-consciousness factors.

In discussing the motivational factors behind hypnotic behavior, van der Walde stressed the diversity of needs that can serve as motivators.

Some of those considered were libidinal impulses, masochistic needs, infantile needs, and dependency needs. Contrary to several earlier positions, no one need or drive state was seen as underlying all hypnotic phenomena. Instead, van der Walde saw ego flexibility as the common theme underlying hypnotic phenomena. Hypnotic susceptibility was viewed as a measure of ego adaptability, as a "dynamic reaction geared toward obtaining individually determined gratifications and not a fixed invariable reaction to specific stimuli . . . the subject enters the hypnotic state to achieve one of many desired for gratifications" (1965, p. 441).

Van der Walde (1965) agreed with earlier theorists on the importance of transference elements and interpersonal factors in hypnosis:

> The hypnotic transference allows the subject to safely relinquish his normal responsibilities, fears, and inhibitions. His individual problems, desires, and needs are given over into the hands of an omnipotent and protective being under whose guidance many previously unaccessible things may now be safely obtained. Under this orientation, the subject is able to shift responsibility for his actions onto the hypnotist and in this situation gratification may be obtained without incurring superego condemnation [p. 442].

While both motivational and interpersonal factors are important, van der Walde noted that these are usually not sufficient to produce hypnosis. He saw a third factor, the "altered ego state known as trance," as needed to complete the acceptance of the specific attitude characterizing hypnosis. This altered state was defined as

> a psychological mechanism by which the ego, usually restricted to reality testing, is now deluded into accepting the fact that normal reality has been replaced by the above [i.e., an altered state], and that in this situation the usual rules of reality no longer apply. Reality and rules of behavior are, therefore, to be defined by the hypnotist. The ego can now allow the desired for gratification because responsibility for the subject's actions is now completely projected unto the hypnotist [van der Walde, 1965, p. 443].

Van der Walde believed that the manner by which the ego is deluded into accepting the belief in an altered state consists of two processes. One involves encouraging the subject to attend to certain phenomena that are usually ignored. For example, a subject might be asked to notice his thighs pressing against the chair, his muscles relaxing, or his breathing becoming regular. Through this process, "the subject accepts his perception of these sensations as resulting from the hypnotist's suggestions instead of as a result of his own innate abilities" (van der Walde, 1965, p. 444). This effect is strengthened by the hypnotist's predictions that what the subject subsequently experiences will come true. Examples of this would be predictions that the subject's eyes will become heavy and start to water and that his vision will become blurry. Such phenomena, of course, inevitably result from a prolonged period of staring at a bright object.

Van der Walde saw the second process through which the altered state is created as the restriction of sensorimotor input. His position here is similar to that of Kubie and Margolin (1944) although he focused more on the consequences of one specific result, body image alteration. He disagreed with Kubie and Margolin that this state, when induced without a hypnotist, is still hypnosis. Regarding these "hypnoidal conditions," van der Walde (1965) wrote: "In those conditions similar phenomena occur, but only in hypnosis are these events used to support a fantasy about another person's omnipotence and, as one step in a complex scheme, to obtain otherwise unattainable gratifications" (p. 445). Thus, according to van der Walde, the specific difference between hypnosis and other hypnoidal states is to be found in the interpersonal and motivational matrix within which traditional hypnotic induction takes place.

A further difference between the theories of van der Walde and Kubie and Margolin involves the former's nondifferentiation of the process of hypnotic induction and the hypnotic state. To van der Walde (1965) "the so-called difference between the hypnotic process and the hypnotic state may be nothing more than expressions of the subject's ambivalence to being convinced of the validity of hypnosis in the former, and final acceptance of it in the latter" (p. 444). In this reformulation all aspects of hypnosis were understood as adaptive functions of the ego.

The most recent contribution to psychoanalytic theorizing about hypnosis has come from Fromm (1972, 1979). Starting from Rapaport's (1953) concepts of ego activity and ego passivity, she proposed an intermediate stage called ego receptivity. During a phase of ego receptivity, the ego "is particularly receptive to stimuli coming from within or without and it lets them influence imagery, thoughts, behavioral action and feelings even if they do not conform to the laws of secondary process logic" (Fromm, 1979, p. 93).

While ego receptivity is the dominant experiential mode in several altered states besides hypnosis (e.g., meditative states), in Fromm's theory it is the interpersonal context within which it appears that distinguishes hypnosis from these states. According to Fromm, the effect of induction procedures, especially those involving eye closing, is to help the subject disattend to environmental stimuli. If this is successful,

> a good deal of attention cathexis is thus released and can be turned on the patient's inner life and on his interaction with the hypnotist. The patient becomes receptive to the promptings coming from his own preconscious and unconscious and to the hypnotherapist's interpretations and suggestions [Fromm, 1979, p. 99].

Fromm's theory is an attempt to explain hypnosis solely in ego psychological terms. Indeed, in her view, suggestibility is equivalent to ego receptivity. While the possibility of unconscious promptings in hypnosis is mentioned, such factors are not given further consideration. Thus, no mention is made of either libidinal or transference elements as being necessary factors in hypnosis. When this theory is compared to such earlier theories as those of Freud (1905) and Ferenczi (1909), with their emphases on unconscious libidinal fixations, one can see how much psychoanalytic theory, both regarding hypnosis and in general, has shifted its focus since its earliest formulations. As a result of these changes in emphasis, hypnosis has been understood from several complementary, as well as sometimes contradictory, viewpoints.

In a forthcoming paper we will examine the extent to which each of the psychoanalytic theories of hypnosis (from Freud's earliest positions through Fromm's) remains a useful framework from which to understand hypnotic phenomena today. This is an important issue since theoretical developments in psychoanalytic views of hypnosis have been, for the most part, responses to paradigm shifts within psychoanalysis; that is, each shift in emphasis brought about a need or a desire to reinterpret hypnotic phenomena within the new framework. What this means to those interested in the validity of the theories is that none of them can be assumed a priori to be more valid than any other. None of the theories was formulated in an attempt to explain empirically derived evidence. Given the renewed interest in hypnosis within the field of psychology, as well as the wealth of data that has accumulated on the topic, it would appear that the time is ripe for efforts at integrating theory with data. Such efforts would not only help clarify some of the issues that have been the source of theoretical conflicts within psychoanalysis, but would serve as starting points for the generation of new theories as well.

References

Bellak, L. (1955), An ego-psychological theory of hypnosis. *Internat. J. Psycho-Anal.*, 36:375–378.

Brenman, M., Gill, M. M. & Hacker, F. J. (1947), Alterations in the state of the ego in hypnosis. *Bull. Menn. Clin.*, 11:60–66.

_____ Gill, M. M. & Knight, R. P. (1952), Spontaneous fluctuations in depth of hypnosis and their implications for ego-function. *Internat. J. Psycho-Anal.*, 33:22–33.

Edmonston, W. E., Jr. (1968), Hypnosis and electrodermal responses. *Amer. J. Clinical Hypnosis*, 11:16–25.

Ferenczi, S. (1909), Introjection and transference. In: *Sex and Psychoanalysis*. New York: Basic Books, 1950, pp. 35–93.

Freud, S. (1888), Preface to the translation of Bernheim's *Suggestion*. *Standard Edition*, 1:75–85. London: Hogarth Press, 1966.

_____ (1891), Hypnosis. *Standard Edition*, 1:105–114. London: Hogarth Press, 1966.

_____ (1905), Three essays on the theory of sexuality. *Standard Edition,* 7:130–243. London: Hogarth Press, 1953.

_____ (1916–1917), Introductory lectures on psycho-analysis. *Standard Edition,* 15 & 16. London: Hogarth Press, 1963.

_____ (1921), Group psychology and the analysis of the ego. *Standard Edition,* 18:69–143. London: Hogarth Press, 1955.

Fromm, E. (1972), Ego activity and age passivity in hypnosis. *Internat. J. Clin. & Exp. Hypnosis,* 20:238–251.

_____ (1979), The nature of hypnosis and other altered states of consciousness: An ego-psychological theory. In: *Hypnosis: Developments in Research and New Perspectives,* 2nd ed. ed. E. Fromm & R. E. Shor. New York: Aldine, pp. 81–103.

Gill, M. M. & Brenman, M. (1959), *Hypnosis and Related States: Psychoanalytic Studies in Regression.* New York: International Universities Press.

_____ (1972), Hypnosis as an altered and regressed state. *Internat. J. Clin. & Exp. Hypnosis,* 20:224–237.

Gruenwald, D., Fromm, E. & Oberlander, M. I. (1979), Hypnosis and adaptive regression: An ego psychological inquiry. In: *Hypnosis: Developments in Research and New Perspectives,* 2nd ed. ed. E. Fromm & R. E. Shor. New York: Aldine, pp. 619–635.

Hilgard, E. (1986), *Divided Consciousness: Multiple Controls in Human Thought and Action (expanded edition).* New York: Wiley.

Jones, E. (1923), The nature of auto-suggestion. In: *Papers on Psychoanalysis.* Boston: Beacon Press, 1961, pp. 273–293.

Kihlstrom, J. F. (1985), Hypnosis. *Ann. Rev. of Psychology,* 36:385–418.

Kris, E. (1952), *Psychoanalytic Explorations in Art.* New York: International Universities Press.

Kubie, L. S. (1961), Hypnotism: A focus for psychophysiological and psychoanalytic investigations. *Arch. Gen. Psychiat.,* 4:66–80.

_____ (1972), Illusion and reality in the study of sleep, hypnosis, psychosis, and arousal. *Internat. J. Clin. & Exp. Hypnosis,* 20:205–223.

_____ Margolin, S. (1944), The process of hypnotism and the nature of the hypnotic state. *Amer. J. Psychiat.,* 100:611–622.

Morse, D. R., Martin, J. S., Furst, M. L. & Dubin, L. L. (1977), A physiological and subjective evaluation of mediation, hypnosis, and relaxation, *Psychosom. Med.,* 39:304–324.

Rado, S. (1925), The economic principle in psychoanalytic technique. *Internat. J. Psycho-Anal.,* 6:35–44.

Rapaport, D. (1953), Some metapsychological considerations concerning activity and passivity. In: *The Collected Papers of David Rapaport.* New York: Basic Books, 1967, pp. 530–568.

Schafer, R. (1958), Regression in the service of the ego: The relevance of a psychoanalytic concept for personality assessment. In: *Assessment of Human Motives.* ed. G. Lindzey. New York: Rinehart, pp. 119–148.

Schilder, P. & Kauders, V. (1927), *Hypnosis.* New York: Nervous & Mental Disease Pub.

Van der Walde, P. H. (1965), Interpretation of hypnosis in terms of ego psychology. *Arch. Gen. Psychiat.,* 12:438–447.

_____ (1967), Trance states and ego psychology. *Internat. J. Clin. & Exp. Hypnosis,* 15:95–105.

A Model of Affect Using Dynamical Systems

JEROME I. SASHIN
JAMES CALLAHAN

Since 1983 we have collaborated on the development of a model of the mind to understand affect. We seek to be comprehensive in treating the psychoanalytic evidence and scientific in approach by using recently developed tools from the theory of dynamical systems. In this chapter, we summarize some of the psychoanalytic ideas that guide our thinking, show how we model affect, and demonstrate the benefits of our approach.

By affects we mean subjectively experienced feelings; an affect-response is any response to a stimulus that one ordinarily expects to evoke affects. We call such a stimulus an affect-evoking stimulus. In fact, affect-responses are enormously varied, and indeed, an affect-evoking stimulus may produce no affects at all in certain circumstances. So we ask: what determines the specific response to an affect-evoking stimulus, and what, in particular, enables the feeling response to occur? We want to know what the crucial variables are and how they act, separately and in concert.

Our model accomplishes the following: First, it synthesizes disparate clinical material in a coherent framework. This framework is visual in form; it allows us to grasp the situation as a whole and to see how the different aspects of affect-response are related to each other. Second, it gives us insights about affect in the form of unexpected predictions and new therapeutic strategies, all empirically testable. By having such descriptive and predictive power, our model meets the most stringent demands of a scientific theory.

This collaboration was funded in part by research grants from the Boston Psychoanalytic Society and Institute, Inc., whose encouragement and support we gratefully acknowledge.

James Callahan dedicates this work to the memory of Jerome Sashin, who died in January 1990.

Background

Currently there are more than 100 theories of emotion (Kestenbaum, 1980), but no comprehensive psychoanalytic theory of affect (Compton, 1972a, b, 1980; Panel, 1974, 1982). There are certain requirements for a comprehensive theory: It should include both normal and pathological states (Zetzel, 1971). It must cover phenomena observed in the fully mature person as well as those pertaining to earlier developmental states (Panel, 1974). It must explain "normal" and adaptive states as well as pathological conditions.

Though human behavior is unlimited in its variety and complexity, everyday experience and clinical observation reveal discernible patterns. The need to find effective treatments for a wide range of disorders urges us to understand these patterns. The methods of 19th-century science give us one language to describe patterns, of course, but those methods were intended for variables that change continuously and can be measured with arbitrary precision.

But the psychoanalytic variables we consider are not like this. For one thing, they can undergo sudden and pronounced change. Ordinary language reflects this abruptness of change; we speak quite naturally of "a mood shift" or a "burst of anger" or a "flash of inspiration." Second, the intensity of an affect-response is assessed not by instrument readings but by clinical judgments. Individual assessments may differ in detail, but the common training and experience of clinicians tend to produce consensus about overall patterns. To model affect, with its volatile and subjective features, we have turned to the recently developed method called catastrophe theory, from the larger field of dynamical systems.

This field considers the behavior of a system as it evolves over time. It applies equally to all the sciences—the human, as well as the physical. It is, in fact, a theory of the *structure* of behavior. Catastrophe theory is the simplest part of the field; it deals with systems that evolve to a steady state. It emphasizes the visual over the numerical, and it concentrates on the qualitative aspects of change. It takes discontinuities in stride. The term catastrophe is just a whimsical, but evocative, name given to a sudden—but not necessarily calamitous—change in behavior. Zeeman (1977) presents numerous models of behavior using catastrophe theory, and Galatzer-Levy (1978) calls attention to the usefulness of the subject in psychoanalysis.

To begin, we use the psychoanalytic literature to identify the variables that constitute affect-response behavior and the factors that control or influence the behavior. Then, using catastrophe theory, we describe the relationship between the control factors and the behavioral variables. Catastrophe theory provides us with a catalogue of models that describe patterns of behavior. The description is visual. The models we select form a natural sequence from the simple to the complex; each later model naturally incorporates all its predecessors while capturing some new feature of affect-response. The three principal models in our sequence are called the *cusp*, the *butterfly*, and the *double cusp*. The first two models were introduced by Sashin (1982, 1985), the third by Callahan and Sashin (1986); they are described in the sections immediately following.

Normal and Abnormal Affect-Response: The Hysteresis Model

Affects are subjectively experienced feelings in response to affect-evoking stimuli. Some people have little or no subjective feeling response. Instead, they may exhibit impulsive action, somatic dysfunction, or personality disorganization; they may even have no apparent reaction whatsoever. In order to limit the number of variables we have to work with, we shall restrict ourselves to a *single* emotion—anger, sadness, or anxiety, for example—in constructing our models. Our analysis is independent of the affect chosen; different affects would produce similar results. The normal response to an affect-evoking stimulus then has the form illustrated in Figure 1. This graph is the simplest pattern in the catastrophe theory catalogue. It says that, however stimulus and response are measured, response directly "follows" stimulus as it increases or decreases. In particular, a moderate stimulus produces a moderate response.

By contrast, the most distinctive features of abnormal affect-response are shown in Figure 2. Suppose we start at the lower left corner of this

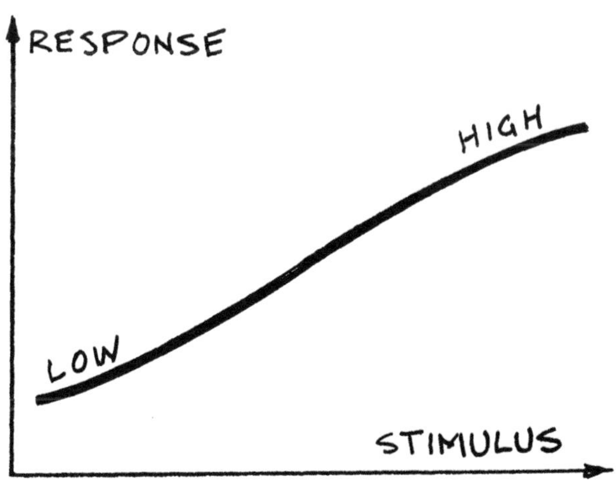

FIGURE 1. *Normal affect-response.*

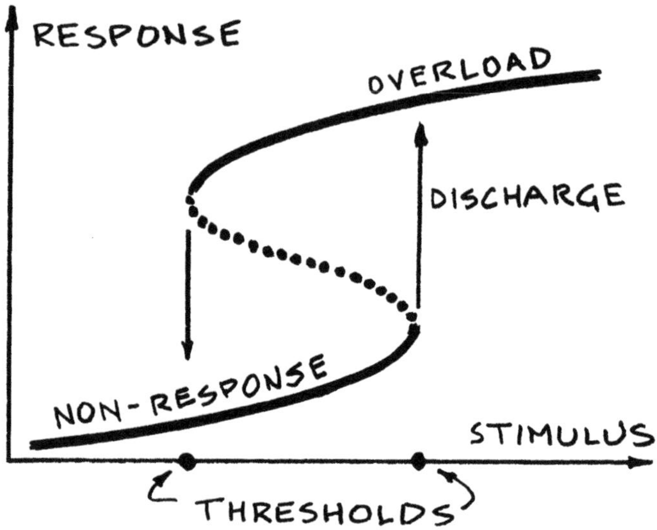

FIGURE 2. *Abnormal affect-response.*

graph and watch what happens as stimulus increases. Response is noticeably lower than in the normal case, and it remains low until a threshold is reached. At that point there is a sudden and extreme overload response—such as impulsive action, somatic dysfunction, or personality disorganization—called *discharge*. Once it has been evoked, the overload response persists, even when stimulus is reduced below the threshold level at which the discharge was triggered in the first place. Only when stimulus continues downward to a second threshold, lower than the first, does response drop; and once again the change is sudden and relatively large. The pairing of large delayed responses in this way is called *hysteresis* (from the Greek for "lagging behind").

Perhaps the most striking difference between these two graphs is found in the mid-range: whereas the normal response to a moderate stimulus is itself moderate, the abnormal response is extreme—either high or low, depending on how that stimulus level was reached. The possibility of two distinct responses for a given stimulus is called *bimodality*. As we see, bimodality in the abnormal case is coupled with the loss of the middle range of affect-responses; only the extremes are possible. The hysteresis model says that abnormal affect-response involves four things: an absence of feelings, bimodality, surges between apathy and overload, and delays.

It should be emphasized that jumps, delays, bimodality, and the absence of mid-range responses, while *abnormal* for affect-response, can be *normal* for other sorts of behavior. The most familiar example is sleep. Wakefulness and sleep are two distinctly different states that can be regarded as extremes of alertness. There are states in the mid-range of alertness, but we do not normally spend much time in them. Furthermore, the onset of sleep is relatively sudden, and so is waking up. Finally, the fact that a level of environmental distraction that would keep us awake can be insufficient to wake us up once we are asleep demonstrates hysteresis in sleep patterns. An even more striking example of the benevolence and utter normality of jumps and hysteresis in human behavior can be found in our thought processes: a problem we have been brooding on for a long time can be solved by a flash of inspiration.

Jumps, hysteresis, and the absence of mid-range responses are aspects of human behavior that can be normal or abnormal, depending on the context. We identify them as abnormal within the study of affect-response because that is how the psychoanalytic literature, on balance, characterizes them.

Synthesis of the Patterns: The Cusp Model

Abnormality is a matter of degree, and one can imagine a whole series of graphs to fit between Figures 1 and 2, representing responses that vary continuously from normal through mildly abnormal to extremely abnormal. The next graph in the hierarchy of catastrophe-theoretic models provides us with precisely such a series. It is called the *cusp catastrophe* and has the form of a surface in three dimensions (see Figure 3). If one thinks of this shape as a solid, like a loaf of bread, then the series of individual graphs just described are vertical slices of this loaf. At one end, we find the slice corresponding to normal response, and at the other, the abnormal (illustrating what was said earlier about simpler graphs being embedded within those further up the hierarchy). As we move along the axis perpendicular to the slices, abnormality level increases. We can see, by allowing the eye to travel from the back of the loaf to the front, how responses drift toward the extremes, and how, at a certain level, hysteresis and bimodality arise. The jumps are small at first, but they grow in size—and the corresponding threshold stimuli spread apart—as abnormality increases. Moreover, their growth creates an ever-larger gap in the mid-range of possible responses.

The cusp model expands our view of affect-response because it shows simultaneously the effects of abnormality and stimulus on response.

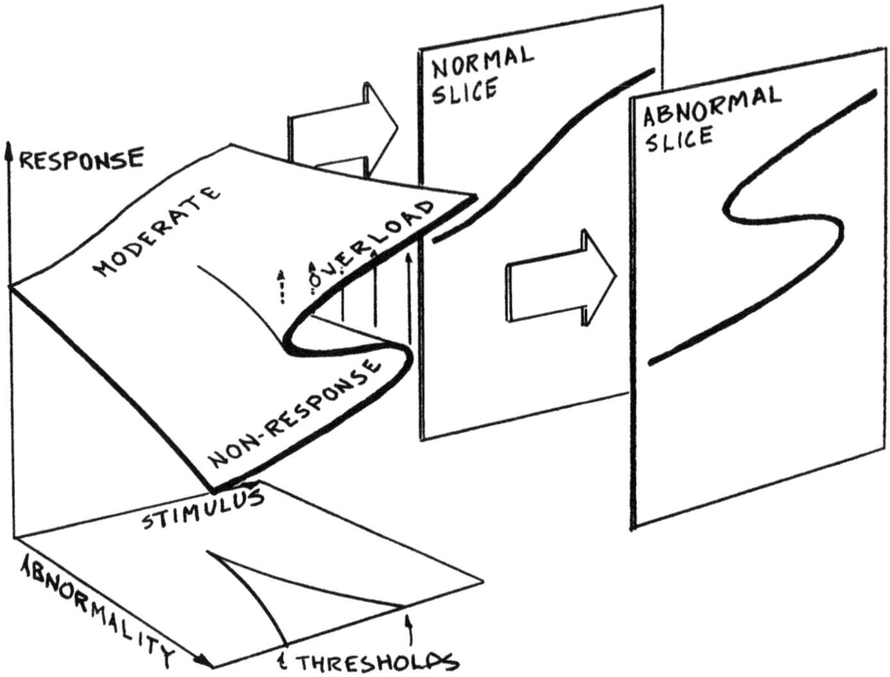

FIGURE 3. *Synthesis of affect-responses in the cusp model.*

Stimulus and *abnormality* are called the control factors of the model; and the horizontal plane on which they are plotted in Figure 3, the *control space.* Affect-response is the behavioral variable of the model and is indicated as *response* on the vertical axis of the graph. Any alteration of stimulus and abnormality level corresponds to a motion in the control space. Particularly important are those changes that move the controls across a threshold point for jumps. These points form what is called the *bifurcation set;* the cusp shape of the bifurcation set in Figure 3 gives this graph its name. By referring back to the hysteresis model, we can see that behavior is bimodal within the cusp and unimodal outside.

We shall use the term *bifurcation of behavior* to describe the effects that increasing abnormality level has on affect-response. Those effects can be summarized as follows: (1) loss of feeling responses in the moderate range; (2) drift toward a bimodal pattern of extreme responses; (3) thresholds for jumps between extremes; and (4) hysteresis when stimulus is restored to its initial level.

The cusp model underscores the tentative conclusions we drew with the hysteresis model, namely, that the loss of feeling responses and sudden dramatic, even violent, swings in behavior can be modeled as aspects of a single overarching pattern of disorder. The model has therapeutic implications. Treatment must seek to recover moderate responses as well as eliminate sudden dramatic mood shifts. In the plainest geometric terms, we must get out of the cusp.

Identifying Abnormality Factors: The Butterfly Model

The cusp model is one of the simpler ones in catastrophe theory. Clearly, affect-response has many more components than a cusp can account for. The next step in this research was to break down *abnormality* into specific components and to find a suitable model that could incorporate them. In 1982 Sashin showed that at least three factors are needed to model the clinical situations in a minimally adequate way. Thus, a model was needed in which the control space had four variables instead of two, and a new graph from the catalogue was needed. This led to the development of the butterfly model of affect-response (Sashin, 1982, 1985).

Considerable clinical evidence shows that three additional factors besides *stimulus* intensity influence the form of affect-response (Sashin, 1985). They are impairment of the inner container (*inner container*), the capacity to fantasize (*fantasy*), and the capacity to verbalize affect (*language*). *Inner container* is our term for the inner psychological structure that has been described by Brazelton and Als (1979), Kohut (1971), Krystal (1975), Settlage (1977), and others. This structure is based on self- and object representations and enables a person to experience, contain, modulate, and bear his feelings.

Let us now turn to the butterfly model. It has a single behavior variable governed by four controls. We identify the behavior variable with *affect-response* (just as we did in the cusp model), and we identify the model's four controls with *stimulus, inner container, language*, and *fantasy*. The graph of the butterfly model lies in a five-dimensional space and therefore cannot be shown in a single picture, but we can visualize it nonetheless.

Here is our approach. First, we fix the values of the controls that correspond to *language* and *fantasy*. Then *affect-response* depends only on *stimulus* and *inner container*. The butterfly model then displays this relationship as an ordinary (that is, three-dimensional) graph. Figure 4 shows one such graph. It is similar to the graph of the cusp model (Figure 3), with two notable differences. First, the axis labelled *abnormality* in the

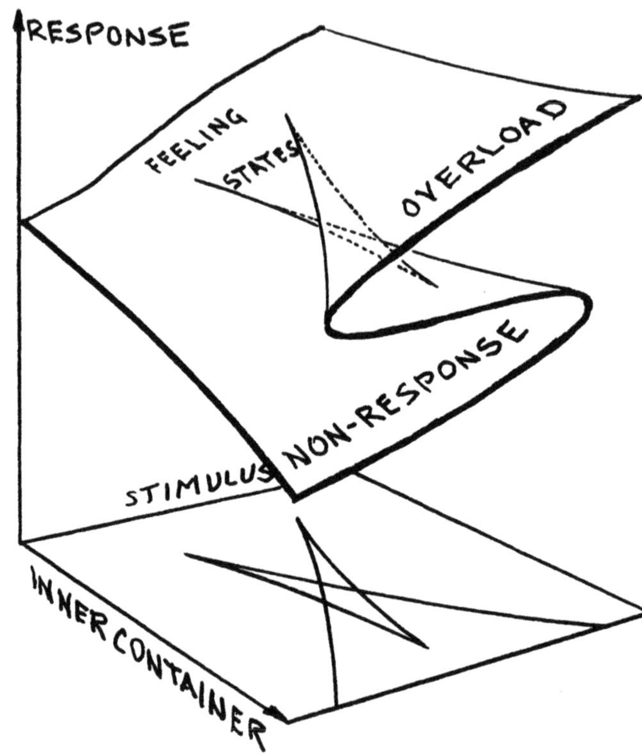

FIGURE 4. *The characteristic picture of the butterfly model.*

cusp graph is now called *inner container*. This labelling is consistent with our goal of having the butterfly model extend and refine the cusp: we replace the broad notion of abnormality with more specific factors, in particular, with the notion of loss of the inner container. The second striking difference between Figures 3 and 4 is in the shape of the graphical surface itself. In the butterfly picture, the surface has acquired two extra folds, creating an additional sheet in the middle, where the feeling response occurs.

To draw Figure 4, we fixed the values of two of the controls (namely, *language* and *fantasy*). To see the full butterfly model, we must allow these controls to vary. The results are simple to describe. When *language* increases, the middle sheet grows, and invades the cusp region; when it decreases, the middle sheet shrinks and eventually disappears. An increase in *fantasy* pushes the middle sheet to one side of the surface; a decrease pushes it to the other. With a sufficiently large push (in either direction), the middle sheet again shrinks up and vanishes. Of course, whenever the middle sheet in Figure 4 shrinks up, we are left with the plain cusp model of Figure 3. In other words, the cusp model appears as an aspect of the butterfly model.

The middle sheet is the crucial new factor in the butterfly. It implies that behavior becomes *tri*modal for some values of the control factors, specifically, in the diamond-shaped region inside the cusp in Figure 4. Anywhere inside the cusp, two distinctly different extreme responses are possible. Within the smaller, diamond-shape portion, the feeling response is possible as well. In effect, the model says that an affect-intolerant person may have access to feeling responses, at least in these very special circumstances. Access cannot be guaranteed, however. The feeling response can be very elusive: in Figure 5, which is a two-dimensional slice of Figure 4, we see how a jump from one extreme state may carry all the way to the other extreme, bypassing the intermediate feeling state entirely. In spite of this difficulty, we consider the "intrusion" of a feeling response into the region where bifurcation of behavior has occurred to be one of the keys to treatment of affect-response disorders. Such an intrusion is unexpected; it is a testable prediction made by this butterfly model of affect-response.

In studying the butterfly model, Sashin (1985) showed that the model effectively describes many of the observed clinical features of affect-

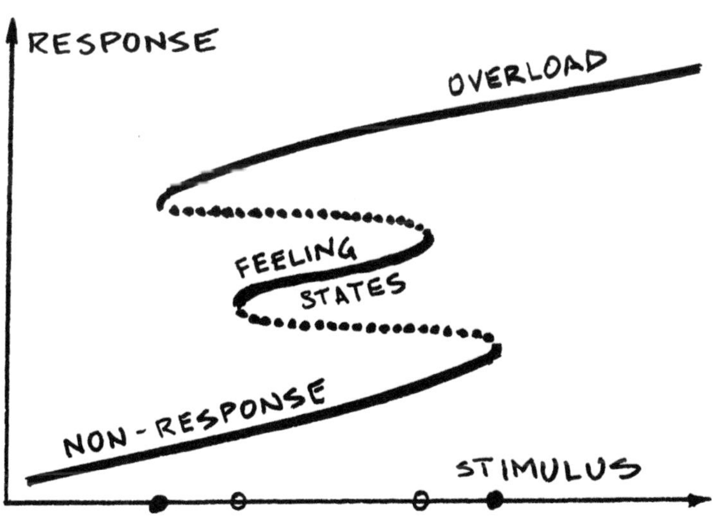

FIGURE 5. *Inaccessibility of the feeling states.*

response, including multiple states, sudden jumps between states, inaccessibility of the feeling response, and hysteresis. It provides a coherent synthesis of data from many areas of psychoanalysis. It has predictive power, and it can generate experimentally testable hypotheses. The model suggests approaches to clinical assessment and treatment, and it stimulates ideas about a comprehensive psychoanalytic theory of affect.

Elaborating Response: The Double Cusp Model

The butterfly model was introduced to take a more realistic account of abnormality factors. We must do the same for the behavioral variable *affect-response*, because it clearly has many components. But how many, and what are they? That depends on whom you ask. Valenstein (1983) points out that since earliest times all responses have been described using the familiar, traditional three-dimensional system of affective, cognitive, and conative variables (for feelings, thoughts, and volitions). To these he adds a fourth, for action. Horowitz (1972) has described a different three-dimensional system of modes of representation: images, thoughts, actions. Standard psychiatric texts suggest an even larger system of scales, including cognitive, conative, affective, perceptual, intellectual; and each of these has many subscales. In fact, all these systems are simplifications; the actual behavioral space is genuinely complex. Any choice we make is inevitably incomplete. Investigators choose those factors which seem most relevant for their purposes.

Our own choice is to split affect-response into two components: *feelings*, a measure of the intensity of experienced affect, and *activity*, a composite measure of all nonfeeling responses, including expressions in the cognitive, somatic, and action realms. Inevitably, very different mixtures of mental and physical activity will still be represented as the same *activity* level. However, we can consider many more clinical situations than before—for example, high affect with high activity, as in manic states; low affect with high activity, as in some psychosomatic states; low affect with low activity; and in fact all the combinations of affect and activity that are seen in the different neurotic states and in normal persons.

How should the elaborated response be modeled? According to the catastrophe theory catalogue, the simplest full-scale model that encompasses two separate response variables, each controlled by a cusp, is the catastrophe graph called the *double cusp* (Zeeman, 1977). The double cusp involves eight control factors, so its graph is 10-dimensional. When we began our collaboration, little was known about the geometry of this graph. However, because the double cusp model promised to go even further beyond the butterfly than the butterfly went beyond the cusp, we decided it was important to try to develop it.

This meant we had to work on two fronts: we had to determine the geometry of the double cusp, and we had to identify eight control factors for affect-response that would be consistent with that geometry. The four factors of the butterfly model—namely, *stimulus, inner container, language,* and *fantasy*—would naturally appear, because the butterfly is embedded in the double cusp in the same way that the cusp is embedded in the butterfly. For the remaining factors, we had to consider what the butterfly did *not* take into account. From the many possible factors cited in the psychoanalytic literature, we selected the following four because they corresponded well with factors that naturally appear in the double cusp itself. For a start, we saw that the butterfly model did not distinguish affect as signal from affect as trauma; hence it did not include an adequate consideration of defense mechanisms. The role of *defenses*, as so beautifully described by Bellak, Harvich, and Gedemen (1973), corresponded well with one of the four remaining control factors of the double cusp. In its functioning, a second control matched *constitution*, a factor having to do with general overall reactivity, disposition, and temperament. This factor was also absent from the butterfly model, but Thomas and Chess (1977) and Priband (1980) have argued it is crucial. For the remaining two geometric variables we found a good correspondence with the clinical variables *frustration intolerance* and *vigilance*. *Frustration intolerance*, which indicates the inability to delay action and to postpone expected satisfaction, is crucial in disorders involving the regulation and control of drives and impulses, as Bellak *et al.* (1973) point out. *Vigilance* indicates the degree of attention being paid to the outer, rather than the inner subjective, world. It has been shown by Marty and de M'Uzan (1963), in their beautiful description of *pensée opératoire* in patients with major disorders of affect-response, to be an extremely important factor in determining the way a person responds to an affect-evoking stimulus.

We now have a usable picture of the double cusp in which the control variables have been identified with the eight factors *stimulus, inner container, language, fantasy, defenses, constitution, vigilance,* and *frustration intolerance*. For the purposes of visual display, we replace *inner container* and *frustration intolerence* by two new factors, called *intolerance* and *imbalance*, which measure their sum and their difference, respectively. The double cusp describes how the two behaviors, *feelings* and *activity*, depend on the eight control factors by a ten-dimensional graph. We study this graph the same way we studied the butterfly—by fixing the values of most of the controls, in order to reduce the picture to one we can draw in three dimensions.

Which control factors should be fixed? The psychoanalytic literature is a useful guide: for a given person at a given time, most of the factors we are considering show little fluctuation from day to day. In fact, only *stimulus* and *vigilance* vary on a short time-scale. If we combine these two with *intolerance,* which is one indicator of what we called *abnormality* in the cusp model, we get a three-dimensional control space. This space is shown in Figure 6. *Stimulus* is high in the foreground and low in the background; *vigilance* is high at the right and low at the left; and *intolerance* is high at the top of the picture and low at the bottom.

Notice that in Figure 6 all three variables are control factors, unlike in Figures 3 and 4, where one of the variables described behavior, and the surface was a graph that showed how behavior was determined by the control factors. The surfaces in Figure 6 have a different meaning: they separate regions in control space where the behavioral possibilities are qualitatively different. Specifically, at the bottom of the picture, behav-

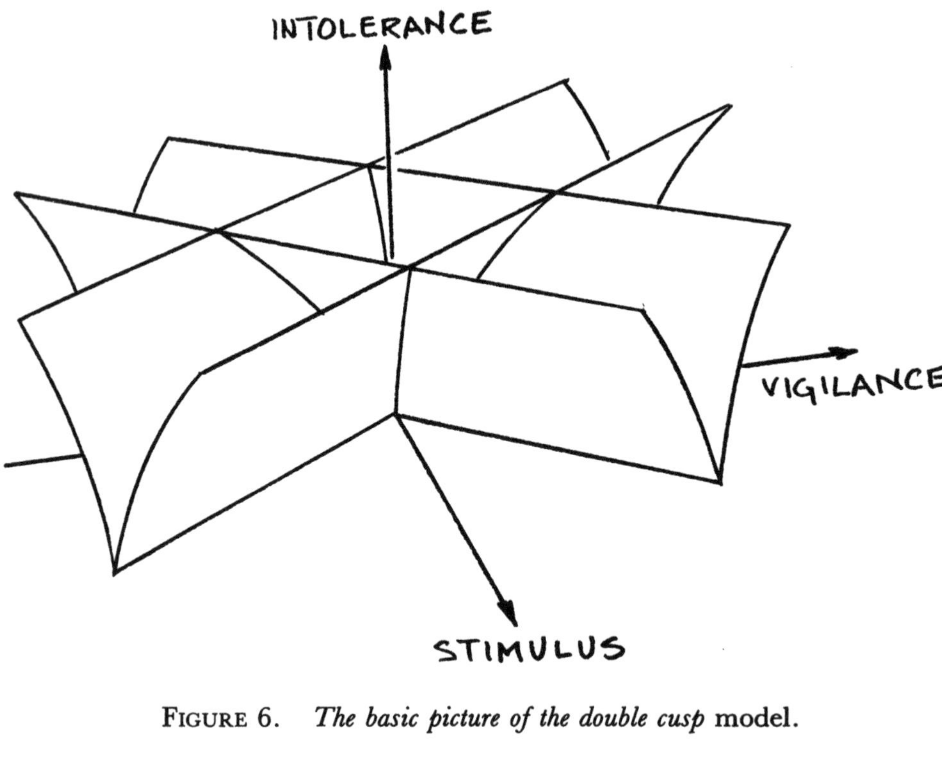

FIGURE 6. *The basic picture of the double cusp* model.

ior is unimodal: each of the behavior variables *feelings* and *activity* has only a single value. Higher up, inside the cusp-shaped "wings" or "troughs," bifurcations of behavior occur: the *feelings* response is bimodal inside one wing, the *activity* response bimodal inside the other. Finally, where the two wings cross in the central core, there are four responses, extreme for both behavior variables. Roughly speaking, abnormal response is found inside the wings, and the goal of therapy is to get out of the wings by lowering intolerance level. However, this cannot be done directly; the analyst's problem is to find a way to do it. Here the model really helps us, by providing us with guidelines for therapeutic strategies, as we shall see presently.

Remember that Figure 6 depicts how behavior depends on the three control factors *stimulus, vigilance,* and *intolerance*, while the other five controls are held fixed. If any of these five controls is altered, the basic picture in Figure 6 is changed. Figure 7 shows what happens to the basic picture when a single one of the five controls goes either above or below the neutral value it has for the basic picture. Of course, changing several controls simultaneously produces still more variations in the shape of the basic picture, and we had to determine all such variations in order to construct a complete double cusp model. When we did, we discovered a most remarkable thing. Some of the pictures that we found contain, in the central core (where *intolerance* is high), a small tunnel-shaped region (see Figure 8) where another behavioral mode exists side-by-side with the abnormal modes. In this new mode, *feelings* and *activity* take moderate values. The new mode therefore represents a normal response, though it is different in some ways from the one evoked below the cusp region. We have named it the therapeutic response.

The therapeutic response differs from the ordinary normal response because it occurs at higher *intolerance* levels and hence is accessible—in theory, at least—to someone suffering from an affect-response disorder. According to the model, however, the therapeutic response is not easy to realize, for two reasons. First, the tunnel does not always appear; it occurs for only a very limited range of control variables. Here we are particularly interested in the "pliant" controls, that is, the ones that can be more or less readily altered. Besides *vigilance* and *stimulus*, these are *language, fantasy*, and *defenses*. Second, even when the pliant controls fall within the tunnel, we must reckon with the fact that the therapeutic state coexists with the abnormal states and is dominated by them. That is, the therapeutic response does not occur spontaneously, and when it does appear, it is often quickly replaced by one of the abnormal responses. Hence, in order to activate the therapeutic response, the abnormal states must be overridden.

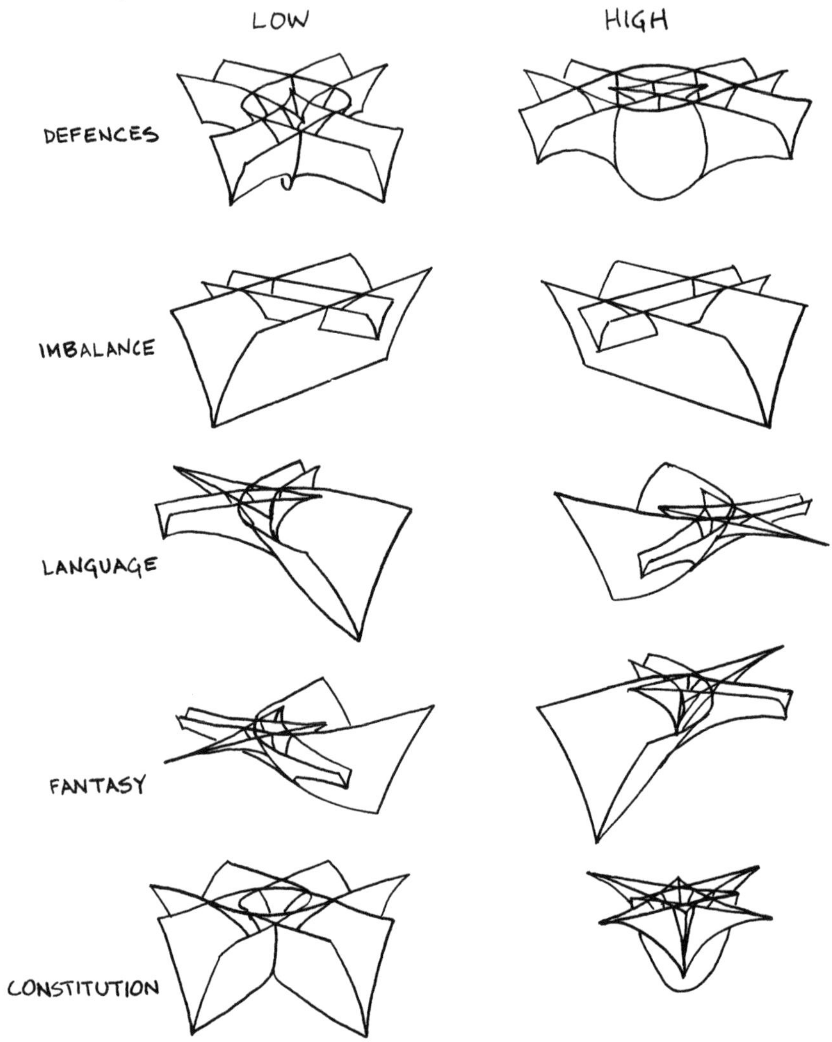

FIGURE 7. *Modifications to the basic picture produced by the other factors.*

To explain how to override these states we invoke a convention called *focusing of attention*. This is one of several conventions used in catastrophe theory to decide how to choose a particular state when the model provides several alternatives, that is, when behavior is multimodal. Focusing of attention was introduced by Zeeman (1982) specifically to deal with models of human behavior based on catastrophe theory. It says that

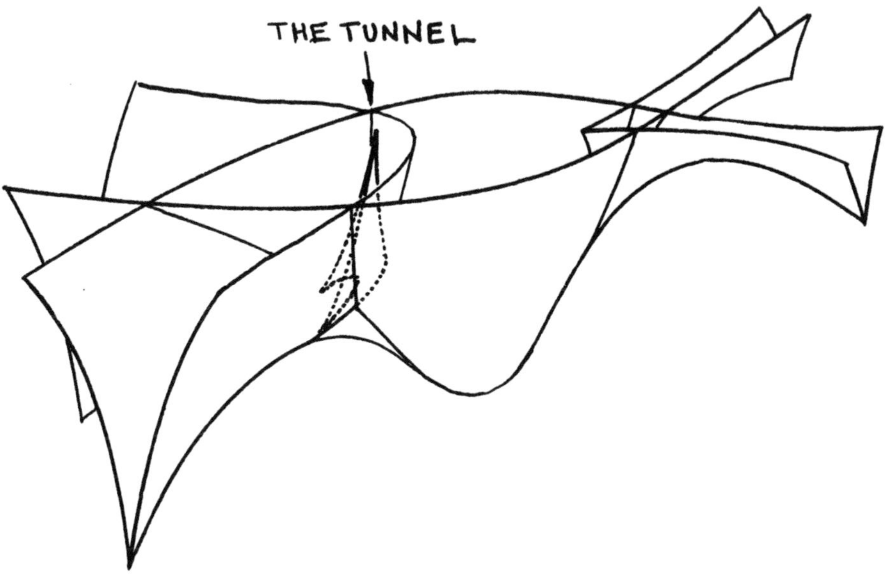

FIGURE 8. *The therapeutic tunnel.*

learning and experience permit a person to gain access to any one of the behavioral modes provided by the model. In our case, the focusing convention tells us there is an aspect of the patient's behavior that is not already a part of the model, and it explains the role of the analyst.

According to the model, the analyst's job is to modify the pliant controls to suitable values and then to encourage the patient to focus on the therapeutic state. The value of the therapeutic state is that, for increasing periods of time up to the duration of a session, the patient's responses will include moderate levels of *feelings*. It is through this process of the patient's actually experiencing moderate feeling responses that the patient's inner container is gradually repaired, resulting ultimately in a cure of the affect-response disorder. If we take Figure 6 as a representative picture of the control space, repairing the *inner container* means moving down a path from higher levels of *intolerance* to lower ones; in other words, repairing means getting beneath the cusp.

The model says that the situation just described will occur, in one form or another, for any values of the three "nonpliant" variables: *constitution, inner container,* and *frustration intolerance* (and therefore in the factors *intolerance* and *imbalance*, which are combinations of them). Thus, even if one of these variables undergoes gradual change—say, in response to treatment—the therapeutic state remains accessible. However, for different values of the nonpliant controls, the tunnel's size and location can be quite different. Nonetheless, by studying the richly complex geometry of the double-cusp model, we can discover many therapeutic strategies that would otherwise have gone completely undetected.

Our final observation about the therapeutic state is that it arises from the double-cusp model as a prediction; it is not one of the hypotheses about affect-response that we used to construct the model in the first place. Likewise, the role of the analyst, as it devolves from the focusing convention, is a prediction.

Discussion

While psychology tries to describe and understand manifest human behavior, psychoanalysis has as its goal the investigation of the general laws of the human psyche. In this project we used Zeeman's outline (1977, p. 267) of the interplay between science and mathematics as a guide to indicate how psychoanalysts and mathematicians could work together. We began by examining the psychoanalytic clinical situation to identify our basic assumptions, that is, the initial data for our model. We made five assumptions:

(1) The mental apparatus is governed by an optimizing principle—the basic "pleasure-unpleasure" regulatory principle of psychoanalysis as described by Sandler and Joffe (1969).
(2) Psychoanalytic variables can be measured on continuous scales.
(3) Affect-response can be split into two components of behavior.
(4) Catastrophe theory can be used to model affect-response, and in particular, each affect-response component can be modelled by a cusp.
(5) The two affect-response behavior components are coupled.

Having identified our psychoanalytic premises and the bases for a mathematical treatment of them, we then looked to the mathematics—specifically, to elementary catastrophe theory—to find the simplest stable model consistent with our premises. That model turned out to be the compact double cusp (Zeeman 1977, p. 564). Little was known about the mathematical structure of this model when we began our project, so we had to make a thorough study of the double cusp and obtain an essentially complete description of its geometry. It is worth emphasizing that the work in this stage was pure mathematics, not connected in any way to affect-response. The geometric properties of the compact double cusp were proven in the same way that any mathematical result is proven.

This process led to the discovery of certain properties of the double cusp that translated into three nontrivial and previously unsuspected predictions about affect-response. First, we learned that the behavior we were studying was controlled by eight—not by one or two or three, but also not by 10 or 100 or 1000—underlying variables. Second, by determining the characteristics of each control variable (as shown in Figure 7), and seeing how each affected the mathematical model, we were able to make a plausible correspondence between the model's control variables and the clinical variables described in the affect-response literature. The result was a 10-variable, psychoanalytic, compact double-cusp model of affect-response. And, third, the discovery of a tunnel in the mathematical model indicated that, for certain values of the clinical variables, we would expect moderate behavior to coexist with extreme affect-responses. This discovery thereby generated a startling clinical hypothesis, suitable for experimental testing. The coexisting moderate state is a refutable prediction, demonstrating that our model satisfies the most stringent of demarcation criteria for a theory to be scientific.

Catastrophe theory provides us with an important tool for developing psychoanalytic theory. It tells us, in a well-defined way, the "simplest sort" of mechanism in the psychodynamic system we are studying. It gives us a coherent synthesis of much disparate data and serves as a visual metaphor of considerable heuristic value, enabling us to grasp and think creatively about the situation as a whole. And, as we have seen, it has potential implications for psychoanalytic treatment. Finally, by providing us with a universal language for expressing our psychoanalytic theory and a model that generates hypotheses suitable for clinical testing and possible refutation, catastrophe theory gives our work a scientific basis.

The 10-variable double-cusp model is an extremely powerful vehicle for enhancing our understanding. It is twice the size of the butterfly model: we now have two behavioral factors instead of one, and eight controls instead of four. Clearly, we can go much further. The behavioral space and the control space are still oversimplified; many crucial variables, such as the quality of object relationships, reality testing, and memory are still missing. But by studying this model in detail, we can learn much about deeper mechanisms, dynamics, possible therapeutic strategies, and make progress towards our ultimate goal of developing a truly comprehensive, explanatory, and scientific psychoanalytic theory of affect.

References

Bellak, L., Harvich, M. & Gedeman, H. K. (1973), *Ego Functions In Schizophrenics, Neurotics, and Normals*. New York: Wiley.

Brazelton, T. B. & Als, H. (1979), Four early stages in the development of mother—infant interaction. *The Psychoanalytic Study of the Child*, 34: 349–370. New Haven, CT: Yale University Press.

Callahan, J. & Sashin, J. I. (1986), Models of affect-response and anorexia nervosa. *Ann. N. Y. Acad. Sci.*, 504: 241–259.

Compton, A. (1972a), A study of the psychoanalytic theory of anxiety, I: The development of Freud's theory of anxiety. *J. Amer. Psychoanal. Assn.*, 20: 3–44.

_____ (1972b), A study of the psychoanalytic theory of anxiety, II: Developments in the theory of anxiety since 1926. *J. Amer. Psychoanal. Assn.*, 20: 341–394.

_____ (1980), A study of the psychoanalytic theory of anxiety, III: A preliminary formulation of the anxiety response. *J. Amer. Psychoanal. Assn.*, 28: 739–774.

Galatzer-Levy, R. M. (1978), Qualitative change from quantitative change: mathematical catastrophe theory in relation to psychoanalysis, *J. Amer. Psychoanal. Assn.*, 26: 921–935.

Horowitz, M. J. (1972), Modes of representation of thought. *J. Amer. Psychoanal. Assn.*, 20: 793–819.

Kestenbaum, C. J. (1980), The origins of affect—normal and pathological. *J. Amer. Acad. Psychoanal.*, 8: 497–520.

Kohut, H. (1971), *The Analysis of the Self*. New York: International Universities Press.

Krystal, H. (1975), Affect tolerance. *Ann. Psychoanal.*, 3: 179–219.

Marty, P. & de M'Uzan, M. (1963), La "pensée opératoire". *Revue fr. Psychoanal.*, 27 (suppl.): 345–356.

Panel (1974), Towards a theory of affect. P. Castelnuovo-Tedesco, reporter. *J. Amer. Psychoanal. Assn.*, 30: 197–213.

_____ (1982), New directions in affect theory. E. Lester, reporter. *J. Amer. Psychoanal. Assn.*, 30: 197–213.

Priband. K. H. (1980), The biology of emotions and other feelings. In: *Emotion Theory, Research, and Experience Vol. 1 Theories of Emotion*, ed. R. Plutchnik & H. Kellerman. New York: Academic Press, pp. 245–270.

Sandler, J. & Joffe, W. G. (1969), Towards a basic psychoanalytic model. *Internat. J. Psycho-Anal.*, 50: 79–90.

Sashin, J. I. (1982), Catastrophes in psychodynamics. Presented at American Psychoanalytic Association Scientific Meetings, Boston.

_____ (1985), Affect tolerance: a model of affect-response using catastrophe theory. *J. Social Biol. Struct.*, 8: 175–202.

Settlage, C. F. (1977), The psychoanalytic understanding of narcissistic and borderline personality disorders: advances in developmental theory. *J. Amer. Psychoanal. Assn.*, 24: 805–833

Thomas. A. & Chess, S. (1977), *Temperament and Development*. New York: Brunner/Mazel.

Valenstein, A. F.. (1983), Working through and resistance to change: insight and the action system. *J. Amer. Psychoanal. Assn.*, 31: 353–373.

Zeeman, E. C. (1977), *Catastrophe Theory: Selected Papers, 1972–1977*. Reading, MA: Benjamin.

_____ (1982), Sudden changes of perception. In: *Logos et Théorie des Catastrophes*, ed. J. Petitot. Geneva: Foundation Patiño, 1988.

Zetzel, E. (1971), The relationships of defense to affect and its tolerance. In: *The Unconscious Today*, ed. M. Kanzer. New York: International Universities Press, pp. 137–146.

AUTHOR INDEX

M

N

O

P

R

SUBJECT INDEX

D

T

For Product Safety Concerns and Information please contact our EU representative GPSR@taylorandfrancis.com
Taylor & Francis Verlag GmbH, Kaufingerstraße 24, 80331 München, Germany

www.ingramcontent.com/pod-product-compliance
Ingram Content Group UK Ltd.
Pitfield, Milton Keynes, MK11 3LW, UK
UKHW022001180926
475701UK00003B/145
9780367606473